BEAVERBROOK
A Shattered Legacy

Lord Beaverbrook

BEAVERBROOK

A Shattered Legacy

JACQUES POITRAS

Quotations from *Beaverbrook* by A.J.P. Taylor © Aitken Alexander Associates Ltd. Used with permission. Quotations from *Beaverbrook: A Life* by Anne Chisholm and Michael Davie © David Higham Associates Ltd. Used with permission. Quotations from Beaverbrook Canadian Correspondence used with permission of Archives and Special Collections, Harriet Irving Library, University of New Brunswick. Quotations from the Beaverbrook Papers used with permission of the Parliamentary Archives, House of Lords Record Office. The author gratefully acknowledges permission of the Beaverbrook Foundation to quote from the writings of Lord Beaverbrook.

Cover illustrations: *Lord Beaverbrook* by Yousuf Karsh, by permission of Camera Press, UK; *The Fountain of Indolence*, J.M.W. Turner. Cover and interior book design by Julie Scriver. Printed in Canada.
10 9 8 7 6 5 4 3 2 1

Library and Archives Canada Cataloguing in Publication

Poitras, Jacques, 1968-
Beaverbrook: a shattered legacy / Jacques Poitras.
Includes index.
ISBN 978-0-86492-497-1

1. Beaverbrook, Lord, 1879-1964. 2. Beaverbrook Art Gallery – History.
3. Beaverbrook, Lord, 1879-1964 – Family. 4. Beaverbrook, Lord, 1879-1964 – Art collections. 5. Philanthropists – Canada – Biography. I. Title.
DA566.9.B37P63 2007   971.5'1   C2007-904304-6

Goose Lane Editions acknowledges the financial support of the Canada Council for the Arts, the Government of Canada through the Book Publishing Industry Development Program (BPIDP), and the New Brunswick Department of Wellness, Culture and Sport for its publishing activities.

Goose Lane Editions
Suite 330
500 Beaverbrook Court
Fredericton, New Brunswick
CANADA E3B 5X4
www.gooselane.com

To Zachary and Sophie
and to Giselle

It may be that I shall be recalled chiefly as
the builder and founder of an art gallery.
— Lord Beaverbrook, 1959

Families are absolutely a necessary evil.
— Timothy Aitken, 2007

CONTENTS

BEAVERBROOK

A Shattered Legacy

Lady Violet Aitken arrives to testify, October 23, 2006.

Karen Ruet, *Telegraph-Journal*

"I thought we had friends in New Brunswick"

The muscle arrived first: a beefy fellow who wore a long moustache and a black suit. He would claim later that he was not a bodyguard at all, just "a friend of the family"; if that was true, he was the kind of friend who behaved rather like a bodyguard. He appeared in the front door of the conference centre about twenty minutes ahead of the family, striding out into the large central lobby to scan the room and taking a long look up to the second floor, where reporters lay in wait. He continued his visual sweep, noting the locations of the exits, the stairwells and the corridors, as if identifying possible escape routes. He was clearly a cautious and diligent friend.

He did not spare a glance at the bronze bust encased in glass in a display built into a brick wall just a few yards from the door. The bust of an old man, only slightly larger than life, captured its subject's kindness, that type of kindness that a man can afford only towards the end of a life devoted to becoming wealthy. The old man had accumulated his fortune in the fading days of the British Empire and then decided to give much of it away. He'd set up a foundation as the vehicle for his good works and, thus, his immortality. The bust commemorated the gift of this modern conference centre, tucked into the southeast corner of the University of New Brunswick campus in Fredericton, the provincial capital. His name was over the door.

The journalists waiting upstairs had arrived early, the TV cameramen and newspaper photographers by necessity. They had a sensational story to cover today, but the pictures they needed to tell it would be scant. Though both sides in the bitter feud had agreed that their month-long arbitration would be open to the public — a rarity here in New Brunswick — cameras were not permitted in the rented hearing room itself. The cameramen and photographers would have to make do with what they could get in the corridor: images of the star witnesses coming up to the second floor and walking inside. They'd be able to round out their reports, of course, with archival footage: grainy black-and-white shots of Lord Beaverbrook, the long-dead press baron; perhaps an external pan of the art gallery he had built downtown as a gift to the province where he grew up; and, naturally, close-ups of several of the paintings at the heart of the drama, including the two said to have provoked all the fuss.

Downstairs, on the ground level of the conference centre, behind the two large wooden doors to the Chancellor's Room, hung a portrait that would have provided a wonderful image for the television reports. It was of Lord Beaverbrook's daughter-in-law, Lady Violet Aitken, the wife of his son, Sir Max Aitken, who had served as chancellor of the University of New Brunswick after his father's death. Lady Aitken herself had stepped into the role in 1981, after Sir Max became too ill to continue. Lady Aitken just happened to be the first of two witnesses — two Aitkens, in fact — scheduled to testify that morning. The portrait captured her proud bearing, her narrow features, her bright, clear blue eyes and the steely resolve that hid behind her aristocratic charm.

There was a bustle at the main entrance to the building. The beefy "friend" reappeared, ushering four people into the building: Lady Aitken, now in her eighties; her son Maxwell, who held the title created for his grandfather, Lord Beaverbrook; his sister, Laura Aitken Levi; and Maxwell's son, also named Maxwell, who would one day inherit the title from his father. A second man, trimmer, dark-suited, his salt-and-pepper brush cut set off by a neatly trimmed goatee, followed them in. He, too, would describe himself — with a pronounced Glaswegian accent — as "a friend of the family." As friends went, he was in remarkable physical condition, with the powerful build one might expect a bodyguard to have. His definition of friendship, it became evident as the day unfolded, included shadowing members of the Aitken family each time one of them visited the conference centre washrooms. The Glaswegian would station himself outside, his presence discouraging anyone else from heeding nature's call while an Aitken was doing so.

The cameramen and photographers moved in close as the elevator reached the second floor and the Aitkens emerged. Kent Thomson, the Toronto lawyer representing the family and its charitable foundation, had warned that none of the Aitkens would make any comment, but a few reporters gamely tossed questions their way. All four stared straight ahead and walked into the hearing room, claiming four seats that were marked Reserved: The Beaverbrook Foundation.

The small but modern hearing room had been transformed into a showcase for the very latest in litigation technology. Two long tables for each firm, separated by a centre aisle, were covered with equipment. The hardware belonging to Thomson's firm, Davies Ward Phillips and Vineberg, was cutting edge: laptop computers were connected to large, wide-screen monitors that could display the massive database of more than fifteen thousand documents filed in the case. Each document had been individually scanned and could be called up on the screen with a click of a mouse. Other monitors were linked by a wireless connection to the court reporter, hired from a leading Toronto reporting firm, whose transcript of a witness's words would scroll onto Thomson's screen just moments after they'd been uttered.

These twenty-first-century resources had been marshalled to attempt to peer into the mind of Lord Beaverbrook, who had been born in the nineteenth century, left his New Brunswick home for England before the advent of air travel, became a giant of that quintessentially twentieth-century form of communication, the mass-circulation popular newspaper, and, in his twilight years, zealously collected hundreds of examples of that most traditional and low-tech art form, the oil-on-canvas painting. Now, two institutions named for him — the London-based Beaverbrook U.K. Foundation and the Beaverbrook

Art Gallery of Fredericton, New Brunswick, Canada — were each spending millions of dollars to prove their ownership of one hundred and thirty-three paintings he had sent to the gallery decades before.

This collision of modernity and tradition was also evident in the changing relationship between the House of Beaverbrook and the little Canadian province that the original Maxwell Aitken had called home. Once, newspaper editors here would report Lord Beaverbrook's every movement, pronouncement and charitable gift. Premiers and senior officials of the New Brunswick government would rush to the airport or train station to greet him, hats in hand, showing a deference — a servility, even —normally reserved for royalty. But New Brunswick had changed by 2006: great importance was still attached to trad-ition, but the deference was gone. An Aitken — a Lord Beaverbrook — could no longer arrive in the province and have his will be done without question. Grandson Maxwell had not only been refused what he considered a reasonable request, he had also found himself branded a villain.

One of those who had refused to acquiesce to his wishes sat in the far corner of the hearing room, in the very last of the chairs set aside for curious members of the public. Judy Budovitch, dressed in black, her face betraying a momentary sadness as she watched the Aitkens file in, was no ordinary bystander. She had given years of her life to the Beaverbrook Art Gallery, most recently as the chair of its board of governors, and she'd come to know all of the Aitkens before the ownership dispute had so damaged their ties to New Brunswick. "I'm relieved that it's coming to a conclusion," Budovitch had told repor-ters the day the hearings began. "I would have hoped that we could have resolved it in a more amicable way, but this is certainly one way to do it." She defended yet again the gallery board's refusal to hand over the paintings. "We are public trustees. We are a public board. And we can't give away work that the public may own."

Almost two decades earlier, Budovitch had worked closely with Lady Aitken on a fundraising campaign for the gallery. "She was very nice," Budovitch had testified about Lady Aitken, "and couldn't have been nicer to me personally. She couldn't have been more supportive of the institution. And I have nothing to say about her but the most positive things, both as a person and as a supporter of the gallery. She was as good as we could ever expect to have." That seemed like such a long time ago now as Lady Aitken rose from her seat and walked confidently to the front of the room to begin her testimony. Even the very name of that 1988 fundraising campaign, Cherish the Gift, would be drawn into the dispute as one side tried to use it to chip away at the other's case.

There were actually two Beaverbrook art disputes unfolding in New Brunswick in the autumn of 2006, one prompted by the other. They had become indistinguishable in the public mind: *which* grandson was involved here? Was *this* the dispute that included the works by Dali? The 2003 request by the Beaverbrook U.K. Foundation, run by Maxwell, and the gallery's subsequent refusal to grant it — the dispute coming to a head today — had prompted the second dispute, between the gallery and the Beaverbrook Canadian Foundation, overseen by Maxwell's cousin Timothy, another Beaverbrook grandson. More than two hundred paintings were at stake in the two disputes. The more placid Maxwell had agreed to have his fight resolved in this speedier, less costly hearing under New Brunswick's Arbitration Act; the irascible Timothy had spurned that idea, choosing to let the Canadian battle unfold in the New Brunswick courts. That trial date was still nowhere in sight when Maxwell and his mother arrived in Fredericton to testify at the arbitration on this October morning in 2006.

New Brunswick's arbitration law allows the parties in a dispute to choose their arbitrator; the British foundation and the gallery had gone to the pinnacle of Canada's legal system, selecting Peter Cory, a retired justice of the Supreme Court of Canada, now working in a high-end arbitration firm in Toronto. Cory sat at the front of the room behind a large folding table, under which everyone in attendance could, day after day, catch a glimpse of his pant legs riding up to reveal the pale flesh of the esteemed jurist's lanky shins. A smile crossed his aquiline features as he greeted Lady Aitken and invited her to take a seat. About to celebrate his own eighty-first birthday, Cory would show fondness and sympathy for the more elderly witnesses, of which there would be several. Cory's profile on the federal justice department's web site notes that he was "hardly a 'retiring' judge." Before coming to Fredericton, he'd been engaged in untangling the facts behind a series of sectarian killings in Northern Ireland. Once his work in New Brunswick was done, he'd be off to Afghanistan to help set up that country's judiciary. At times during the Beaverbrook arbitration, that task would seem straightforward compared to divining the intentions of a dead press baron.

Cory looked up at the foundation's lawyer, Kent Thomson, and with a nod instructed Thomson to begin his examination of Lady Aitken.

She told her own story first. Her maiden name was de Trafford, and her family line had been established in Britain "apparently before William the Conqueror, but you never know with these things"; her self-effacing remark drew a little grin from the court reporter. Violet de Trafford had met Lord Beaverbrook's son, Max Aitken, in 1949, when he was a British MP and she was working for another member at Westminster. "Max, for me, at that age — I was quite younger than him — I was absolutely bowled over by him," Lady Aitken said, her eyes as sparkling and her posture as proud as in the portrait downstairs. "He was a war hero. He was someone who had enormous charm." She became his third wife on New Year's Day, 1951. At Lord Beaverbrook's suggestion, the wedding took place at a Presbyterian church in Montego Bay, Jamaica. But Max had a hard time living up to the expectations of his father, she added. Even though Lord Beaverbrook had ceded nominal control of his newspaper empire to his son, Beaverbrook would call Max from anywhere in the world, she said, at any time, to dictate what he wanted done. Max had borne the brunt of his father's never-ending need to be in control.

Thomson carefully led Lady Aitken through the layers of context and meaning that he would need later on. When he asked her about Cherkley Court, she spoke nostalgically of the four-hundred-acre estate in Surrey which Lord Beaverbrook had purchased in 1911, with its "quite big" main house and its smaller cottages, one of which she and Max had lived in after they were married. And she described, at Thomson's request, several of the people who had played supporting roles in the life of the great man: his London assistant, A.G.

Millar, "the original detail man"; his Fredericton courtier, Michael Wardell, who "would have no nonsense from my father-in-law"; and Lady Dunn, known to her friends as Christofor, the widow of Beaverbrook's friend Sir James Dunn. Beaverbrook himself married Christofor in 1963, a year before his death; she thus became Lady Beaverbrook and a bane to her newly acquired family. "She was inclined to alienate," Lady Aitken allowed, "but he liked her, so who were we to say?"

Slowly but surely, Thomson nudged his witness's narrative toward its inevitable conclusion. After Beaverbrook died in 1964, Lady Aitken testified, her husband Max had inherited several of his father's titles. Though he declined to take the peerage itself, declaring memorably that, "in my lifetime, there will be only one Lord Beaverbrook,"[1] Sir Max had become chair of the Beaverbrook U.K. Foundation, chancellor of the University of New Brunswick, and co-custodian, with Christofor, of the art gallery. This brought him and Lady Aitken to Fredericton several times. "We used to go check on our paintings to see if they were displayed and if they were in good condition," she said. Her husband, she added, was disturbed that the works weren't always hanging. "It was very much a worry if they were being properly observed."

Now Thomson brought her right up to the genesis of the dispute. Christofor, Lady Beaverbrook, increasingly eccentric and reclusive, had lived at Cherkley until her death in 1994. Only then did the Aitkens realize just how badly she'd allowed the house to deteriorate. Having regained control of the property, the family, through the Beaverbrook Foundation, now had to decide what to do with it. Given that there was no real memorial to Beaverbrook in England and that Cherkley was "absolutely full of history," the trustees decided to make it a public building, a heritage site that could be rented for conferences, meetings and weddings. By 2002, work was well underway on extensive and expensive renovations.

At the same time, however, a change in British law had forced the foundation to obtain, for insurance purposes, a new valuation of the paintings it owned at the gallery in Fredericton. Upon returning to England, a Sotheby's official informed the foundation trustees that their art — particularly J.M.W. Turner's *The Fountain of Indolence* and Lucian Freud's *Hotel Bedroom* — were worth millions of dollars more than anyone had known. That was going to mean much higher insurance premiums, which the foundation had always paid on the gallery's behalf. "It was costing us a great deal of money for those and the other paintings," Lady Aitken said, and "it seemed to us that perhaps they weren't seen by enough people."

Several of the reporters and other Frederictonians who had crowded into the small hearing room looked at each other knowingly. Lady Aitken's testimony had been worth the wait. From the moment the dispute had erupted in the spring of 2004, there had been speculation, including by the media, that this battle was really about the Turner and the Freud. But no one had ever confirmed that. Until now.

The gallery always needed money, Lady Aitken said, so the trustees had deemed it "sensible" to offer its board of governors a deal: return the Turner and the Freud to their owner, the foundation, which could in turn sell them, reducing the increased insurance cost. The foundation would use the money to fund its charitable works in England, to pay the insurance on its remaining paintings in Fredericton, and to make a large donation to the gallery's endowment fund. This perfectly logical proposition appeared to benefit everyone.

The controversy "could have been resolved," Lady Aitken said, "with a bit of common sense and a bit of forward-looking that would have ensured the future of the gallery." But the gallery's board had decided instead to verify the foundation's supposed ownership of the works. Contrary to what everyone had acknowledged and believed for four decades, the board later reported to Maxwell, the foundation's ownership of the paintings was not clear at all.

*

Turner's *Fountain of Indolence* and Freud's *Hotel Bedroom* are very different paintings, created more than a century apart, but the battle between the foundation and the gallery linked them in the public consciousness. In the language of the dispute, they were now a pair, the-Turner-and-the-Freud. That was what people called them, and that was what people came to see. For the gallery, the bright side of the dispute was the jump in the number of visitors following the 2004 news reports that the foundation wanted to remove the-Turner-and-the-Freud.

Laura Ritchie, the acting registrar of the gallery when the arbitration hearings unfolded in the fall of 2006, told me that Turner's *Fountain of Indolence*, painted in 1834, "is a good example, a prime example, of the romantic Picturesque British landscape," a reference to the Picturesque movement in which artists saw landscape, not as mere background, but as the thematic centre of their works. "We're lucky to have this piece in our collection because it's one of the few masterworks that we have that represents so poignantly a particular time period in art history. . . . That's of real importance: that we can say we contribute to the great chain of art history in terms of British landscape painting." The picture is a realistic depiction of a fanciful scene, a group of Cupid-like figures cavorting around a fountain beneath Greek or Roman pillars. It is based on a poem by James Thomson, "The Castle of Indolence," the first canto of which describes the scene Turner painted:

> *. . . they to the fountain sped*
> *That in the middle of the court up-threw*
> *A stream, high spouting from its liquid bed,*
> *And falling back again in drizzly dew;*
> *There each deep draughts, as deep he thirsted drew,*
> *It was a fountain of nepenthe rare;*
> *Whence, as Dan Homer sings, huge pleasaunce grew,*
> *And sweet oblivion of vile earthly care;*
> *Fair gladsome waking thoughts, and joyous dreams*
>   *more fair.*

> *This rite perform'd, all inly pleas'd and still,*
> *Withouten tromp, was proclamation made:*
> *"Ye sons of Indolence, do what you will,*
> *And wander where you list, through hall or glade;*
> *Be no man's pleasure for another stay'd;*

Let each as likes him best his hours employ,
And curs'd be he who minds his neighbour's trade;
Here dwells kind ease and unreproving joy:
He little merits bliss who others can annoy."[2]

"It's a pleasureful scene," Ritchie said with some understatement. "You would enjoy being there." Its value to the gallery was considerable; it was, after all, part of the original collection Lord Beaverbrook assembled in the 1950s. "The Turner, *The Fountain of Indolence*, that's a name that rings true to a lot of people as a prominent work at the Beaverbrook Art Gallery," she said.

The other half of the-Turner-and-the-Freud pair, Freud's *Hotel Bedroom*, was equally irreplaceable, "one of our best examples of modern British painting," Ritchie said, and the only canvas of the artist's on display in a public gallery in Canada. Beaverbrook had acquired it in 1955, when Freud, the grandson of Sigmund Freud, entered it in the Young Artists Exhibition sponsored by the press baron's flagship newspaper, the *Daily Express*. The jury, which included Graham Sutherland, another painter represented in the gallery, awarded young Freud second place, and Beaverbrook immediately added *Hotel Bedroom* to his collection. "From the get-go Lord Beaverbrook knew that Lucian Freud was going to be a prominent figure in art history, which he has proven to be," Ritchie said. Freud's renown reached such heights that when he asked, in 2000, if he could paint a portrait of Queen Elizabeth to present to her as a gift, she agreed.

Hotel Bedroom, which Freud created just as he was shifting from surrealism to realism, depicts him in shadow at a window, glaring at his second wife, Caroline Blackwood, who lies in bed in the foreground, apparently in distress. "I actually heard that she wasn't that flattered at all" by the painting, Ritchie said. Blackwood herself would recall, "It was the winter, when everyone was freezing in Paris, and that's why I was sort of huddled under the bed clothes. . . . We were tense because [Lucian] didn't have a studio, and the room was so small that Lucian broke the window because he couldn't get distance enough to paint. It was never repaired, and that's why I look so miserable and cold."[3]

"It's personally not one of my favourites, but I think its story is one of the more interesting," Ritchie said, adding that the layout is adapted from another work Freud had done of himself with his first wife. Because *Hotel Bedroom* was smaller than the Turner, Ritchie said, it was visually accessible to gallery visitors. Its size also meant that it was more easily loaned. In 1998, it had been a cornerstone of the Beaverbrook Art Gallery's exhibition *Sargent to Freud*, which had toured internationally until 2000.

In 2005, the gallery's director, Bernard Riordon, had decided to capitalize on the renewed interest that the dispute had provoked in the-Turner-and-the-Freud. He assembled all 211 of the works in both disputes into an exhibition, *Art in Dispute*, that transformed the legal feud into a marketing coup. Gallery staff had filled each wall from ceiling to floor with the paintings, creating a powerful tableau of Beaverbrook's legacy. Thousands upon thousands came to see the show, shattering previous gallery records. It had been a triumph for the New Brunswick-born Riordon, who, after a successful career at the Art Gallery of Nova Scotia, had come home for a short stint at the Beaverbrook before retirement. He had his ambitions for the gallery, calling it "a sleeping giant" that he hoped to awaken. Instead, he found himself caught up in a tangle of court filings, procedural motions and affidavits. In that swirl of rancour, *Art in Dispute* had been a precious moment in which the beauty of the art itself had come to the fore. "Some people said it was very cheeky, in the sense of in-your-face to the other side," Riordon says. "It wasn't meant that way."

Had the director wanted to be truly cheeky or in-your-face, he might have left a large empty space on one of the walls of the exhibition, measuring about five-and-a-half feet by four, to symbolize the third painting at the heart of the dispute, one that no one had seen in New Brunswick for a generation: Thomas Gainsborough's *Peasant Girl Gathering Faggots*. It had been Beaverbrook's favourite, and he had thrilled in its purchase and in its arrival at his Fredericton gallery. Less than two decades later, in 1977, it had been removed, and its fate, as much as that of the-Turner-and-the-Freud, would come to symbolize what the gallery saw as an attack on its collection.

*

Faye Matchett was feeling as besieged as Bernard Riordon in the midst of the battle over Beaverbrook's art. Unlike the gallery director, however, she lacked even the minimal resources to turn the nastiness into something beneficial.

Matchett had been one of five people to apply for the job of caretaker of the Old Manse, the house in the town of Newcastle where Lord Beaverbrook had spent his childhood. The job involved living in and maintaining the Second Empire-style house, built in 1879 and now owned by the city, and sprucing up its small collection of Beaverbrook artifacts. "In the end I was the only one interviewed," Matchett said as she led me through the house in October 2006. "I was interested in coming here because of the beauty of the home and the privilege to live in it. I wish I had got to know Lord Beaverbrook. Unfortunately, I didn't, but it's a very big honour to live here. And I give a hundred per cent to it. I'd love to see it back the way he had it. That is my dream. And I wish he was still living so he could see it. I think he would be very proud."

More likely, Beaverbrook — who devoted a great deal of time and attention to the monuments to himself scattered around New Brunswick — would be appalled and would quickly put in place one of his elaborate schemes to correct the situation. For the Old Manse was in terrible shape during my tour. Some rooms managed to be rough approximations of what they might have been in the last decade of the nineteenth century, but others, such as those still rented out by the city to distance-education programs, utterly lacked historical character. There were water stains on the ceilings where rain had leaked through the damaged roof. Outside, paint was peeling off the walls, and the front steps were so rotten they had been declared unsafe.

Matchett's grasp of the Beaverbrook legend seemed equally ramshackle. She was hired as a caretaker, after all, not a historian. She related, inaccurately, that Beaverbrook's entire family "went back to England" when he was seventeen, when in fact his parents and siblings had remained in Canada. In one of the few rooms with a decent collection of artifacts, she pointed out an ornate walking stick "that belonged to R.J. Bennett. He was prime minister of Great Britain." While Beaverbrook had known several British prime ministers and had even helped remove one from office, the walking stick had, in fact, belonged to his lifelong friend R.B. Bennett, the thirtieth prime minister of Canada.

But how much could one expect, really, when there wasn't enough money for basic maintenance to keep the harsh weather at bay, never mind a few decent display cases or a trained historian to work on the collection? Once, the Beaverbrook Canadian Foundation had given the city of Miramichi — an amalgamation of the old towns of Newcastle, where Max grew up, and Chatham, where he first worked with R.B. Bennett — ten thousand dollars a year, half for the house and half to maintain the small main square a few blocks away, where Beaverbrook's ashes are encased in a plinth topped with a massive bust of the man. In 2004, even that tiny subsidy had vanished when the foundation cancelled all its support of New Brunswick causes to protest the gallery's and the provincial government's intransigence in the art dispute.

"This summer, when we had two students here," Matchett said, "I actually got one of the students to e-mail this grandson who's in the dispute to say, We would love you to come and visit your grandfather's home. Like, come and see what he's doing to his grandfather's home, how it's deteriorating. Of course, we never got any response from him."

She paused to look at a newspaper front page from 1954, commemorating Beaverbrook's seventy-fifth birthday. In a photograph, the aging press baron clutches his grandson Maxwell, just a toddler, on his knee. "He's a darling there in the picture," Matchett said, "but he's not now. Sometimes I think money's the root of all evil. They're not poor by any means and they want to do something like this, take all this art back there."

*

Matchett's understanding of the dispute was no better than her knowledge of Beaverbrook's impressive life story, but she was not alone. Like many other New Brunswickers, she had accepted the conventional wisdom that the Aitkens stood to profit personally from the sale of the-Turner-and-the-Freud. That perception had been shaped in 2004, early in the dispute, by a few acerbic remarks from a former gallery curator, some carelessly written newspaper headlines, and a couple of angry outbursts from Maxwell's cousin Timothy. The perception had stuck. And though most New Brunswickers' lives would not be materially affected at all by the removal of two paintings from an art gallery that most of them had never visited, people in the province were outraged by the very thought of it.

New Brunswickers, particularly those in Fredericton, had rallied to the gallery's side to the extent that the provincial government felt compelled, in 2004, to lend the gallery $1 million of public money so it could hire the very best lawyers to fight the Aitkens. And they would need the very best lawyers, for there was a paper trail dating back forty years that showed, with remarkable consistency and precision, that the gallery did *not* own the paintings. It had, in fact, repeatedly acknowledged for years that they were owned by the very foundation that now wanted them back.

This forced the gallery's lawyers to come up with a rather elaborate explanation for how gallery officials had, for four decades, apparently overlooked the evidence that they now suddenly claimed to have uncovered. This oversight was, according to one gallery document, the result of "a series of abuses" following the death of Lord Beaverbrook.[4] The lawyers were alleging, in effect, a conspiracy by his heirs to deliberately misrepresent the ownership of the paintings to the very gallery staff responsible for the ownership records and to conceal evidence that Beaverbrook had intended all along to give the paintings to New Brunswick as outright gifts.

Kent Thomson, one foot tapping silently behind the podium on which his notes rested, asked Lady Aitken how she'd reacted to that allegation of a conspiracy. "Complete shock and anger," she replied, her words increasingly clipped. "I can't understand the vilification. It's unbelievable, besides being totally libellous." What had angered her and the family even more, however, was the suggestion that she, her son and other members of the Aitken family stood to gain personally from the sale of the two paintings. "It is outrageous to suggest it. There is no question of benefiting."

And then there was the final indignity. In the rush of media coverage after the dispute became public in 2004, when journalists were tracking down anyone they could find with a connection to the gallery, no one — not one person — had even remotely suggested that, just possibly, the Aitkens might be right, that they perhaps could have a case, that the foundations might be perfectly entitled to ask for the return of the paintings. "We thought we had friends in New Brunswick," Lady Aitken said. "We always worked in partnership. There wasn't one single person who stood up in our defence."

"I thought we had friends in New Brunswick," she repeated. "Obviously I was mistaken."

And with that, Thomson thanked her, and the arbitrator, Peter Cory, suggested it was time for a break. Thomson led the Aitkens out of the room, past the reporters again and into a small office off a side corridor that was reserved for his firm's use.

When Lady Aitken returned to the witness chair after the break, the gallery's lawyer, Larry Lowenstein, rose and told Cory that he would not be cross-examining her.

"Nobody is going to ask me any questions?" she asked, her blue eyes darting from Lowenstein to Thomson to Cory.

"There will be no questions," Cory said with a smile, "as much as everyone would have appreciated it."

Lowenstein would explain to reporters later, "Those are the decisions counsel makes, as to whether the witness has said things that are relevant or harmful to the real issues in the dispute, and you can draw your own conclusions." He was suggesting that because Lady Aitken had acknowledged she had never seen the ownership documents for the paintings, her opinions and observations, though entertaining and occasionally sensational, were meaningless to the case. He did not need to challenge her on anything she'd said.

Cory called an early lunch break and again the Aitkens dispersed, retreating to the lawyers' room. Thomson's junior colleagues were sent out to bring them plates of food, which had been laid out on a table as part of the conference centre's services. Reporters spent the lunch break analyzing with each other what Lady Aitken had said, filing early versions of their stories or trying to get the two muscular "friends" to cough up information.

At one o'clock the hearing resumed. Maxwell, his left arm tucked into his pocket to conceal a birth defect, walked up the centre aisle of the room, past the tables of lawyers, towards the witness chair. His grandfather had not left him any money, a fact much commented upon over the years. Fortunately, Beaverbrook hadn't passed on his puckish features, either. Maxwell is handsome, if blandly so, and his eyes that afternoon conveyed a hint of boredom but also a sense of duty.

Maxwell was not in an introspective mood during this visit to New Brunswick. He was here to perform a task, an unpleasant but unavoidable one. "We had a very focused three days," he would explain later.[5] He had not taken the time to travel up to Miramichi to assess the state of the Old Manse or to inspect the little park around his grandfather's ashes. Nor had he paid a discreet visit to the art gallery to gaze at the Turner and the Freud. During the lunch break, he had remained cloistered with his family and the lawyers, choosing not to slip downstairs into the darkened Chancellor's Room to study the portrait of his mother.

And Maxwell had certainly not stopped to look at the bronze bust of the old man behind the glass, the man whose name was above the door of the conference centre. If he had, he might have realized that it, too, said much about the status of the House of Beaverbrook in New Brunswick.

Wu Yee-Sun, the man cast in bronze, had grown up in Hong Kong, rising to become chairman of Wing Lung Bank and then using a considerable portion of his riches to promote his passion, the botanical art of Penjing.[6] He had also established a foundation for charitable works, and because members of his family had studied at the University of New Brunswick, the foundation helped to build the Wu Centre, now the venue for the final unravelling of the Beaverbrook connection to New Brunswick. The bust represented a new benefactor, a new orientation, and a new era for a university and a city peppered with buildings named Beaverbrook or Aitken. The British Empire that Maxwell's grandfather had loved and had sought to revive and sustain was gone; at the start of the new century, New Brunswick was looking to Asia for its future, to Beijing and Hong Kong and Singapore. London was no longer the centre of the universe, and the whims and requests and demands that emanated from that city no longer prompted the worthies of little Fredericton to snap to attention.

Maxwell, who, unlike his father, Sir Max, *had* claimed the title Lord Beaverbrook, settled into his seat. There had been a time when that name had meant something — everything — in this province. No longer. It was now just another name over a door.

His mother's words from earlier in the day still hung in the air: "I thought we had friends in New Brunswick. Obviously I was mistaken."

The Age of Beaverbrook had come to an end.

Cherkley Court, 1925.

Beaverbrook U.K. Foundation

CHAPTER TWO

"This was his hour"

The Aitken family's long journey to that 2006 arbitration hearing began one day in the spring of 1889, as the steamboat *Miramichi*, named for the river on which it travelled, prepared for the five-mile journey upstream from Douglastown to Newcastle, a logging community in northeast New Brunswick. That particular morning, nineteen-year-old R.B. Bennett, the schoolmaster in Douglastown, was waiting at the wharf when he was spotted by a ten-year-old boy with sparkling eyes and a broad, grinning mouth: William Maxwell Aitken. Dick Bennett "was slight of figure, with a freckled face," his new acquaintance would remember. "He was wearing a Derby hat a bit too big for him. His clothes were neat and for our community he would be described as a well-dressed young man." Young Max was returning home to Newcastle, the county seat, where his father, the Reverend William Aitken, was the minister at St. James Presbyterian Church. Bennett paid the ten-cent fare, Aitken boarded for free, and, he would recall, "in that short journey I formed a strong friendship that lasted for more than fifty years."[1]

The two friends were very different. The schoolmaster, a Methodist from Albert County almost a hundred miles to the south, "was noted for rectitude and godliness. I had a bad reputation for mischievous conduct."[2] But Aitken had found a mentor and idol to inspire him. "Bennett, who was marked with distinguished abilities and splendid force of character even in his young manhood, exercised a complete influence on me. He aroused my ambitions and steadied my purpose."[3] Their encounter marked the start of a pattern: for many years, young Aitken would attach himself to older, wiser men to learn the ways of the world. His father later wrote Bennett, "Your influence on him in the past has, I know, been very beneficial. Max is the better for having someone near him, to whom he can look with respect and for guidance."[4] So powerful was the bond that, Aitken later wrote, when Bennett left teaching a year later to pursue a career in law, "I settled that I would be a lawyer too under his influence."[5]

Max did not immediately adopt Bennett's self-discipline, however. At sixteen he sat for the entrance examinations for the law school at Dalhousie University in Halifax. The third day was devoted to "Greek or Latin or both and my hostility to these dead languages overwhelmed me from the very outset. Revulsion set in. The paper was solemnly returned to the examiner with my declaration that a university career held no attractions as it involved unnecessary and even useless labour in futile educational pursuits."[6] In those days, a degree in law was not required, provided that one articled with a lawyer. Bennett had joined the firm of Lemuel J. Tweedie in Chatham, a nearby town on the Miramichi River, so Aitken persuaded Tweedie to take him on as well. Even then, there were indications of how Aitken would reverse his apprenticeships to become the dominant force. "Do you know that after he had been in my office for a month," Tweedie told Aitken's future business partner in Chatham, H.E. Borradaile, "I was not sure whether he was working for me or I for him." And when Chatham was incorporated into a town in 1896, Aitken, then seventeen years old, encouraged Bennett to seek office as an alderman and organized his successful election campaign, using his bicycle to distribute leaflets for the man who would one day become prime minister of Canada. Borradaile recounted how Aitken watched one spring as the current pushed the river ice up onto the banks to snap the trunk of a large tree. "If I could harness that power," Aitken told him, "there would be nothing I could not do."[7]

Remote Newcastle, with its population of 1,500 and its reliance on the logging industry, was not large enough to accommodate the ambitions of young Max Aitken. Throughout his life he would nurture the myth that his early life had been hard. But though the Manse where the Aitkens lived lacked electricity and plumbing, it was one of the first houses in town to have a telephone, and the Reverend Aitken had the means to build up a large library that included Charlotte Brontë and *Don Quixote*.[8] Max, the youngest of ten children, had been born in Maple, Ontario, his father's second Canadian posting after arriving from Scotland, and was a year old when the family moved to Newcastle. He found family life happy but formal, saying it was "difficult to recollect any evidence of warmth in the relations of my parents and yet there is no occasion when a quarrel comes to my memory. My mother invariably spoke of her husband and to him as Mr. Aitken. And I cannot recall any time when my mother was called Jane."[9] While watching his father officiate at funerals, young Max acquired his lifelong preoccupation with illness and death.

Max was something of a loner within the family, and he had a mischievous streak. He would claim that he inherited his high spirits from his mother and received his intelligence from an accident in which a mowing machine struck him in the head. "When I returned to consciousness after the accident, I was a clever boy! . . . The crack which the wheel gave to my skull possibly gave the brain room to expand, which it needed." His penchant for enterprise manifested itself first in journalism, when, at thirteen, he launched a little newspaper called *The Leader*. Reverend Aitken quickly shut it down, however, when delays pushed the Saturday production of the paper into the early hours of Sunday, a violation of the Sabbath.[10] Max then became the Newcastle correspondent and salesman for the *Daily Sun*, a newspaper published in the industrial port city of Saint John, two hundred and fifty miles to the south. When his salary did not arrive promptly, he began paying himself — much to the consternation of the paper's distant managers — out of the subscription fees he'd collected, an early lesson, one biography noted, in the principle that "keeping pieces of paper was an important element of the art of self-defence."[11]

Aitken was disappointed and saddened when Dick Bennett, his idol, left Chatham in 1897 to take an offer from a Conservative law firm in Calgary. Passed over to replace him as a partner in Tweedie's firm, Aitken went through a nomadic phase, heading first to Saint John to try his luck at the law school there. Lonely and homesick, he followed Bennett to Calgary six months later and helped with Bennett's 1898 campaign for a seat in the territorial legislature. Aitken "had sworn off drinking and smoking the year before, but there is no evidence he was able to hold to that." Bennett told him, "'If only your industry equalled your energy!'"[12] Rather than become a lawyer, Aitken invested in a bowling alley, was soon bored, and moved to Edmonton, where he encountered James Dunn, another expatriate New Brunswicker whom he and Bennett had both known back home. When Dunn decided to make his fortune in Montreal instead, declaring that "the west must pay tribute to the east," Aitken followed him and continued on to New Brunswick. In Saint John again, he tried selling insurance.

Then, during a fishing party on his twenty-first birthday, he had his epiphany. He met a young man from Nova Scotia, his name soon forgotten, who had gone to the United States and found great success. "Something in the expatriate lad's manner and way of talking, his delineation of new ideas of effort and achievement set the match to the tow of latent and fiery ambition which must have been present below the threshold in the mind of one of his hearers," Aitken would explain. "I never loafed again. I seemed to shake off in an hour of reflection the careless habits of my early years. My intellectual make-up remained the same, but a sudden and tremendous reinforcement was given to the active and aggressive side of my character. Effort was worth while, labour was rewarding, ambition was a worthy goal."[13]

Aitken settled in Halifax, the commercial centre of the Maritimes. He began selling bonds and latched on to another mentor, the well-connected financier John F. Stairs. Aitken went to work for Stairs, investing his profits in a company he set up, Royal Securities Corporation, with Stairs and other partners. It was soon raising capital for electricity projects in the Caribbean and South America. Aitken's successes mounted, and when Stairs died in 1904, he was able to take over the business and put together ever larger deals. In 1906 he took over the Montreal Trust Company and moved to Montreal with his wife, Gladys, whom he'd married earlier that year.[14]

Three years later came Aitken's greatest coup, the so-called Canada Cement affair, which increased his fortune while at the same time darkening his reputation. Even his most tenacious biographers, Anne Chisholm and Michael Davie, acknowledge the difficulty of precisely reconstructing the sequence of events.[15] The allegation was that, in overseeing the merger of several cement companies to create a near-monopoly, Aitken misled investors and issued himself bonds and shares in a way that vastly padded his profits. At the same time, 1910, he and Gladys and their two young children, Janet and Max, left Canada to live in England; this move was seen as further proof of his guilt. A 1996 analysis by Gregory Marchildon, a professor of economic history, makes a persuasive case that Aitken's profit was not the $12 million alleged by his chief accuser, Sandford Fleming, but was closer to $600,000. "Aitken had a right under the raw logic of capitalism to take a cut" of the successful merger, Marchildon concluded.[16] At the time, however, the deal attracted the scrutiny of the federal government; one cabinet minister warned him he would "incur strictures" if he kept it up.[17]

While the controversy simmered in Canada, Aitken began his remarkable rise in England. His purchase of controlling interest in Rolls-Royce in the summer of 1910 brought him into contact with men of influence in the Conservative Party, then known as the Conservative-Unionists. By the end of the year, with the support of a fellow expatriate New Brunswicker, Andrew Bonar Law, a member of the British House of Commons, he'd been nominated as the party's candidate for Ashton-under-Lyne, near Manchester, and became an MP. Law became Aitken's new Bennett.

The following spring, Aitken was knighted, he said, for "the purposes of rewarding me for services to come."[18] This meant, in Aitken's case, something other than a simple donation to the party in exchange for an honour: his biographer A.J.P. Taylor suggests that Aitken's subsequent investment in the *Globe* newspaper was backed by party funds, making him a conduit that allowed the Conservatives to influence the paper toward their own ends. Though he showed little interest in the running of the paper, it was the first, early sign of the power and influence he would one day enjoy. That he held such a position in England makes it hard to imagine why he still held out hope of returning to New Brunswick and launching a political career there. In any event, that ambition was quashed when the Canada Cement affair was injected into Canada's 1911 reciprocity election, turning him into a liability for the Canadian Conservatives.

*

Five days after the election, in which his Halifax friend Robert Borden became Conservative Prime Minister of Canada, Aitken confirmed that he was in England for good. He paid £25,000 for Cherkley Court, a large grey stone house in the Surrey countryside one hour by car from London. "For the next fifty-three years, Cherkley saw as much political, social and sexual intrigue as any house in England," his biographers would write.[19] The house featured a porticoed entrance, towers and a terrace looking onto the gardens, as well as a stable, a mile-long driveway and a forest of yews and beeches that afforded the new owner the privacy he sought. It lacked central heating, electricity and modern plumbing, all of which Aitken installed, along with a swimming pool and tennis court. "Architecturally it had little to recommend it," his daughter Janet recalled, "but the view from each of its thirty-one rooms was breathtaking." Among the guests in the early years were some of the most powerful men in England, including Andrew Bonar Law, by then leader of the Conservatives, Liberal leader David Lloyd George, and, later, Winston Churchill. Among the writers in Aitken's ever-widening social circle were W.B. Yeats, H.G. Wells and Rudyard Kipling. Janet said her father "was a good host but a bad guest," avoiding social events he could not control and preferring that people come to him.[20] Which they did. "History has been made, conversation has sparkled, thoughts have been bold and ambition has run high" on the veranda at Cherkley, Aitken's acolyte Michael Wardell would reminisce many years later.[21]

At Cherkley, Aitken plotted many of the moves that solidified his power. He had bought into the *Globe* to create a soft landing for the editor of another paper that was floundering, the *Daily Express*; the Conservatives wanted the *Express* to survive, but they wanted its editor, R.D. Blumenfeld, out. When the *Express* went into receivership, Aitken moved to buy it but was outbid by a faction of Tory supporters anxious to maintain their own influence on the paper. In 1916, he finally acquired control, just as a leadership crisis within the British government was reaching a climax. Aitken's friend Bonar Law had agreed to bring the Conservatives into a coalition government headed by Liberal Herbert Asquith. With the First World War going badly for the British, Asquith's position was soon besieged. Aitken sought to manoeuvre Law, his fellow New Brunswicker, into the prime minister's chair, but Law's participation in the coalition had cost him support within his own party. Law "did not possess that supreme passion of patriotism which enables a man to be ruthless for the public good,"[22] in Aitken's words, and another Liberal, David Lloyd George, emerged as prime minister, supported by both Law and Aitken. In the midst of this drama — one that would contribute much to his legend — Aitken was elevated from his simple knighthood to the House of Lords, over the objections of King George V, and took the title Lord Beaverbrook, after a stream near Newcastle.

Beaverbrook joined the cabinet in January 1918 as Minister of Information, a position Lloyd George felt suited him given his success as the quasi-official, self-appointed "Canadian Eye Witness," the Dominion's publicist for its contribution to the war effort. In this role, he fed stories to Canadian war correspondents, brought Canadian authors to Europe to write books, and created the Canadian War Memorials Fund, which commissioned British and Canadian artists to paint scenes of the battlefield. "The function of propaganda is the formation of public opinion," Beaverbrook would explain. "The method is to tell the truth but to present it in an acceptable form."[23] To achieve this, naturally, the minister needed access to all the intelligence of the war, which in turn only enhanced his standing. At the same time, his eminence led to clashes with the Foreign Office; this inability to work peaceably with others in authority demonstrated "that Beaverbrook was ill-suited to be a minister except in abnormal circumstances, a fact he fully appreciated himself. He would not be a subordinate unless he could turn his leader into a hero as he did with John F. Stairs, Bonar Law and later Churchill. He had to be the boss, issuing orders without respect for protocol or the rights of others."[24] He resigned from the cabinet in October, a month before the armistice.

The fall of the Lloyd George coalition government in 1922 gives another glimpse of the extent to which Beaverbrook, in just over a decade, had mastered the Byzantine workings of British politics: he orchestrated Andrew Bonar Law's return from retirement and ascension into the prime minister's chair. When Law was diagnosed with cancer and resigned only seven months later, however, Beaverbrook's leverage was gone. He was no admirer of Law's replacement, Stanley Baldwin, and declared his independence from Baldwin's Conservative government. "If I am expected to conform blindly to anything that executive may choose to do, however wrong I may think it," he told Churchill, "I would rather go back to my own little village in Canada — where there is good fishing."[25] Instead of returning home, he devoted his full attention to the *Daily Express*, having sold the money-losing *Globe* in 1914. "What we want," he once explained, "is a newspaper which fulfils neither the desires of the extreme highbrow, nor of the groper in the mud of life, but of the ordinary men and women of culture in any walk of life who require sound news and good views put before them in an attractive manner."[26] He invested more money in the paper, gave it a flashier appearance, and installed better managers, though he was forever looking over their shoulders, barking instructions.[27] He inspired fear but also affection and loyalty, creating "an atmosphere that reflected his own combative nature: here on the sunny side of the street was the Beaverbrook press, and on the other side was the rest of the world. His staff knew they had to satisfy one reader only."[28]

In coordination with his friend Lord Rothermere, owner of the *Daily Mail*, Beaverbrook used the *Express* to champion the cause of Empire Free Trade, the belief that Britain and its dominions, including Canada, should lower tariffs against each other but raise them to keep out the goods of other nations. The power of the press to advance a cause, Beaverbrook said, was "a flaming sword which will cut through any political armour." Even some great newspapers, he continued, could not influence policy or break governments because "they do not know how to strike or when to strike. . . . They are in themselves unloaded guns. But teach the man behind them how to load and what to shoot at, and they become deadly."[29]

Beaverbrook's efforts went far beyond a mere editorial crusade: in 1930, he established a new political party, the United Empire Party, designed to contest by-elections and thereby harass the Conservatives into adopting a more robustly pro-Empire policy. But the crusade backfired by giving Baldwin an opening to make Beaverbrook and Rothermere the issue during a 1931 by-election. In a fiery speech, he denounced their papers as "engines of propaganda for the constantly changing policies, desires, personal wishes, personal likes and dislikes of two men. . . . What the proprietorship of these papers is aiming at is power, but power without responsibility — the prerogative of the harlot throughout the ages." Baldwin's Conservative candidate won and a truce was declared, with Beaverbrook ending the crusade and Baldwin adopting some quotas and duties on agricultural imports.[30]

Beaverbrook's single-mindedness on Empire Free Trade nearly cost him the friendship of his onetime mentor, R.B. Bennett, who had become leader of the Conservatives in Canada. In May of 1930, Beaverbrook gave an interview to the Toronto *Globe* praising the budget of Bennett's Liberal opponent, Prime Minister Mackenzie King, because it lowered the tariff on British goods. But the newspaper held the interview until the election campaign later that year, making it appear that Beaverbrook was intervening against his old friend.[31] Bennett won the election but felt betrayed, and at an Imperial Conference later that year declared that Empire Free Trade was "neither desirable nor possible."[32] Instead, he offered a modest tariff deal to Baldwin, who accepted it, marginalizing Beaverbrook. "He was hitting back and, according to his life-long practise, he was hitting hard," Beaverbrook concluded.[33] The two old Chatham friends reconciled, but Bennett still would not embrace the cause, rebuffing Beaverbrook's offer to advise him as chairman of the 1932 Imperial Conference, held in Ottawa. The bond endured, however: following

Bennett's stinging, Depression-induced defeat in the election of 1935, he exiled himself to England, buying Juniper Hill, a sixty-acre estate adjacent to Cherkley, and becoming a frequent guest of his former protégé.

*

Beaverbrook often found himself on the wrong side of history, crusading to save an empire that was destined to wither away, arguing against modern notions such as independence for India, or declaring Joseph Stalin "an excellent character." In the abdication crisis of 1936, his dislike of stuffy, puritanical British manners led him to side with the King.[34] Beaverbrook agreed to Edward's request that the *Express* not report on his relationship with Wallis Simpson, nor on her divorce — her second — and he persuaded other proprietors to do likewise, even though American and European newspapers were carrying these stories. When it became clear that Edward intended to marry her, Prime Minister Stanley Baldwin told the monarch that the British people and the government were opposed, raising the possibility of a constitutional crisis if the King defied the will of Parliament. Beaverbrook, en route by ship to the United States as the controversy broke, disembarked in New York and promptly turned around and sailed home. He urged the King to play for time and sought in vain to meet with Mrs. Simpson to persuade her to withdraw. Instead, Edward abdicated on December 10. "I thought he made the wrong decision," Beaverbrook said much later. "I think he should have stayed. [The British people] would have accepted her. . . . Responsibility would have made her, I think. She would have been a different character altogether, probably. He was wrong to run away from his responsibilities. If he wanted to marry the woman of his choice, why not?"[35] Given Edward's apparent disdain for the will of Parliament and his subsequently revealed sympathy for Adolf Hitler, many came to see the abdication as a fortunate turn of events.

Beaverbrook's most profound error, though he was hardly alone in it, was his opposition to war with Germany. Ribbentrop, Hitler's foreign minister, dined at Cherkley in 1936 and invited Beaverbrook to the Berlin Olympics. He accepted, accompanied by his daughter Janet and son Max. During the opening ceremonies, Janet was summoned to meet Hitler. His hand "felt boneless, like a piece of wet meat, clammy and soft," she remembered. "There was nothing there; no warmth, no voice, not even an awareness. The eyes were unfathomable, the jaw strong enough, but the man himself seemed totally lacking in any sexuality; without substance, inhuman."[36] Beaverbrook would say how he hated "the regimentation of opinion" he witnessed during the trip, but nonetheless he split with Churchill over Germany, calling his friend "a war monger" and instructing an *Express* journalist, "He must be stopped. Go get him."[37] He predicted repeatedly that there would be no war, congratulated Chamberlain on his Munich agreement with Hitler, and declared Poland, the day after it was invaded by Germany, "no friend of ours."[38] Two decades later, he would explain, "I thought we shouldn't have any truck with Europe at all. We should stand aside and let them fight it out amongst themselves. We should stick to our own people and in companionship with the United States have nothing to do with their squabbles. But when Britain was dragged into the war, naturally, all British citizens were dragged into the war too."[39]

Beaverbrook was dragged, in fact, into another episode that would become part of his legend when Churchill, two days after being named prime minister, appointed him minister of aircraft production, splitting that responsibility away from the air ministry. Churchill had appreciated for a quarter of a century Beaverbrook's "power to inspire and drive, his ability to get at the heart of a problem at speed, his refusal to despair or admit defeat."[40] Their differences over the case for war were forgotten now as the minister, refusing to draw a salary, tossed aside bureaucratic niceties and pushed his factories to catch up to the Luftwaffe. "This was no time for red tape and circumlocution," Churchill himself would say in his memoirs. "He did not fail. This was his hour. . . . His personal force and genius, combined with so much persuasion and contrivance, swept aside many obstacles. Everything in the supply pipe-line was drawn forward to the battle. New or repaired airplanes streamed to the delighted squadrons in numbers they had never known before. All the services of mainten-

ance and repair were driven to an intense degree."[41] His reputation as
a war hero was secure.

*

Beaverbrook was not nearly as sure-footed in his relationship with his
family. In the 1930s, not long after Gladys's death in 1927, he said
that she "had a more lively interest in me than I had in her. I had my
business, my affairs, my liabilities, all pressing on me every hour of the
day. . . . I had not married under any very compelling desire for marriage. It had been to some extent a matter of convenience with me. I
had been moved by two factors, (1) I was eligible as it is called, and
a good deal sought after, and (2) a statement by I.C. Mackintosh that
if I was to have a permanent place in Montreal, I must have a family.
And so I made what I thought to be the best marriage. I do not say
that I made her life easier for her but I can claim that I made it more
interesting and exciting." Beaverbrook's biographer A.J.P. Taylor for-
gives this callous comment by suggesting that Beaverbrook "was being
unfair to his younger self," yet he acknowledges that Beaverbrook
was at heart a loner, "switching people on and off according to his
mood," for whom his friends and his wife "ceased to exist" when he
turned to other things. He "could never quite understand that people,
especially those close to him, wanted steady, quiet affection rather
than a shower of gifts and the occasional excitement of his stimulating
company."[42] In his memoir published in *The Atlantic Advocate* and,
posthumously, in book form as *My Early Life*, Beaverbrook describes
Gladys as "simple, though clever, and most beautiful, with charm and
sympathy," and he edits his earlier dismissal to the more benign statement that "my wife had a lively interest in me."[43]

As did many other women. He had several affairs, not bothering
to conceal them from Gladys or his children. His daughter Janet confronted him about his dalliance with the actress Tallulah Bankhead.
"Father was defiant, telling me to shut up and mind my own business." Janet was forgiving, writing in her memoirs that he was "caught
up in Tallulah's web." She could barely acknowledge that "it was as if
he *wanted* to do what he did." The affair with Bankhead ended when

an acquaintance, Richard Norton, introduced Beaverbrook to his wife, Jean; that introduction launched a long and serious relationship. Appallingly, he even brought Jean to Cherkley, compelling Gladys to play hostess to his mistress.[44]

Beaverbrook's serial philandering intersected with his dysfunctional family life again in 1935. He had had a brief affair with a model named Catherine Koopman, nicknamed Toto, who had Dutch and Javanese ancestry. When his son Max began seeing her, Beaverbrook took to calling her "that black woman" and banned mentions of her from the *Express*. He tried to bribe Max into giving her up, offering him first a car and then an important job and unlimited money. When Max refused, Beaverbrook shipped him out of London to a position at the *Scottish Daily Express*, prompting the couple to flee to Spain. When they returned to England, Beaverbrook offered Max "a lot of money" not to marry Toto. She told him to take it, and they lived together, unwed but in financial comfort, for four years.[45]

Young Max never had an easy relationship with his father. Beaverbrook's second son, Peter, was quieter and closer to his mother; he "developed a habit of retiring into himself and saying nothing," Janet remembered, and eventually cut his father out of his life almost completely.[46] Max, though academically not a success, was tall and dashing, and he found himself oppressed by his father's expectations, longing to please him but unable to make himself into what his father wanted: an heir apparent who shared his father's passions. Beaverbrook would regularly recruit other young men as protégés, then threaten Max that he planned to groom one of them, not him, to take over the newspapers. At the same time, it seems, Beaverbrook, "like many men who have become rich by their own efforts . . . resented his children's advantages, and something in him despised them for being what his wealth had made them." Max wrote to one girlfriend, whom his father was trying to stop him from marrying, "He is frightfully jealous of you because he used to be the only person I would go to the ends of the earth for. . . . He is the loneliest man I know. Everyone is frightened of him because he has such unlimited power. And I seem to be the only person he will confide in and who he enjoys having around." Beaverbrook, in collaboration with his friend Lord Castlerosse, even used his own newspaper to take an extraordinary public swipe at Max, publishing an article, "Pity These Great Men's Sons," in which Castlerosse compared Max and other heirs in London society to "pigeons . . . aping the habits and fine feathers of peacocks. . . . They seem to think that fate and fatherhood have ordained them to immediate importance and command. . . . History proves almost indisputably that major fathers as a rule breed minor sons, so our little London peacocks had better tone down their fine feathers and start trying to make a name of their own."[47]

Beaverbrook's daughter Janet fared little better. He could be cruel to her, choosing when she had a problem "to stand back, offer no advice and let me work things out for myself," patching things up "with a present of money or too much praise for something I didn't deserve, and a hug and a kiss." Her most searing memory is her description of how her father was "constantly taking my ponies and horses away from me throughout my childhood and early teens. As far as I was concerned, it was the ultimate punishment and he knew it. Just as suddenly as one pony was taken away, another, or maybe two, would appear in the stables. Sometimes the slightest misdeed on my part would be enough; at other times, he would be indulgent and forgiving. I never knew where I was with him, from one pony to the next."[48]

*

The war allowed young Max to redeem himself in his father's eyes: his exploits as a fighter pilot earned him deserved praise for bravery, and he would become known as the only pilot who had been in the air on both the day the war began and the day it ended. Beaverbrook himself showed no such consistency. Ever mercurial, he resigned as minister of aircraft production in 1941, his task complete, then left Churchill's cabinet altogether in 1942 to lead a public campaign for a second front to relieve the pressure on Soviet Russia. Many have speculated that he was angling to replace Churchill, whose prestige was suffering at that moment after the British defeat at Singapore. But Churchill survived and restored Beaverbrook to cabinet in 1943 after promising him that the Allies would launch the liberation of western Europe in the spring of 1944.[49]

As Allied troops and the Red Army converged on Berlin early in 1945, Beaverbrook's reputation and influence were at their height. Many would see his efforts in aircraft production as the turning point that allowed Britain to survive a war of attrition until it could turn the tide. When Churchill prepared to dissolve Parliament shortly after V-E Day and call an election for July, Beaverbrook was part of a triumvirate put in charge of campaign strategy. They chose, naturally, to base everything on the prime minister's leadership, which had won the war.

The British people had other ideas. The Conservatives were soundly defeated by Labour, a party with which Beaverbrook enjoyed few ties and over which he exercised no influence. A major phase of his life, a great adventure, had come to a crashing end. During his three-decade climb to the pinnacle of British politics, he had often mused, particularly when bored or discouraged, about retiring to Canada. So it was that in 1945 his thoughts turned once again to the little seaside province that he called home.

Michael Wardell, Colin B. Mackay, Robert Tweedie, Lord
Beaverbrook and Premier Hugh John Flemming, 1950s.

CHAPTER THREE

"We must remember the greatness of the man"

For Lord Beaverbrook, nothing was certain in 1945 except death and New Brunswick. Taxes would be another matter.

In England, he found himself deprived of the access to power to which he'd become accustomed. Restless, he bought more houses and travelled more, as if seeking out new frontiers for his empire. He was pondering as well how to ensure that that empire would survive him: at sixty-six, he was increasingly aware of his mortality. Preoccupied with his own death since childhood, he ruminated now about how he might ensure that his name and his achievements would endure after his passing. His thoughts turned, not surprisingly, to New Brunswick.

This was not a sudden inspiration. Quite the contrary: it dovetailed perfectly with the conceit Beaverbrook had consistently nurtured that he'd remained "domiciled" in Canada during all the years he lived in England. "I intend to return to Canada and spend the rest of my days in peace," he wrote to one friend as early as 1929. The following year he told another, "I want a handful of New Brunswick soil on my bosom at the end." He purchased land in the province, ostensibly for retirement. Like all Canadians, he was a British subject, but he obtained his Canadian citizenship and acquired a passport as soon as Ottawa legalized the distinction in 1947. And he maintained a large portion of his fortune in Canadian investments overseen by his brother Allan, ensuring they were exempt from British income tax.[1] This paper trail would allow his eventual executors to advance a compelling argument that his estate should be exempt from England's large death duties.

One of the earliest and most bizarre manifestations of Beaverbrook's interest in creating memorials in New Brunswick was his quixotic attempt in 1952 to dig up the remains of his old friend R.B. Bennett and repatriate them to Canada, where he envisioned incorporating them into a monument to Bennett's greatness. The fact that Canadians did not share his glowing assessment of their Depression-era prime minister was of only passing concern to Beaverbrook. "He was good. He was great," he wrote of his friend. "And in the fullness of time his reputation will grow and expand. His name will rank with those Prime Ministers of his country whose deeds thrill and inspire the youth of the Dominion."[2]

After retreating to Juniper Hill, adjacent to Cherkley, after his 1935 electoral defeat, Bennett had been named a viscount in 1941. At Beaverbrook's urging he had served the war effort by visiting British factories to address the workers. He clearly felt at home in Mickleham, a nearby village, and put a lot of money into fixing up his home, even installing a movie theatre where he would screen films for villagers on Saturday nights. Unlike his old friend Max, he made no pretence of planning to return to New Brunswick at the end of his days. "I would not leave this house for anywhere else in the world," he told his secretary when his friends urged him to flee as the Germans bombed England during the war.[3] He died in the house on June 26, 1947, in his bath, after having declined Beaverbrook's invitation to come to dinner. Beaverbrook arranged for his burial in the Mickleham village churchyard, but he later became convinced that it should not be Bennett's final resting place. The scheme was only one of many to honour his friend: his first attempt at a tribute was to try to recruit a reputable biographer to write Bennett's life, and he arranged for Bennett's papers to be transferred to and archived at the University of New Brunswick. There were also plans by the federal government for plaques to honour Bennett in both Calgary, where he had practised law, and Hopewell Cape, New Brunswick, near his birthplace. But Beaverbrook favoured the grand gesture, and nothing would be grander than the ceremonial homecoming of Bennett's mortal remains.

Bennett's former secretary, Alice Millar, was at first willing to defer to Beaverbrook and Bennett's brother, who still lived in New Brunswick. "Whatever you and Captain Bennett agree upon for the return of Lord Bennett's body to New Brunswick will decide what is to be done," she wrote. But she added that she was quite certain Bennett "expected to be buried in Mickleham churchyard, where he often said he had many good friends." She acknowledged that she was motivated in part by her loyalty and her own bitterness about Bennett's 1935 defeat at the polls. "I am influenced by a narrow resentment against my fellow-countrymen who don't deserve to have back so great a man." Beaverbrook, not surprisingly, was undeterred, convinced — wrongly, at least as of 2007 — that history would redeem his friend and recognize his place in the pantheon of Canadian prime ministers. "I still think it would be a good thing for the province of New Brunswick if Bennett's body was brought back and buried there," he wrote. "He is an example to youth, and he will be valued more and more highly as the years pass by, and as his conduct during the panic is discussed and determined."

Millar dug in, as gently and politely as she could, throwing up a number of questions that, she hoped, might cause Beaverbrook to slow down: where exactly Bennett would be buried, how the Church of England might react, and whether Canadians would treat his grave with as much respect as the people of Mickleham. Beaverbrook brushed these aside, explaining that, though the grand vision was his, these mundane details of how to execute it would be left to others. "The Province of New Brunswick would have to take responsibility for reburial. I should think the best place is in Fredericton. There is an old graveyard in the centre of the town. Personally, I would prefer a site near the government buildings."

Tellingly, Beaverbrook had put off consulting Bennett's brother, a step he finally took almost a year later, in October 1953, as the unveiling of the plaque in Hopewell Cape drew near. "It is past time that we brought Dick home. He should be buried in Fredericton near the Parliament building. I hope this Conservative administration [in New Brunswick] can be persuaded to work out a programme. Do you approve?" Captain R.V. Bennett did not. "The last time I saw R.B.," he wrote, "was at Christmas time 1946, when he brought up the matter as to where he was to be buried, and he was quite definite that he wished to be buried in Mickleham Churchyard, as he was, and I would not like to go against his wishes now." Beaverbrook dropped the matter then and there. "I see your point," he wrote in a letter on October 21, 1953, "and I will not ask again to change the resting place of Dick."[4] He quickly switched gears, returning in the very next paragraph to his ultimately vain quest for a suitable Bennett biographer. Beaverbrook's own memoir of Bennett, *Friends: Sixty Years of Intimate Personal Relations with Richard Bedford Bennett*, published in 1959, makes no mention of his aborted repatriation plan. But the effort reveals the Beaverbrook of which New Brunswickers would see more and more over the next decade: sentimental, stubborn and audacious in his desire to enrich the life of the province.

*

Beaverbrook's other schemes would prove more successful. "I put in the first sixty-eight years of my life making money," he told *Maclean's* magazine. "Now I want to spend it — here in New Brunswick."[5] In fact, he had already been doing so for more than three decades. Only a few years after his move to England, he had created seven scholarships for high school students entering the University of New Brunswick. Beaverbrook followed that with the construction of a men's residence and a gymnasium on campus, both named for Lady Beaverbrook, as well as an arena. The university's librarian, Alfred Bailey, who had once lent Beaverbrook's father a hundred dollars, was told to draw up lists of books the library needed, and over the course of three years the collection grew from fifteen to fifty thousand books — courtesy of Beaverbrook. In Fredericton, legend had it that he gave so much to UNB to take revenge on Dalhousie, where he had started but not finished the entrance exam. He set up more scholarships so that UNB students could do postgraduate work in London, thus intellectually stimulating and changing the lives of young New Brunswickers in ways they had never dreamed possible. Dalton Camp, later one of Canada's most influential political strategists and columnists, so impressed Beaverbrook when he delivered the UNB valedictory address in 1947 that Beaverbrook ordered he be given an overseas scholarship on the spot, without having to apply, write a test, or submit letters of reference.[6] In London, Camp was taught by Harold Laski, the great socialist thinker whom Camp called "one of the greatest teachers I have ever known" and whom Beaverbrook called "Anti-Christ!" when young Camp came to dinner at Cherkley.[7] "He was the first man that ever frightened me," Camp later wrote of the press baron.[8] Beaverbrook later had second thoughts about the entire program. "If I could make my plans again," he wrote, "there would not be any overseas to Britain scholarships, except teachers. The money would be diverted to sending students from England out to Canada. I am almost persuaded to make the change."[9]

Beaverbrook dispensed other gifts to Saint John, where he'd briefly worked, and to Newcastle, where he'd grown up. The latter even received a new town hall courtesy of his Lordship. He also bought a large recording device for a Miramichi folklorist, Louise Manny, so that she could record the traditional songs of lumbermen and fishermen on the Miramichi River, an effort that eventually inspired Manny to launch a local folk festival. And he provided her with additional money to restore the Old Manse, his childhood home, and convert it into a library. He funded pensions for retired Presbyterian ministers and trips to England for New Brunswick politicians and school teachers. One of his own former teachers from Newcastle, Philip Cox, was treated, along with twenty-four colleagues, to a five-week, all-expenses-paid party that wound its way through England, Scotland and Ireland. "When the teachers went to fancy functions, such as an entertainment by the Lord Mayor of London, the formal clothes they needed and most of them lacked appeared out of nowhere. For underpaid schoolmarms from small communities, it was all like a beautiful dream," *Maclean's* reported more than two decades after the fact. "They're still talking about it."[10]

New Brunswickers knew little of the controversies and the secret dealings so essential to Beaverbrook's life in England. In their mind, he had earned every honour and then some. "I, like every other kid in Fredericton, was brought up with the idea that Lord Beaverbrook was close to God," recalls Colleen Thompson, a Fredericton travel writer who became well acquainted with him. "He was revered." One day Thompson slipped on some ice on a sidewalk, scattering her parcels in every direction. She looked up to see Beaverbrook bending over her. "Are you all right, young lady?" he asked, helping her with her packages. "I remember my awe, and his big grin. You could practically see his back molars," she remembers. "My father, who was originally from the Miramichi area, was particularly impressed with my experience and the family passed it on to interested neighbours and friends. Lord Beaverbrook was our star." When a new downtown hotel was built in 1948, the Fredericton Chamber of Commerce asked citizens to write in with suggestions for its name. Nine out of ten said it should be called the Lord Beaverbrook Hotel, and it was. He was "the son of the manse made good, with the other sides of his character well concealed. . . . He was treated like a tribal chief, and behaved like one, too."[11]

Fredericton was and remains the smallest and sleepiest of New Brunswick's three main cities; but for an accident of history that led to its selection as the capital, it might have remained just another of the small towns along the majestic Saint John River. Its postwar population was around sixteen thousand, including, thanks to the government and the university, a provincial elite that appreciated Beaverbrook's importance and willingly accommodated his whims. He had been invited to become UNB's first chancellor, a position that would formalize his role in New Brunswick, and was installed at Encænia, or convocation, in May 1947. He soon decided that an annual ceremony in the spring, when he preferred to be in England, did not suit him. The university obligingly began holding convocations in October, which fit his usual travel cycle: Fredericton in October, with a week in Montreal tacked on; New York in late fall, Jamaica for Christmas, then Nassau, then back to New York, and then to England for several months, the schedule punctuated with jaunts to his estate in the south of France, La Capponcina, before the cycle began again with his journey to New Brunswick for convocation. Fredericton became an important base for the itinerant press baron.

The university bent to Beaverbrook's will again in 1953, with the provincial government equally compliant. The university's president had resigned, and its senate, following convention, set up a nominating committee to recommend a candidate to the provincial government, which, by law, had the power to make the appointment. While this was happening, the premier of New Brunswick, Hugh John Flemming, was in England with Hugh Mackay, a member of the university senate. When they called on the chancellor, Beaverbrook suggested that Colin B. Mackay, Hugh Mackay's nephew, be considered for the position. Returning to Fredericton, Flemming passed this recommendation on to the committee, which considered Mackay too young and inexperienced. There was a flurry of letters, during which Beaverbrook made clear that while he favoured Mackay, he would accept the committee's choice. But Flemming let it be known that the government would exercise its power to appoint Mackay regardless of the committee's recommendation. There was grumbling at the university, which got back to Beaverbrook. He became angry that the nominating committee hadn't sent a name to the government, a circumstance which, he believed, created the appearance that he was dictating the choice of Mackay. "It is not correct," he wrote. "When the Senate and Chancellor diverge, it is detrimental to the well-being of the University. I now resign my Chancellorship."[12]

Thanks to Flemming's browbeating and his effort to curry Beaverbrook's favour, the university now faced losing its most generous benefactor. Flemming, Mackay and Michael Wardell, one of Beaverbrook's lieutenants in Fredericton, held a clandestine meeting in a men's room at the Legislature during a ball given by the lieutenant-governor. Flemming had come up with the notion of creating a new position, honorary chancellor for life, and offering it to Beaverbrook. Mackay and Wardell agreed, and Flemming, with no writing paper on hand, drafted a cable to London on a scrap of toilet paper. It asked him to accept the post "in consideration of your great services to the Commonwealth in two world wars and of your help and generosity to the University and to New Brunswick generally covering a period of many years." Members of the university senate, Flemming wrote without having consulted them, "concur unanimously in this decision."[13] When Beaverbrook accepted, a bill creating the position — including the erroneous statement that he was "a native son of New Brunswick" — was rushed through the Legislature. The crisis was over, and Mackay went on to preside over the university for sixteen years, a period in which its enrolment increased fivefold. He was eventually seen as the single most influential administrator in its history.

Flemming was not the first premier to defer to Beaverbrook: his predecessor, Liberal John McNair, was Beaverbrook's guest in Jamaica. He wrote from Montego Bay in 1948, "My attachment for Lord Beaverbrook grows with each passing day. He's just grand." When Flemming defeated McNair in 1952, the new premier instructed Bob Tweedie — McNair's long-time assistant and another Beaverbrook courtier in Fredericton — to "do all that I possibly could be helpful to the province's greatest benefactor."[14] Tweedie took this to include advising the premier on the proper deference; two weeks before Beaverbrook was to arrive in Fredericton on his annual visit, Tweedie wrote to Flemming, "It occurs to me that it would be a kindly gesture if you and one or two members of your Government would take the time to meet him at the airport."[15] It was hardly surprising that the premier of a small Canadian province would prove susceptible to the same charms that had so influenced successive British governments. Some of Flemming's actions, however, seem overly fawning to the modern observer. "Flemming is especially proud of a birthday letter from you," Michael Wardell would write to Beaverbrook in 1956; he "carries it always."[16]

*

Michael Wardell knew all about servility. In 2006, the lawyers for the U.K. Foundation would call him "a fiercely independent man," and Lady Aitken claimed when she testified at the arbitration hearing that Wardell "would have no nonsense from my father-in-law. If something was wrong he would stand up to him." She clearly hadn't seen the extensive correspondence between Beaverbrook and Wardell, which makes clear precisely who dominated whom. New Brunswick was the newest outpost in Beaverbrook's empire, and Wardell was his regent; there was no question of where the ultimate authority lay. "Beaverbrook collected men and, for that matter, women, in lieu of artifacts," wrote one essayist. "He was an enabler, a facilitator who liked to create opportunities to help in the moulding of his protégés, thereby enhancing their ineluctable bond to him.[17] Helen Parker, a young Fredericton woman who observed the relationship with Wardell and was later a secretary at the Beaverbrook Art Gallery, believed Beaverbrook was a lonely man. "He knew people were nice to him because of what he could give them. But he also took whatever he could get."

Wardell had been educated at Eton and the Royal Military College at Sandhurst, and he had fought at Ypres in the First World War. With the eye patch he was forced to wear after a fox-hunting accident, his larger-than-life persona, and his own connections in London society as a confidant of the Prince of Wales during his courtship of Wallis Simpson, he fit well into Beaverbrook's circle, which he joined after leaving the military in 1925.[18] Eventually put in charge of the London *Evening Standard*, he became part of the press baron's entourage, and he was one of the few acquaintances invited along when Beaverbrook was Hitler's guest at the 1936 Olympics. Wardell rejoined the military for the Second World War, earning the rank of brigadier, though Beaverbrook would always refer to him as "Captain."

During a fishing trip to New Brunswick with Beaverbrook in 1950, Wardell, who had been en route to South Africa to go into the newspaper business, decided instead to set up shop in Fredericton. He formed a company, University Press, to buy three enterprises: the Fredericton *Daily Gleaner*, a company called Wilson's Printing, and McMurray's, a family-owned store that sold books, stationery and printing services. The three businesses had co-owned a printing plant, which also became Wardell's. He would claim the decision was completely spontaneous. "It's not a story of logic and a planned decision at all," he once said. "I didn't originally intend to stay."[19] Beaverbrook's biographers Anne Chisholm and Michael Davie say Beaverbrook orchestrated the move because Wardell was impossible to work with at the *Daily Express*, where he'd landed after the war, and several executives had threatened to quit if he was not removed.[20] "Beaverbrook used to laugh at Wardell," says Jackie Webster, a Fredericton journalist befriended by Beaverbrook when she was a young student. "I had the feeling he just brought him over here for amusement — someone to pal around with whenever he was in town." Whatever the explanation, Wardell's foray into Canadian journalism suited Beaverbrook. Despite his "long, thin forearms the colour of milk" and "a face of utter mystery,"[21] his tall, aristocratic bearing guaranteed that he would easily impress and intimidate the provincial power-brokers around Fredericton when he conveyed the press baron's wishes. But he would rarely, if ever, defy his patron, particularly after Beaverbrook began lending him large amounts of money and even setting up trust funds for his mother and two of his sons.[22]

In November 1950, Wardell proposed to Beaverbrook that the two of them invest in the *Gleaner*, splitting the $555,000 price so that each man would pay $227,500 — an incorrect calculation by Wardell, as a memo from A.G. Millar to Beaverbrook noted. The actual figure would be $277,500, and Wardell had forgotten the annual Canadian Press membership fee, which would cost each man an additional $5,000. Beaverbrook suggested to Wardell that he reduce their investment to $455,000, to which Beaverbrook would contribute half. He would also buy the printing press for $100,000 and lease it back to Wardell. Wardell was ready to jump into business on New Year's Day 1951 — "I am putting myself through some intensive study into the general principles of retailing," he wrote Beaverbrook — but their financial agreement remained frustratingly ill-defined. He accused Beaverbrook, who refused to take any shares in the enterprise, of leading him on. "I'm here because you talked me into it," Wardell wrote. Beaverbrook rejected the accusation. "Advice foolishly given by me in conversation cannot be interpreted by you as anything more than that." He charged Wardell with trying to draw him further into the business, a responsibility he did not want. "You will have a great venture if you get a newspaper," Beaverbrook wrote. "That should be your first and only objective."[23]

Wardell finally gave in, accepting that his patron's role would be limited to a $100,000 loan for the printing press. "Confidence ebbs and flows," Wardell wrote to Beaverbrook when the matter was finally resolved. "At the moment you are critical of my powers and doubtful of the enterprise. I think it will succeed. I have had a good and respectable list of successes. This may sound boastful, and you know them well enough; but it is right to run over them at this time because they have a bearing on this new endeavour." He listed bringing the *Evening Standard* out of the red and saving the *Scottish Express* "when it was under the sentence of death. . . . I shall be surprised if University Press is my first failure."[24]

No sooner was Wardell established, however, than it became clear Beaverbrook saw him less as a fellow newspaper proprietor and more as a glorified errand boy. In one letter he is checking Beaverbrook's Fredericton house to make sure repairs are being done as ordered. In the next, he is off to Newcastle, where Beaverbrook plans to build a theatre and a new town hall. No wonder Wardell came to see himself as a sort of colonial exile and to cherish his Beaverbrook-funded trips to England, where he was often a guest at Cherkley. "Every yard I walk there is alive with memories. I feel like crying . . . at the thought of banishment again on Wednesday," he wrote in one letter. Apologizing for the poor framing job done on a copy of the legislation designating Beaverbrook honorary UNB chancellor for life, Wardell wrote, "This is an example of the wretched workmanship one encounters here when any hand operation is called for."[25] His attempts to launch Beaverbrook-style editorial crusades in the *Gleaner* only spawned resentment. "Staid Fredericton, for instance, wasn't ready for his newspaper campaign for open bars," recalls Colleen Thompson. "And when the River Room opened at the Lord Beaverbrook Hotel, and women were allowed in, too, he was totally blamed for introducing such a wicked practice."

Beaverbrook added insult to injury in the summer of 1954, informing Wardell by telegram that he was offering him £3,000 in compensation for his removal from the board of the *Express*. Wardell was stunned. "I had not the glimmer of an idea that you wanted me off the board. I don't want to go at all." The loss of income would be a terrible blow, given the poor performance of the *Gleaner*, from which he was drawing no salary and no dividends. More dispiriting was the realization that his removal meant his exile in Fredericton might not be as temporary as he'd imagined. "I should not have come back to you," he wrote. "I understood that you wanted me as a standby, and the New Brunswick adventure seemed part of that plan. I would not have considered it on any other basis, having just returned to your board. I have no doubt greatly disappointed you in its execution. I have disappointed myself, grievously. Knowing what I know now, I know that this is just about the last place on earth to go to, to set up a business like this. There are no skilled men, no businesses with printing requirements." Wardell begged Beaverbrook to hold off and give him some "breathing space," then he would resign from the board. To Beaverbrook, it seemed perfectly logical that, based in Fredericton, Wardell could not attend board meetings in London. "There is nothing going to be held against you, even if there is cause. If you retire you will get more compensation than you require for years. . . . I wish you wouldn't make such a fuss about a reasonable and ordinary proposal which carries with it obvious advantages. You must really take life as it comes."[26]

"If I had gone to Canada and neglected my duties at the *Express*," Wardell answered, "I could understand the demand for my removal from the board. But the truth is otherwise. I entirely re-made my life to return to the *Express*, and undertook the Fredericton venture *to carry out your will and intention* before ever I had started to work at the *Express*." Beaverbrook did relent, allowing Wardell to retain his directorship at the *Express*, but he had A.G. Millar send Wardell a stern warning. "Lord Beaverbrook takes the view that he has tried to dissuade you from your programmes of expansion," Millar wrote. He reminded Wardell that he had defied the conditions Beaverbrook had attached to another $100,000 loan in 1952: he used part of it to settle a legal dispute with a former investor, but spent half the sum on an expansion to his printing plant, contrary to Beaverbrook's wishes. This made Wardell more dependent than ever, and everyone knew it. Beaverbrook "hopes you do not write any more complaining letters," Millar told him. "Let good feeling prevail."[27]

Wardell quickly reverted to grovelling. "Dear Max, Thank you for not kicking me off the Board," he wrote. "Nothing will alter my regard and affection for you." But he tried one last time to restate his case, telling Beaverbrook he would not have gone into business in Fredericton "had you not pointed the way. . . . That is not to say that I blame you for any lack of capacity or errors of judgment that I may have displayed." Despite the pathetic tone, Beaverbrook could not let even this impudence stand. "You know that your newspaper venture had my approval, and I recommended against your extensive printing project. Whatever happened after January, 1950 cannot be due to any 'pointing' from me."[28]

Even Beaverbrook's quashing of this minor rebellion, one of the very few the "Captain" ever dared mount, did not shake Wardell's loyalty, nor his readiness to use the *Gleaner* as a pro-Beaverbrook pamphlet. When former *Daily Express* journalist Tom Driberg published a biography, *Beaverbrook: A Study in Power and Frustration*, in 1956, Wardell went on the attack. Never mind that Beaverbrook had given Driberg a free hand, then changed his mind and decided to vet the book, then lost interest and allowed the author to publish as he saw fit; Wardell devoted forty-two column inches to his review of what he called a "dull and disagreeable" book, "much of it . . . tedious and some of it wildly inaccurate." Driberg — an ex-communist, Wardell noted — had not devoted sufficient attention to Beaverbrook's "many acts of kindness" nor to his achievements, such as the "brilliant manoeuvring" that allowed him to conquer "the impregnable citadel of conservatism in London within a matter of months."[29]

If Wardell was hoping these endearments would earn him a commutation of his Fredericton exile, he was mistaken. When E.J. Robertson, the general manager of Beaverbrook's newspapers, became ill, Wardell was quick to offer his assistance. "If you wish me at this stage to take some part in the conduct of the *Daily Express*, I will come home and visit Fredericton periodically. The business here is now developed to a point when I can leave it for periods with equanimity." Beaverbrook decided, however, that his London operations could prosper quite well without Wardell's intervention. Still, he threw the Captain a bone now and then. In 1956 he offered to let

Wardell serialize his memoir of his early days in Newcastle and the launch of his Canadian business career in Wardell's magazine, *The Atlantic Advocate*, which he had bought and relaunched. "To me it is the most entrancing, unbelievable and extraordinary story," Wardell gushed during the editing.[30]

Wardell had purchased the magazine following a tip that its predecessor, *The Maritime Advocate and Busy East*, was up for sale. The tip had come from Bob Tweedie, Beaverbrook's other agent in Fredericton and Wardell's occasional rival for the great man's approval. He and Wardell were very different men, making them unlikely allies in the effort to promote Beaverbrook's agenda in Fredericton, but they shared one important, defining characteristic. "Some are destined to work for others," Tweedie wrote in his memoirs. "I was one of these."[31]

Unlike Wardell, Tweedie was not born to privilege. The Tweedies were Liberals in the little village of Centreville, New Brunswick. In 1935, young Bob landed the job of secretary to the new premier, Allison Dysart; when John McNair succeeded Dysart, Tweedie held on to his position. One day Beaverbrook complained to McNair that the university's system of assigning young professors as his local assistants was faltering. McNair, worried that Beaverbrook "might lose interest in the province and curtail, if not eliminate, all future benefactions," offered Tweedie's services. Soon the premier's secretary was at Beaverbrook's disposal, responding to urgent summonses, organizing banquets, serving on the scholarship committees, chairing another group overseeing the construction of a rink, and badgering federal and provincial governments for sales-tax rebates on various projects. "Every transaction I carried out for him was executed with extreme care; I drove far harder bargains for him than I ever did for myself." When Tweedie complained to McNair — who had in effect loaned him to Beaverbrook — the premier told Tweedie to be patient. "We must remember the greatness of the man," he said. Tweedie's appeal to Beaverbrook was rooted in the latter's long memory: Tweedie's father was a cousin of Lemuel J. Tweedie, the lawyer who had been a demanding taskmaster when Beaverbrook articled in his office as a young man. "I made up my mind," he once told Bob, "that one day I would have a Tweedie of my own to bounce around, and that is why I have you."[32]

Tweedie's services to Beaverbrook continued after Flemming's Conservatives defeated McNair's Liberals in 1952. Like Wardell, he performed tasks ranging from the grand and vital to the mundane and ridiculous. Beaverbrook would demand that Tweedie, secretary to three committees that awarded his scholarships, explain why the New Brunswick students he was meeting in London "cannot measure up to the type of scholars who are flowing into this educational centre from several countries." He would request updates on municipal elections, particularly curious about results in Chatham, Newcastle, Fredericton and Saint John. "I see that the mayor in Newcastle is retiring. Is that because he could not get elect[ed] again?"[33] He had Tweedie scout out parcels of land that he might purchase for his often-promised retirement in New Brunswick and travel to Newcastle often to supervise work on the town hall or the Old Manse or the Square, all of which Beaverbrook was funding. "He liked Bob Tweedie, but he sort of abused him," says Jackie Webster. "He was awfully hard on him."

Occasionally, Beaverbrook found Tweedie too eager to please. One January, he wrote from Nassau, "A consignment of oatmeal has arrived from you. Now I have plenty to see me through my present stay in Nassau. So please do not send any more to me here."[34] An acquaintance of Tweedie says, "Beaverbrook was terrible to him, but Bob admired him anyway. He loved the old man and how exciting it was when he came to New Brunswick. The air was charged." Beaverbrook and Wardell "had this dream that New Brunswick would become this cultured, English-affected paradise. Bob just loved being part of the project." Colleen Thompson agrees. "I didn't get the feeling that they were friends. Bob Tweedie was enamoured with his role. . . . He was pleasant, personable, but became — let me see, how shall I say it — sort of crazed when his Lordship came town. He had everyone around him running in circles. . . . The connection with Lord Beaverbrook seemed to be Tweedie's reason for being."

Beaverbrook paid Tweedie $3,000 a year, the equivalent of $22,000 in 2006, an amount that kept him compliant. "Your confidence in me is a prized possession," he wrote one January after the money had arrived. "I intend to do everything in my power to retain it." In another letter, Tweedie explained that he did not consider the money to be a salary. It "has always been treated as a gift. I make no mention of it on my Income Tax Return, but assume that all the gifts you make are listed on yours. When you gave me the first $3,000, you made it very clear that it was a gift and was to be so regarded by me."[35]

Yes, Tweedie was different from Wardell — they had vastly different origins and experiences — but they were also very much alike: both were men of some ambition and achievement who were nonetheless fated to work in the shadows of better-known men — for Wardell, the Prince of Wales; for Tweedie, John McNair — and to be pulled into the orbit of the same master manipulator. Beaverbrook stripped them of their independence, their pride and their dignity, deploying them as foot soldiers, pawns even, in his campaign to enshrine himself as New Brunswick's greatest benefactor. And if this campaign was designed mostly to feed his ego or reduce his taxes, it was still an irresistible adventure, one that would make the province an undeniably more interesting, lively and liveable place.

No project fits that definition better or more grandly than the one Beaverbrook began to advance in the mid-1950s: the creation of a collection of fine paintings to be housed in an art gallery for all New Brunswickers to enjoy. Wardell and Tweedie would soon share the single-mindedness their patron devoted to what would become his greatest legacy and, decades later, his most contentious.

Lord Beaverbrook in the Beaverbrook Art Gallery
with Thomas Gainsborough's *Peasant Girl Gathering Faggots*, 1959.

CHAPTER FOUR

"The rich man loose in the art market has a lot to learn"

The idea of an art gallery in New Brunswick had been gestating in Beaverbrook's imagination for decades. During the First World War, before he had been granted his peerage, he created the Canadian War Memorials Fund and asked his friend Lord Rothermere, another future press baron, to chair it. They commissioned many paintings, which Beaverbrook donated to Canada, though a plan to hang them in a suitable gallery collapsed. In 1928, Beaverbrook agreed to lend a painting by William Orpen to his friend Robert Borden, a former prime minister of Canada, "for so long as I do not require it myself. . . . But it is quite possible that I might want it back — in connection with some public building."[1] This is the first documented reference to the project that would consume his attention three decades later. Between the wars, his flagship newspaper began sponsoring the *Daily Express* Young Artists Exhibitions to promote the next generation of British artists. He became a patron of several prominent painters, including Orpen, Graham Sutherland, Walter Sickert and Augustus John. By 1945, the dining room at Cherkley Court was, according to Michael Wardell, "stacked with paintings heaped round the walls and reposing on seats and tables."[2] Beaverbrook's friend Sir James Dunn, who had built an impressive collection, lost it during rough times, and amassed a second one, had become a generous art patron of Dalhousie University in Halifax. Beaverbrook "took up the chal-

lenge to be an art patron in his turn. He had run through the interest
of providing books for the University of New Brunswick and the
town of Newcastle. Pictures would be a new field of endeavour."[3] He
moved ahead with his usual impetuosity. "When he started working
on that gallery, he was like a kid," says Jackie Webster. "He was so
wrapped up in it."

The vehicle for the project would be a foundation, which would
help him address his other preoccupation: how to protect his heirs
from estate taxes, which were as high as eighty per cent in England
at the time. No tax would be levied on any gift he gave more than
one year before his death. Additionally, Beaverbrook could transfer
his shares in the newspapers to the foundation, rather than to his
son Max, who would inevitably be forced to sell them to pay the
death duties.[4] With Max as chairman of a foundation that owned the
shares, however, and other family members and friends as trustees,
the House of Beaverbrook would continue to control the newspapers,
and dividends from the shares would fund charitable work.

The primary beneficiary would be New Brunswick. The draft trust
deed drawn up to govern the foundation would see Beaverbrook give
832,572 shares — representing fifty-one per cent — of the *Daily
Express* to the trust. The trustees would use the income from the
shares' dividends to establish scholarships at the University of New
Brunswick, buy books for university libraries in the Maritime provinces, and, the deed said, fund "other charitable purposes . . . for
the benefit of any persons resident in the Maritime provinces."[5] But
British law placed limits on what a resident of the United Kingdom
could give away outside the country, a restriction put in place after
the Second World War to protect the value of the currency.[6] The Bank
of England approved the deed but said it would likely approve only
gifts from the foundation that allowed teachers or students to visit
the United Kingdom. It was, the bank said, "unlikely . . . that permission to use Trust income for the benefit of non-residents . . . would
be given in his Lordship's lifetime."[7] This stymied the entire point of
Beaverbrook's effort, and he abandoned his plan for the time being.

He was not deterred for long. He soon began sending paintings to
New Brunswick for display at Mount Allison University in Sackville or

22nd October, 1953

I propose to make a change in our plans. Instead of doing three books of photos, I intend to prepare a gallery of photographs, prints and pictures.

Maybe we will set up a gallery in Saint John, or, possibly in Fredericton.

Will you let me know what is existing in Saint John.

If we are to have a successful gallery of photographs we must set up some system of securing photographs of distinguished leaders in various offices, such as Prime Ministers, Ministers in the Government, Post-masters, and other office holders.

Perhaps an appeal for photographs of this type would bring in a response from the families concerned who would wish that their relatives' photos should be displayed in such a gallery.

Then again I want to know what goes on at the New Brunswick Museum. It might be that an excellent gallery of photographs exists at that venerable institution.

This letter is, of course, private, but there is no reason why you should not get information from Mary Louise Lynch, who has my confidence.

Yours sincerely,

R. A. Tweedie, Esq.,
New Brunswick Travel Bureau,
Fredericton.

Beaverbrook's letter to Bob Tweedie
proposing a gallery in New Brunswick.

Beaverbrook Art Gallery, exhibit G001242

at the Old Manse in Newcastle. By October 1953, he was writing to Bob Tweedie that he would "prepare a gallery of photographs, prints and pictures" either in Saint John or Fredericton,[8] and the following year he revived plans for a foundation. He created two: the first was devoted exclusively to scholarships, education trips and other means for New Brunswickers to visit the U.K. — all in complete conformity with what the Bank of England had stipulated in 1950. The second, however, had much broader objectives. Its trust deed allowed for a wide range of charitable work both in Britain and in Canada, and one clause, 2(e) — a clause that would become a critical focus of the dispute half a century later — allowed for "the purchasing for or providing funds for the purchase by libraries museums or art galleries in the Province [of New Brunswick] . . . of books manuscripts papers letters periodicals maps paintings prints statuary and other documents or works of art . . ."[9] At first, the Bank of England raised the same objections as in 1950: many of the "substantially wider" goals of the second foundation[10] would benefit non-residents of the U.K. But the bank's objections faded in the weeks that followed. It is not clear why, though Beaverbrook's old friend Winston Churchill, not in office when the bank took a tough line in 1950, had returned to power by 1954, when it was more accommodating. The trust deed was eventually approved.

At least in theory, Beaverbrook was no longer in charge of the newspapers. The words "Controlling shareholder: Lord Beaverbrook" were removed from the *Express* masthead, though the trust deed required that the trustees maintain his Empire policy and that they hire employees who supported it. And senior executives still sought his approval for even tiny matters. "I no longer control. I still dominate," Beaverbrook wrote to his friend Henry Luce.[11] But he could proceed now at full speed to build a collection of paintings to display in New Brunswick. In Canada, he used the fortune he had left in the country to buy paintings there, while in England, the foundation made the purchases — ensuring gift taxes and estate duties would never apply — and then had the works shipped to New Brunswick. His own paintings in England he handed over to the foundation for dispatch to Fredericton. "You will be surprised, astonished and perhaps pleased to hear that I have decided to build a picture gallery for the farmers and fishermen near my home," Beaverbrook wrote an acquaintance in June 1954, in a rare example of explicit paternalism. "It will be a small gallery, and I propose to confine the collection to English painters after the turn of the century."[12]

Beaverbrook's taste in art could hardly be called refined. He admired Cornelius Krieghoff, whose work his friend James Dunn did not consider art. He liked English landscapes and "the luscious females of Boucher and Fragonard." Otherwise he treated his collection as an investment portfolio, avoiding too many purchases of works by the same artist, except when the artists were friends, such as Orpen, Sickert, Sutherland and Winston Churchill himself. "I've got enough of that fellow," he said, refusing a Turner. "We must have big pictures in the gallery," he decreed. Beaverbrook turned to curators, dealers, experts — anyone he could charm or cajole into helping — to make up for his own lack of knowledge about or interest in the visual arts. "His passionate obsession is with the concrete, the 'human,' the financial, the topical," wrote an early biographer, Tom Driberg. "Partly this may be because, after a boyhood little of which was devoted to formal education, the single-minded pursuit of worldly power has left him no time to turn aside and develop wider intellectual resources and cultural interests."[13] He was always seeking out bargains, haggling with dealers, and withdrawing when a competitor bid up the price, to the exasperation of his loose network of advisors.[14] "The art galleries of London, Paris, New York, Toronto and Montreal are littered with the bodies of discarded experts, some in chagrin, some in anger, and some, it must be said, in relief," Wardell once wrote.[15]

One consultant was Marie-Edmée Escarra de Ribes, Beaverbrook's French-tutor-turned-mistress, who was credited with sparking his interest in paintings when she took him to the National Gallery in London. When she fell deeply in love with Beaverbrook, however, he quickly cast her aside.[16] Another art advisor was Le Roux Smith Le Roux, a South African who had been deputy director of London's Tate Gallery until he was fired for trying to oust and replace the director, Sir John Rothenstein. Bob Tweedie would note with awe that Rothenstein devoted 145 pages of his memoirs to his troubles at the Tate, most of them brought on by Le Roux. "He succeeded," Rothenstein wrote, "in inflicting upon me more harm and more distress than I have suffered from all others together who have wished me ill in the course of my whole life." Hired to write for Beaverbrook's *Evening Standard*, Le Roux soon found himself scouring the art market for his boss and having paintings sent to his Arlington House flat for inspection. This led him inevitably to Fredericton, where he made an impression on Tweedie. "I liked him immediately," Tweedie wrote. "It would have been almost impossible not to have — such was the force of his personality. . . . He was a great companion and a witty conversationalist. To the best of my knowledge he made many friends and no enemies in New Brunswick."[17]

Le Roux helped organize what would prove to be New Brunswick's first glimpse of the future greatness of the Beaverbrook Art Gallery. In November 1954, the paintings that Beaverbrook had been shipping to Fredericton for storage were put on display at the Bonar Law–Bennett Library at the University of New Brunswick. The show, officially opened by the lieutenant-governor, was a sensation, with hundreds of visitors cramming into the building each day to see Beaverbrook's collection, augmented by five works from the private collection of Sir James and Lady Dunn. The Dunn collection included several works by Walter Sickert as well as a portrait of Lady Dunn by the Spanish surrealist Salvador Dali.[18]

On the eve of the exhibition, Beaverbrook, persuaded after "a very great effort" by Le Roux that the provincial capital was a more appropriate location than Saint John,[19] formally offered to build a gallery in Fredericton. In a letter to Premier Hugh John Flemming, he outlined his vision for the building and the collection it would house and display. Flemming was effusive in his thanks. "I feel that the people of the whole Province will be most gratified to learn of this wonderful boost to cultural development."

The success of the exhibition and the premier's gratitude were tempered by Beaverbrook's growing disenchantment with Le Roux, whom he saw in New York later that fall. Beaverbrook "was in an extremely odd mood," Le Roux wrote to Tweedie, "one moment

From Lord Beaverbrook

Fredericton

New Brunswick

Canada.

28th October, 1954

Dear Prime Minister,

The Province may be willing to offer me a site for an Art Gallery.

The building would be of modern fireproof construction with capacity for housing more than 100 paintings which I would propose to give to the Gallery.

There would be a collection of more than 200 prints.

Facilities would be provided for the housing and exhibiting collections of art available on loan.

The New Brunswick Universities would be given ample space for carrying on studies and courses of instruction.

You may wish to show this letter to the Mayor of the City of Fredericton.

Yours sincerely,

Beaverbrook

Premier Hugh John Flemming,
Fredericton,
New Brunswick.

*copy from Premier's Office to:
Miss Rosenberg - Lord Beaverbrook's Sect
& Hon. W.J. West.*

Beaverbrook's first suggestion to the premier of New Brunswick
that he build an art gallery and supply its collection.

Beaverbrook Art Gallery, exhibit G001311

threatening to abandon the whole art gallery scheme, the next to
build something more ambitious and complaining pointedly throughout that he lacked reliable advice. So I told him that he had too many
advisers and from my point of view seemed only interested in advice
which agreed with his own preconceptions. That cleared the air considerably but may also hasten my own demise as a member of the
set-up!" Le Roux wrote in the same letter that Beaverbrook "had
quibbled endlessly about my accounts," a sure sign, in Tweedie's view,
that Le Roux's light-hearted prediction of his fall from favour might
not be far from the mark.[20]

In the short time he had left, Le Roux made two other major contributions to Beaverbrook's gallery. One was the site itself.
Beaverbrook had first conceived of putting it on the university campus because he envisioned it as a venue for art classes. The province
offered him Officer's Square, a park in the centre of the city adjacent
to historic garrison buildings, and assigned the provincial architect,
Doug Jonsson, to the project. But Beaverbrook rejected Jonsson's
proposal[21] and hired local architect Lynn Howell and his partner, Neil
Stewart, who had designed the Lady Beaverbrook Rink for him. The
square itself presented a problem: the old officers' quarters adjacent
to it housed the Fredericton branch of the Royal Canadian Legion,
and Beaverbrook did not want to appear heavy-handed in forcing the
Legion out. Therefore he engaged Wardell to attempt to delegate the
unpleasant task to Premier Flemming. "Lord Beaverbrook is determined not himself to ask for the removal of the Legion nor to make
any suggestion which might result in their ejection," Wardell wrote to
Flemming in May 1955. "In other words, if he is to proceed with his
plans . . . it can only be after independent action by the Government
to terminate the Legion's occupation of the building. No doubt excellent alternative sites are available to them."[22]

This vicarious arm-twisting proved unnecessary, however. Le Roux
objected to the way the Howell and Stewart design would fit into the
site, and he recommended another location, then occupied by the
Fredericton Boat and Bicycle Club, on the Saint John River facing the
Legislative Assembly. Wardell would later report to Beaverbrook that
there was "no opposition to the riverside site," though few would

have dared complain to Wardell, knowing from whom he derived his power. A year and a half later, King Hazen, a former Member of Parliament for Saint John and the son of a former premier, revealed that there had been dissent about the site. The gallery "will destroy forever a million dollar view and the present beauty and attractiveness of Fredericton will be injured," he wrote to Beaverbrook. "Although there was resentment about the site no one wanted to come right out and say so because they did not want to do anything they thought might offend you as you have been so great a benefactor to the Province of New Brunswick."[23] By then it was far too late to choose yet another location, even if Beaverbrook had been so inclined.

Le Roux's other contribution was to organize the 1955 *Daily Express* Young Artists Exhibition, the show that would send Freud's *Hotel Bedroom* on its fateful journey to Fredericton. The jury at that year's exhibition was composed of Le Roux himself, the artist Graham Sutherland, the poet and art critic Sir Herbert Read, and the distinguished art historian Anthony Blunt, later unmasked as a Soviet spy. They chose two artists to share the first prize, Bryan Kneale and Geoffrey Banks, awarding them each £750. Lucian Freud was the second place winner, a choice that struck Beaverbrook as unfair to other artists because Freud was already well established. "Of course he is a good artist, an experienced artist. It is no competition at all when a boy like Lucien [*sic*] is able to enter. . . . It is no encourage-ment to young people at all. How can a lot of lads who have never had any success at all in painting compete with Lucien [*sic*] Freud?"[24] Beaverbrook may have been right; Le Roux persuaded him to buy several of the best paintings for the gallery in Fredericton, including *Hotel Bedroom*.

The painting is disturbing, showing Freud partially in shadow at the window of a room in the Hotel Louisiane in Paris, while his sec-ond wife, Lady Caroline Blackwood, lies in bed. The critic David Alan Mellor would call it a "melancholy crisis painting . . . with its conflicted gazes. Here, a surveilling stare of pent-up and dandified male mastery is directed to the painting's spectator, over against a wounded female pathos."[25] The image is said to be a recreation of an earlier Freud etching, *Ill in Paris*, done six years before, which

portrayed his first wife. Lady Blackwood, the great-granddaughter
of Lord Dufferin, would write decades later, "When I used to sit for
him nearly forty years ago the portraits he did of me in that period
were received with an admiration that was tinged with bafflement. I,
myself, was dismayed, others were mystified as to why he needed to
paint a girl, who at that point still looked childish, as so distressingly
old." Yet Blackwood also acknowledged that Freud's work cut to the
very core of his subjects. "Lucian Freud has always had the genius
ability to make the people and objects that come under his scrutiny
seem more themselves, and more *like* themselves, than they have ever
been — or will be. . . . When Lucian Freud paints a sink, it gives off
a 'sinkishness' so powerful, it seems to exceed what even sinks can
exude. If there are visual odors, his pictures make one smell them as
they rise putrid from his drain. If there are visual noises, one is forced
to hear the maddening drip of the water as it relentlessly releases itself
from his rusted faulty taps. God pity the unfortunate housewife con-
demned to 'do time' at the sink that is given us by Lucian Freud."[26]

Hotel Bedroom would come to be seen as a milestone in Freud's career, "marking the end of his linear, quasi-Surrealist paintings and his
move toward a more 'painterly' application of pigment," Ian Lumsden
remarked in 1998, when he was the director of the Beaverbrook Art
Gallery. "Although Beaverbrook was aware of the deflected glory to
his collection by acquiring such an important work, I suspect that
the subject matter was not compatible with his taste, and he would
not have acquired it for any of his seven residences. Beaverbrook
gravitated to the portrayal of women in a more ideal, if not to say
romanticized mode, whereas the image of Caroline Blackwood in
Freud's painting borders on the cadaver."[27]

The painting was soon shipped to Fredericton for the second exhibition of Beaverbrook's collection — also organized by Le Roux — at
the Bonar Law–Bennett library at UNB. This 1955 glimpse at the
gallery's potential was another success: almost a thousand people saw
Alan Jarvis, the director of the National Gallery in Ottawa, officially
open the exhibition. The mayor of Fredericton, H.S. Wright, told a
newspaper reporter, "Rarely has a city the size of Fredericton had
such an artistic treat as is being afforded them at the present time."[28]

Several of Beaverbrook's important friends, including Sir James Dunn and Viscount Bracken, a former British minister of information and, briefly, first lord of the admiralty, would attend the exhibition and praise it. John Steegman, the director of the Montreal Museum of Fine Arts, who was fast becoming yet another Beaverbrook advisor, wrote to tell him the collection "as it already stands gives a first-class impression of contemporary painting in England."[29]

The adoration of New Brunswickers, the approval of his peers, the endorsement of the experts, and the acquisition of paintings by several of England's highly regarded young artists: Beaverbrook could hardly have wished for more. But Le Roux's days were numbered. Beaverbrook began to doubt the authenticity of two paintings he had bought on Le Roux's advice, *Flatford Mill* by John Constable and *View from the Giudecca* by J.M.W. Turner. "I wish Lord Beaverbrook hadn't bought that Constable," John Rothenstein of the Tate remarked uneasily to Beaverbrook's secretary, Margaret Ince, after seeing it in London. "It has had a lot of things done to it."[30] When Beaverbrook pushed Le Roux to account for the provenance of the two works and for his own spending, Le Roux resigned, claiming he was ill. This aroused Beaverbrook's suspicions even more, and he asked a crime reporter for the *Daily Express* to investigate. He also wrote to several dealers himself, asking whether Le Roux had charged them commissions. He would later tell Rothenstein that Le Roux had defrauded him of forty thousand pounds in addition to the commissions.[31] *Flatford Mill* and *View from the Giudecca* would both prove to be fakes.

The entire affair left Beaverbrook discouraged, but he reacted in character, quickly recruiting other dealers and experts to his cause, mixing a touch of humility with that old pluck. "I am ashamed to come to you so soon after having launched my project for a new picture gallery such a short time ago," he wrote to Hugo Pitman, a director of the Tate. "But I am in real difficulty with errors and mistakes due to ignorance. I would so welcome your advice and counsel in my attempts to straighten out my muddle." He provided a list of what he was looking for. "(1) Ten or twelve masterpieces. I already have four I can count on. (2) 150 modern English paintings. I hope

I have 65 or 70 worthy of a place in the Gallery. (3) 100 Canadian paintings. Here I seem to be better placed, and my present collection is more than halfway to my goal." Pitman wrote back quickly, applauding the fact Le Roux was gone and soothing Beaverbrook's bruised ego. "I think you have made a splendid start," he said, offering his assistance.[32]

Pitman was not alone. No one was too busy or too important to rally to Beaverbrook's cause. Chester Beatty, the mining magnate and art collector, was asked for his views on the decision to focus on English and Canadian painters. "I hope you will continue to take an interest in my amateurish efforts to build up a sensible gallery in New Brunswick," Beaverbrook wrote.[33] W.G. Constable, the curator of paintings at the Museum of Fine Arts in Boston, had been recommended by Le Roux, and Beaverbrook came to rely on him considerably, despite the fact that he had endorsed Le Roux's purchase of the *Flatford Mill* and *View from the Giudecca* fakes. Constable would view Beaverbrook as "a deeply interesting man with wide experience and pity, and very tough. . . . People were rather frightened of him. I never was." Constable also found Beaverbrook uncultured, ignorant of everything from the right amount of rum in a Daiquiri to the proper size of doors for an art gallery. There was no rhyme or reason to his purchase of paintings, either. "I happened to say quite casually, 'There's a first rate Sir Joshua [Reynolds] coming up at Christie's.' He said, 'What is it?' I told him it was a very good portrait. I knew it. 'Oh,' he said, 'I'll get it.' Then and there, on the telephone, he got hold of one of his people in Fleet Street and told them exactly how much he'd go, and it was a big sum. He got it and there it hangs in the Fredericton Gallery. All this was done, I would say, in a quarter of an hour. . . . When he made his mind up he didn't hesitate and he knew enough, I suppose, about me to know that this [Reynolds portrait] was a good thing and anyhow it had a beautiful history. It was a really good buy and I gave him a price within which he wouldn't be swindled if he went quite high. He just went ahead and got it. . . . I could quite see how Winston Churchill had a great faith in him because, when you set him on doing something, nothing could hold him back and God forbid that the guy should ever be a

Prime Minister. . . . 'We must get this done!' And Heaven and Earth would be moved."[34]

It was Constable whom Beaverbrook chose as his surrogate in unveiling details about the gallery: he arranged for Constable to be awarded an honorary degree by the University of New Brunswick and deliver the convocation address in the fall of 1956. Once again the great propagandist orchestrated praise for himself from others in this well-choreographed production. Constable used the speech to acclaim "a noble gift of a collection of works of art and of a gallery to house them, which is being made to Fredericton by that great citizen of Canada, and of the Commonwealth, Lord Beaverbrook." Constable told the graduates and dignitaries that the gift marked "an epoch in the history of the Maritime Provinces." He went on to describe the collection, which was then "still in the process of growth," and listed several of the paintings and artists by name. And he gave a brief tutorial in how the people of Fredericton and New Brunswick should view the paintings. "A work of art does not yield up all it has to give at a casual glance any more than does a piece of music or literature. When looking at the work of art, treasure its first impression, the impact upon the innocent eye; you will never quite recapture what you then obtain, but to this first impression must be added a long and more intensive study. . . . Remember that the more you bring to a work of art, the more it will give to you."[35]

*

As important as W.G. Constable was, Beaverbrook's most important agent — and an unsung hero in the creation of the collection, until the 2004 dispute revealed her role — was his long-time secretary, Margaret Ince. Her first job had been with the *Express*, as one of Beaverbrook's secretaries, and she never worked for anyone else except for a stint with his first wife, Gladys. After Gladys died in 1927, Margaret Guthrie married journalist Cedric Blundell-Ince, and they lived briefly in South Africa. When they came back to England, Margaret — from that point on known forever as "Mrs. Ince" — returned to work for Beaverbrook. Her desk was next to that of A.G.

From Lord Beaverbrook

The Towers

THE
WALDORF-ASTORIA
NEW YORK 24, N.Y

4th December, 1956

Dear Premier Flemming,

I offer to convey to the Province of
New Brunswick, subject to the following
terms and conditions, an Art Gallery to be
erected on the ground known as "The Green".
The Gallery will be fully equipped, and will
contain a collection of paintings, prints,
books, sculpture and other works of art.
The terms and conditions are as follows:

(1)   I am to be sole custodian for life,
       and will be succeeded by William
       Maxwell Aitken.

(2)   Gallery acquisitions and withdrawals
       can be made only with the consent of
       the custodian. Thereafter, acquisitions
       and/or withdrawals can be made only on
       the written authority of a corporate body
       or individual to be named by the custodian
       (such as - National Gallery of Great
       Britain, Boston Museum of Fine Arts during
       tenure of office of Dr. Constable, Sir
       Alec Martin) acting on the recommendation
       of the Board of Governors. TheCorporate
       Body or individual shall have absolute
       right to accept or reject such recommendations.

(3)   It is proposed that the following shall be
       permanent members of the Board of Governors:

       (i)   Premier of New Brunswick
       (ii)   Member of the Executive Council
               to be nominated by the Government
               of the Province.
       (iii)   Leader of the Opposition in the
               Legislative Assembly.
       (iv)   President of the University of
               New Brunswick
       (v)   Chairman of the Board of Governors
               of Mount Allison University.
       (vi)   His Excellency Camille, Bishop of
               Bathurst, Chancellor of the
               Universities of St. Thomas and

Beaverbrook's detailed proposal for a gallery.

The Towers

(-2-)

Sacre Coeur and his successor
in office.

(vii) Representative of the New
Brunswick Teachers Association
(such representative to serve
for three year term only and to
be ineligible for succeeding term.

(viii) Art clubs functioning in the four
cities of the Province to be
represented by one member on the
Board of Governors who will hold
office for one year. Representation
shall alternate in the following
order: Saint John, Moncton,
Fredericton, Edmundston.

The following representative citizens to
be named by the Custodian for three (3) year
terms. Vacancies to be filled by the custodian.
Thereafter, vacancies to be filled by a majority
vote of the Board of Governors.

Mrs. K. C. Irving, Saint John
Mrs. J. Leonard O'Brien, South Nelson
Mrs. Hugh John Flemming
Mr. J. Michael Wardell, Fredericton

I should be obliged if you would consult
with your colleagues and let me know, please,
if you approve of the foregoing plan.

Yours sincerely,

Premier Hugh John Flemming,
Fredericton,
N.B.

Millar, the Edinburgh-born accountant who oversaw Beaverbrook's personal life. Mrs. Ince dealt with everything else, including the selection of paintings for the gallery, and thus she acquired a strong lay person's expertise in art.

Mrs. Ince was the gatekeeper, the funnel, the clearing house, as Beaverbrook accelerated his buying spree in the second half of the 1950s. She knew exactly what he wanted. In response to a query from one dealer, she explained that he was seeking English Old Masters, contemporary English works and any Canadian paintings. "The proviso in each of course," she said, using a phrase she would repeat over and over, "is that the works shall be first rate examples." When dealers offered paintings that didn't fit, she would put them off gently. Beaverbrook had a "programme" for buying paintings, she would explain, "and from this I know he will not diverge." If, on the other hand, a painting might interest him, she would arrange for it to be delivered to his Arlington House flat so that he could view it himself. "I have a rule which governs all my purchases — that is that I do not buy a picture until I have seen it and only then if I like it beyond any doubt," he said. And if someone was naïve enough to offer a work without mentioning the price, she would admonish him or her to please let her know. "That is very important when dealing with Lord Beaverbrook," she said.[36]

Mrs. Ince knew, for example, that Beaverbrook wanted a painting by Thomas Gainsborough. By the end of 1956, she had helped him acquire two, in both cases owing to a bit of luck. The venerable London gallery Thomas Agnew and Sons had acquired *Lieutenant-Colonel Edmund Nugent*, a 1764 portrait. Beaverbrook wanted it badly, but Agnew had promised to hold it for an American buyer. However, when the American asked for another extension, Geoffrey Agnew wrote to Beaverbrook on June 12 that the painting was now "free."[37] Beaverbrook bought it the next day.

But the greater Gainsborough, perhaps the greatest, at least in Beaverbrook's mind, was a later work, *Peasant Girl Gathering Faggots*. His interest in it underscores what Ian Lumsden wrote decades later when he speculated that Beaverbrook would not have liked the Freud: the old man "gravitated to the portrayal of women in a more ideal, if not to say, romanticized mode." When one dealer offered him another painter's portrait of an admiral, Beaverbrook replied that he already had several "of old gentlemen," and wrote in longhand on the page, "I want a pretty, young and colourful girl."[38]

He had already been forced to give up one such girl, a portrait by Fragonard called *Mlle Marie Catherine Colombe*. It, and Beaverbrook himself, had been caught up in a tangled legal dispute involving a Manhattan widow, Mrs. Watson Dickerman, who claimed she had given the painting to a New York dealer, Anthony Seaton, to sell. When she changed her mind and asked him to return it, he'd "converted the Fragonard to his own use" and given her an imitation, she claimed. Seaton had sold the original to Hirschl and Adler Galleries of Park Avenue, who then sold it to Beaverbrook for $17,500. Compounding the problem was Seaton's death in the midst of the turmoil, which put an end to criminal charges against him but which drew an insurance company into the mix.[39] Hirschl and Adler wrote to Beaverbrook, pleading with him to return the painting for a full refund, including expenses, and assuring him that "this is the very first incident of this kind that we have had in our business careers."[40] Presumably the painting's return was the key to a settlement of the whole affair, and Beaverbrook complied, but it left him seeking another "pretty, young and colourful girl" to replace her.

Gainsborough's *Peasant Girl Gathering Faggots* fit the bill. It was part of a group of paintings the artist created late in life that his contemporary, Sir Joshua Reynolds, the first president of the Royal Academy, called "fancy pictures." One might even consider these portraits of anonymous rural characters to be propaganda, given that their "idealized mood of humility and gratitude appealed to picture-buying landowners [at a time when] new legislation had left the rural poor more dependent on the generosity of employers and local charities."[41] As Beaverbrook pulled Tweedie's and Wardell's strings and prepared his great gift to "the farmers and fishermen" of New Brunswick, perhaps he saw something reassuringly familiar in the *Peasant Girl*'s acquiescent demeanour: acceptance of his own tendency to dominate, to control.

Gainsborough was a favourite of the Royal Family and a crowd-pleaser, producing unpretentious works such as the ubiquitous *Blue Boy*. He and Reynolds were "businessmen with an eye to the main chance of the contemporary market; indeed it could be said that between them they made acceptable the idea of the professional artist in Britain," and Gainsborough seems not unlike Beaverbrook himself: "an outwardly sociable, quick-witted, garrulous, generous, intelligent, and promiscuous man." He had little formal education, rarely read books and was hardly an intellectual, which may account for his "surprisingly weak grasp of the rudiments of mixing and applying paint,"[42] a shortcoming that would one day haunt the Beaverbrook Art Gallery.

Gainsborough painted the *Peasant Girl* in 1782, toward the end of his life. The Abdy family, with whom the artist lived for a time at their country house in Essex, would claim that one of their children had been the model, though experts doubt the claim. It was believed for years that Gainsborough himself had given the work to the family, though it later emerged that they'd bought it from his widow in 1797, nine years after his death. It dropped out of sight for a time, was rediscovered in the attic of the house in Essex in 1880,[43] and remained in the family until 1956. The trustees of the estate of Sir Anthony Charles Sykes Abdy let it be known that they might sell the work, but — anathema to Beaverbrook — they would not name a price. "The Trustees are not unanimous in a desire to sell the picture," their solicitors wrote to Mrs. Ince. "One of the trustees is a grandson of the late Sir A.C.S. Abdy and also an ultimate beneficiary. In the circumstances we must leave it to you to make an offer which will be put before the Trustees for their consideration."[44]

Beaverbrook was beside himself. He wanted the *Peasant Girl* badly, but he was determined not to pay more than fair market price for any painting. The problem was that the market knew he was buying — and he knew that the market knew. "How can I be on both sides of the table, a buyer and a seller," he fumed to Mrs. Ince. "But if they will be so good as to tell me if they want to sell the painting and what price they put upon it, that I will give an immediate answer." Mrs. Ince spoke to the solicitors again, but to no avail. "I am afraid we are not going to make any headway with these people. They simply reiterate that they leave it to you to make an offer. The Trustees' attitude seems to be that if Lord Beaverbrook wants the painting he should suggest a figure for it. They are not even agreed amongst themselves that they want to sell the picture." Nor was Beaverbrook willing to budge. "Mrs. Ince you will tell them that I am certainly interested in the picture, but I will not, cannot be persuaded to make an offer," he barked into his Soundscriber, a rudimentary recording device that allowed him to send audio memos on small plastic discs. "They are the vendors. They must decide amongst themselves whether they want to sell or not. If they should want to sell, and if they name a price I will be very glad indeed to have the opportunity of buying in case I can meet their price." It is not clear who finally gave ground, but within weeks, Beaverbrook was receiving letters of praise from dealers and collectors. He had acquired the *Peasant Girl* for £17,500. "I want to send you my warmest congratulations," Geoffrey Agnew wrote. "It is the perfect complementary picture to your Gainsborough portrait of Colonel Nugent, showing another side of his genius as an artist. If I could not own the picture, I am delighted that you should, and I hope it will give you long and lasting pleasure."[45]

Beaverbrook revelled in the knowledge that his purchase had sent a ripple of excitement through the art market. "I am so pleased you approve of the picture of the *Peasant Girl Gathering Sticks*," he wrote to Agnew. "I like it very much. In fact, it is the most pleasing picture I have seen since I lost *Mademoiselle Colombe*." He assigned Mrs. Ince to track down references to the painting in old catalogues, and when one gallery — to which the Abdy family had lent the painting in 1909 — sent him a copy of its exhibition catalogue, Beaverbrook thanked the gallery profusely and again revealed his love for the work. "It is one of my pictures of which I am very fond. I find it quite beautiful."[46] He would later refer to it and the portrait of Nugent as "possibly [the] finest examples" of Gainsborough's work, and he had the *Express* publish a story on his acquisition of the *Peasant Girl* for the gallery he would build in Canada.

This urge for self-promotion had an unintended consequence: Beaverbrook and Mrs. Ince were soon deluged with Gainsborough-related offers, some credible, some anything but. A man named L.G.A.

Thomas, for example, wrote the following August that he, too, had a Gainsborough, *Peasant Girl Burning Sticks*, which was "reputed to be one of a pair."[47] Mrs. Ince noted in a memorandum to Beaverbrook that Thomas's painting was about one-fifth the size of *Peasant Girl Gathering Faggots*, "so there is no chance" of the two being a pair. Still, Beaverbrook indulged the man, having Mrs. Ince request a photograph of the smaller work. Thomas, encouraged, obliged and wrote, "My wife and I think that the model is the same in both and that the girl, possibly his daughter, was say 6 years younger in my picture." He told Beaverbrook to keep the photo — he had "a few copies in reserve" — and also enclosed photos of two miniature oil paintings. "Any ideas as to the age and origin of these would be welcome." Amused, Beaverbrook told Mrs. Ince, "You will deal of course with the letter from Mr. Thomas. Write him a nice reply. Plainly his picture is not a Gainsborough." As instructed, Mrs. Ince was the very model of diplomacy when she thanked Thomas for the photograph of *Peasant Girl Burning Sticks*. "I have to thank you also for giving Lord Beaverbrook the opportunity to borrow your picture at any time for exhibition purposes," she wrote. " Lord Beaverbrook was much touched by your kindness. Unfortunately Lord Beaverbrook is unable to help you in deciding the age and origin of the miniatures. These are something quite outside his knowledge."

Thomas was followed quickly by a Mrs. E.N. Brown, who informed Beaverbrook that she had seen him once "very, very, many years ago" when he arrived at the Haymarket Theatre to see John Barrymore in *Hamlet*. "You arrived with a most beautiful woman, so very beautiful that she made me think you were the most ugliest man I had ever seen (please do forgive me if this seems very rude)." Given Beaverbrook's purchase of the Gainsborough, she wondered if he might also help "some of our struggling artists of today" by buying their paintings as well. She knew of one amateur who painted "extremely good landscapes" but "he just is not in the position to meet the *Right* people to put him on the road to success." She asked if Beaverbrook would be willing to see some of his paintings. "Oh what encouragement it would give him." Fortunately, Mrs. Ince was in this case able to use her standard reply to unsolicited offers of paintings, saying Beaverbrook had his "programme" from which he would not "diverge."

Then came Sir Alfred Munnings, an artist whom Beaverbrook had commissioned to contribute to the Canadian War Memorials Fund. He suggested Beaverbrook buy the house where Gainsborough was born and turn it into a tourist attraction. Beaverbrook begged off, citing a full plate of projects, but he did make sure the *Express* published Munnings's appeal for government funding, which had been rejected by the *Times*. The house was eventually restored and turned into a tourist attraction without Beaverbrook's help. And there were other more bizarre entreaties. A man named Wilfrid Benham offered to put at Beaverbrook's disposal his ability to distinguish real Gainsboroughs from fakes by taking what he called "bimetic" readings of the painting's surface. This involved dangling a small crystal ball on the end of a short piece of thread in front of a painting to detect "waves reflecting an artist's personality [that] radiate from the paint on the canvas." The following spring, a man named Roger Hooper offered to sell Beaverbrook another Gainsborough because he needed the money to fund his work as what he called a "Keeper of the Testaments." This secret order, Hooper explained, was dedicated to receiving "the political testaments of heads of state." Hooper himself had received the testaments of King George V, Hitler and Stalin, which had to be read using the same code book that revealed the "secret secondary messages" concealed in the Bible. Mrs. Ince responded politely that Beaverbrook's two Gainsboroughs were all he needed. She avoided commenting on Hooper's testament assessing and Bible-code cracking.[48]

None of this diminished Beaverbrook's delight in his *Peasant Girl*. He guarded the painting jealously, refusing a 1957 request from the National Gallery to borrow it for an exhibition being mounted in conjunction with a gallery in Toledo, Ohio. He still hoped to open his Fredericton gallery early in 1958, and "we will be in a dreadful difficulty if the *Peasant Girl Gathering Faggots* was missing from the collection." He did part with it long enough for one of London's top restorers, Horace Buttery, to clean it up, but he clearly missed it. "I hope to call on you very shortly to see the *Peasant Girl*," he

9th April, 1957.

Dear Mr. Buttery,

      I believe a cheque has been sent off to you and no doubt you will receive it tomorrow.

      Lord Beaverbrook is delighted with the PEASANT GIRL. He feels it is the loveliest painting he has and since it has been cleaned it is a joy to see.

      We are going to miss her terribly when she goes!!!

      Thanking you once more for your very great kindness to me in coming to Arlington House on that afternoon when I was absolutely certain Colonel Nugent was ruined!!!

      Yours sincerely,

      (Mrs.) M. Ince.

Horace Buttery, Esq.,

Mrs. Ince praises the *Peasant Girl*.

Beaverbrook Canadian Correspondence (BCC), case 25, file 1, no. 15421

wrote to Buttery, "which I understand is looking magnificent." Even the normally taciturn Mrs. Ince developed a fondness for the work. "We are going to miss her terribly when she goes!!!"[49] She was finally sent on her way to Fredericton in the spring of 1958. Almost half a century later, Beaverbrook's travelling secretary, Josephine Yorke, would remember his love for the Gainsborough. In a 2004 interview, she said, "He *loved* his little girl gathering faggots."

*

Not long after the *Peasant Girl* was shipped to New Brunswick, Beaverbrook acquired another of the most important paintings in his collection, J.M.W. Turner's *The Fountain of Indolence*. He had been pursuing Turners for some time, assigning another of his agents, Paul Duval, to scour auction records at Sotheby's, Christie's and other houses to find out whether a good one would become available. In October, Duval reported that only two Turners had come up for sale recently, a small oil sketch and a decoration painted on a tea tray. Neither, he said, "would have been worth consideration for a gallery collection." Duval reminded Beaverbrook that Turner had left "much of his great work to the nation, and the balance has since been bought by public collections. Sale by a public institution . . . is a rare event." A second letter from Duval on the same date pointed out that the American auction house Parke-Bernet was selling a significant Turner, *Staffa, Fingal's Cave*. It was too late: Geoffrey Agnew, the art dealer, told Beaverbrook later that month that he'd purchased the painting, "one of the great landscapes of the world. . . . If I had know [*sic*] I would have acted on your behalf instead of buying it for myself." Then in May 1958, shortly after Beaverbrook had shipped his smaller, inferior Turner, *Warkworth Castle, Northumberland*, to Fredericton, he was offered a chance to view *The Fountain of Indolence*. "This is a picture of great importance both in regard to subject, period (1834 R.A.), merit and provenance," wrote a Mr. Johnson from Leggatt Brothers, another dealer, "and it would seem to me very unlikely that I would have another opportunity of offering a picture of this import-ance by Turner for Your Lordship's collection."[50]

Beaverbrook had his "first-rate" Turner at last. He might have been surprised that such a great work by a great artist had received mixed reviews when it was first displayed in 1834 at the Royal Academy of Arts. A critic for the weekly literary review *The Athenaeum* quoted from the poem that inspired Turner, James Thomson's "The Castle of Indolence," to describe the painting: "fond to begin, but for to finish loth." Other critics, recognizing the scene as fantasy, allowed Turner some licence in his bold use of colours, but grudgingly. The

Spectator critic wrote of both *The Fountain of Indolence* and another new Turner, *The Golden Bough*, "The purity, harmony and transparency of Turner's colouring, redeem his pictures from the reproach of being wholly unnatural: but not all the magic of his pencil, nor the poetry of the scene, justifies him in o'erstepping the modesty of nature." The *Literary Gazette* likewise offered qualified praise. No other painter's imagination was "so replete with rare and gorgeous landscape imagery," it said. The cupids were "indistinct and unintelligible when closely inspected, but, when viewed at proper distance," assumed shape and meaning, delighting the eye "with the finest poetical and pictorial beauty." *Arnold's Magazine* was unequivocal, however: "A more gorgeous specimen of his genius never came before the public."[51]

The provenance of *The Fountain of Indolence* is sketchy from 1834, when Turner painted it, until 1882, when Thomas Agnew and Sons of London bought it from "H. Lumley" and then sold it to a member of New York's Vanderbilt family, which kept the painting until Beaverbrook bought it in 1958. This gap in its history has contributed to a Turner mystery: is it the same painting as a "lost" work by the artist called *The Fountain of Fallacy*? The latter painting is recorded as having been exhibited in 1839, and Turner referred to it in a letter the same year as the only picture of that size among the works he had to sell. Turner's remark bolsters the theory that there was only one painting, which Turner may have altered and renamed between 1834 and 1839. The second title echoes one of the artist's own poems, "Fallacies of Hope," leading one expert to speculate whether "he had the idea — perhaps in a jocular mood — of reinforcing his claims as a poet by changing the title from one which referred to Thomson the poet to Turner the poet." A description of *The Fountain of Fallacy* in *The Athenaeum* is an uncannily accurate description of *The Fountain of Indolence* as well. But believers in the two-paintings theory note that there is no explanation for the title reverting to the original, nor why the critics who reviewed *The Fountain of Fallacy* in 1839 didn't recognize it as the same, albeit altered, canvas they had seen five years earlier.[52]

Though the major works in Beaverbrook's collection were now

in place, he continued to seek more paintings. "Had I been wise and started my collection when you began yours," he wrote to the American financier and art collector Joseph Hirshhorn just two months after buying the Turner, "I should not now have the problem of equipping the art gallery in Fredericton. My progress is slow. I reject all but the very best." There would soon be another casualty of this impatient desire for excellence. Beaverbrook had asked Paul Duval, who had worked at *Saturday Night* magazine, to check on some of the prices paid by Le Roux. Beaverbrook had called him "the best authority I can find on Canadian paintings." But Duval, too, would falter under his patron's scrutiny. His offence was not nearly as serious as Le Roux's, but for Beaverbrook it was still infuriating: Duval simply didn't move quickly enough. In 1956, Duval wrote to Beaverbrook that several works were coming up for sale, including two by Sir Thomas Lawrence. Though the letter was dated December 3, the envelope was postmarked December 11, Beaverbrook noted. "The pictures were exhibited and sold on December the 12th," he wrote. "Therefore, I had no advice from you and nothing was done. It is a pity." The following year Beaverbrook would complain of Duval, "I can't get him to answer my letters. He is a very good man at everything except paperwork and keeping appointments. I have written him about ten letters since I have come to Nassau, and I have not had an answer to any of them. I suppose I must give him up." He held off, noting Duval had acquired several good paintings for him "without resort to secret commission," which was Le Roux's crime.[53] But when Duval failed to turn up on time in Fredericton the following year, Beaverbrook ended the relationship.

For Canadian art, Beaverbrook turned next to Claire Watson, who had worked at the Montreal gallery of her father, William Watson, whom she described as a "pioneer" in the art world.[54] Beaverbrook had bought a Horatio Walker from her, so she wrote to him as a courtesy when her father decided in 1958 to retire and liquidate the business. Beaverbrook immediately asked her to work for him, buying Canadian art for the gallery. "This appeals to me very much; your undertaking will surely enrich the Maritimes, and the whole of Canada," she replied. She warned him that paintings of museum quality were scarce, but "given a reasonable amount of time, I feel sure that I can find some treasures for you." He invited her to London at his expense and offered to pay her $500 a month from July to October for examining the paintings in Fredericton, choosing what should be discarded, deciding what he lacked and tracking it down, and writing biographies —"as lively as possible," he said — of the artists in the Canadian collection.⁵⁵

There followed an intense four-month exchange of correspondence on buying, selling, exchanging, restoring and reframing paintings. "He loved art," she said five decades later. "He really did. He wasn't collecting as an investment. He was collecting because he loved it, and his dream was to pass this on to his people, in New Brunswick." But Watson's role collided with Beaverbrook's traditional views. When she suggested that there would still be plenty of work for her after the end of her contract in October, he vetoed the idea on the grounds that she was getting married. "I am very deeply grateful for all your help and I would like you to remain with me," he told her. "But I have learned that married women are not as efficient as those who have yet to enjoy the state of marital bliss with the blessing of the Church." When she told him a month later that her wedding had been postponed until 1959, and that her fiancé offered his "full approval and encouragement" to her continuing to work after the wedding, Beaverbrook insisted he knew better than her own future husband. "You have commitments leading to your marriage which have to be taken into account." When she asked what she should do if dealers continued to contact her with paintings to offer him, Beaverbrook instructed her to stay in touch with them and to let him know if there was something worth buying.⁵⁶ He may not have wanted to employ a married woman, but he seemed willing to avail himself of her services for free.

Beaverbrook also added to the growing collection for the gallery by cajoling his wealthy friends to offer gifts. Mining magnate James Boylen donated twenty-two paintings from his Cornelius Krieghoff collection. Lucile Pillow, a Montrealer who summered in St. Andrews, gave a collection of British porcelain and two paintings; Beaverbrook appointed her to the gallery board. And though Beaverbrook's friend

Sir James Dunn had died on New Year's Day 1956, his widow, Lady Dunn, who controlled the foundation created in his name, gave the gallery several paintings, most importantly Salvador Dali's *Santiago El Grande*. The Spanish surrealist, who had befriended the Dunns, had created the massive depiction of Spain's military patron saint for the Spanish pavilion at the 1958 world's fair in Brussels. Measuring more than thirteen feet high and ten feet across, it was destined to become the gallery's signature painting. "This picture is the favourite piece in the gallery and commands intense attention from every section, young and old together," Beaverbrook later wrote. "Many visitors sit for long looking in silence and profound meditation upon *Santiago*."[57]

It made for an impressive collection. Constable would praise the "outstanding examples" of Reynolds, Gainsborough and Turner and the way in which the collection represented "the illustrative story-telling phase" of British art in the nineteenth century as well as the "imaginative and sensitive treatment of abstract forms" by contemporary artists such as Graham Sutherland and the "social realism of a younger generation still." The Canadian works, he wrote, included examples of the European tradition, such as the works by Krieghoff, as well as the development of a distinctively Canadian style inspired by the country's landscape, seen in works by members of the Group of Seven. The inclusion of younger artists, Constable said, "demonstrates the importance of painting as a living art." On the other hand, Sir Alec Martin, the chairman of Christie's auction house and another advisor, recommended some paintings not be hung. They would be "all right for a small private house in a far distant town but not up to the standard of a public gallery even in a small town." John Steegman of the Montreal Museum of Fine Art agreed that too many paintings were "poor by almost any standard, especially as some others are very good by any standard." He recommended only the best paintings be hung, lest the new gallery be the subject of negative reviews. "Any hint of derision would be a poor return for your vast generosity and public spirit."[58]

Beaverbrook sent Steegman back to Fredericton to draw up a list of paintings that ought to remain in the vault. Master propagandist that he was, he would want to avoid negative reviews at all cost. With

27447

THE BEAVERBROOK FOUNDATIONS

P.O. BOX 36
FREDERICTON, N.B.

SECRETARY:
R. A. TWEEDIE

June 25, 1958

Rt. Hon. Lord Beaverbrook
121/8 Fleet Street
LONDON, E. C. 4, ENGLAND

Dear Lord Beaverbrook:

On April 25th last, I wrote you giving particulars concerning my TRUST ACCOUNT.

At that time the CREDIT BALANCE was $ 6392.01

Since then the following transactions have occurred:

April 30	Stuart Trueman--Story on Art Gallery for Canadian Art	100.00	
April 30	N.B. Telephone Co.--Somerville House	9.17	
May 2	Hayward Allen & Crew--cleaning grounds Somerville House	46.00	
May 12	Maritime Electric--Somerville House	13.25	
May 13	Imperial Oil--Somerville House	96.04	
May 13	City Fredericton--Water, sewerage Somerville	23.40	
May 26	Zeta Rosenberg--Filing Clerk	38.00	
May 30	Zeta Rosenberg--Filing Clerk	38.00	
June 3	Hayward Allen--Grounds Somerville..	13.00	
	(Carried Forward) ...... $ 376.86		6392.01

The first page of Bob Tweedie's expense report showing payment
to Stuart Trueman for his favourable article about the gallery.

Wardell under his thumb, he was naturally guaranteed effusive coverage in the *Daily Gleaner*. He was also able to finesse positive attention elsewhere, through methods that would be scorned by mainstream journalists today. *Newsweek*, for example, sent him a draft of an article that was to appear in January 1957 and invited him to make any "factual corrections." He found little to quarrel with, either in the description of how he "bounces back to that impoverished land" of his youth once a year to dispense his largesse or in the statement that the gallery would have "the best collection of English and Canadian art in Canada."[59] The article was so fulsome in its praise that both Beaverbrook's *Daily Express* and Wardell's *Daily Gleaner* saw fit to reprint it.

An article published in *Canadian Art Magazine* in November 1958 by journalist Stuart Trueman not only predicted, correctly, that the gallery would become "an integral part of New Brunswick's cultural heritage," it also referred to Beaverbrook's "much-written-about qualities of vigour, impetuosity, tenacity, intuitive genius and extraordinary resourcefulness." Beaverbrook thanked Trueman for the article, calling it "a brilliant account, although altogether too favourable to me," a remarkable expression of false modesty from a man who, according to Bob Tweedie's expense records, paid Trueman $100 — the equivalent of $715 in 2006 — to write the piece.[60]

With his old instinct for propaganda kicking into high gear, Beaverbrook knew the collection would reflect well on him. And not without reason: it contained many weak paintings but also many treasures. Considering the speed and haphazardness with which it was assembled, "the batting average was rather high," Ian Lumsden, a later curator, would remark.[61]

And it had all been terribly instructive. "The rich man loose in the art market has a lot to learn," Constable would say of him years later.[62] Beaverbrook's tutelage went beyond the mere buying and selling of art. Before he finally opened his gallery, he would also endure lessons in architecture, construction and, most painfully, the arcane world of lighting.

The Beaverbrook Art Gallery shortly after
it opened on September 16, 1959.

Beaverbrook Art Gallery

CHAPTER FIVE

"The way is dark, and the dark is very dark"

"This lovely little building, 'a gem' some experts have called it, was from the very beginning, ill-starred."[1] So wrote Bob Tweedie in his memoirs when he turned to the tumultuous origins of the Beaverbrook Art Gallery. John Steegman in his report to Beaverbrook on the collection of paintings assembled in Fredericton, also praised the structure itself, saying the architect had done an excellent job: "The internal proportions on the main floor are perfect."[2] Beaverbrook must have been relieved, for the design and construction of the gallery gave him many more headaches than the amassing of his collection.

The first disaster came even before Beaverbrook had abandoned Officer's Square as a possible site for the gallery. In May of 1956, Wardell sent Beaverbrook an urgent telegram, informing him that his chosen architect, Lynn Howell, was gravely ill. Lung cancer was suspected; "condition probably hopeless," the telegram said. "I am indeed sorry that his illness is so serious," Beaverbrook replied in a letter on May 17. "It seems I am now faced with the problem of what is to be done about the work on the Art Gallery." Before that letter reached Fredericton, Wardell cabled him again. "Lynn Howell died working drawing[s] uncompleted." He elaborated in a letter the same day. "His wife told me yesterday that he had been trying desperately to finish them." Neil Stewart, Howell's partner, took over the project, with

Beaverbrook decreeing that half the fee would go to Howell's widow.[3]

Stewart called the job "the chance of a lifetime,"[4] but he found it hard to please Beaverbrook, who complained to his friends about how long it was taking Stewart to finish his plans. "I surely enjoyed buying pictures and building up a gallery, but the way is dark, and the dark is very dark," he said. Sir Alec Martin, another in his ever-growing collection of advisors, said, "Make it as simple as you can — I think there is great dignity in simplicity — See that the Galleries are day-lighted by top lantern lights; that your entrance doors are imposing and that the Hall is spacious and welcoming."[5] When W.G. Constable eventually visited the nearly completed building, he discovered that Stewart had made serious errors. "He'd never built a gallery before, so a good many changes had to be made," he remembered. "You've got to have doors big enough for a big picture to get in and the same way for a big picture to get out. He hadn't thought of that kind of thing. He didn't know what gallery work was."[6] Stewart's standing dropped again when he began to dispute the terms of his contract, asking for payment for work that, he argued, was not covered by the original flat fee. "The architect seems to be a very silly fellow," Beaverbrook wrote to Tweedie, who was serving as secretary to the gallery board. "I suppose if we employ an auditor, then we are reflecting on his honesty. As soon as this job is finished, you should replace him by a more sensible man."[7]

Stewart was only one of many problems. Early in 1958 Wardell told Beaverbrook that the quarry cutting the stone for the gallery was teetering on bankruptcy, with only half the stones delivered. A week later, word came that "delivery is assured," but Beaverbrook was skeptical. "This is not the first time I have had that assurance about the stone," he told Wardell. "Nor the second, third, fourth, or even fifth. I am extremely grateful to you for pressing deliveries. And I shall never be content until I hear the stones are there."[8] Wardell himself was the source of another headache when, in a rare moment of rebellion, he protested Beaverbrook's tardiness with an advance payment for printing the gallery catalogue. When Beaverbrook told him to negotiate with Tweedie, Wardell exploded. "I'll do no such thing. Why should I negotiate with Tweedie? I'll negotiate with you and no one else." Wardell later told Tweedie, "How angry he could make me and how he enjoyed doing it."[9]

Beaverbrook also clashed with Hugh John Flemming after the premier discouraged his plan for a fine arts program at the University of New Brunswick because it would compete with an existing program at Mount Allison University. "What did Flemming think I was driving for when I . . . built an art gallery in Fredericton?" Beaverbrook raged to Tweedie. He contemplated abandoning the gallery "as large segments of the population were opposed to it" and making the whole controversy public. The disagreement became tangled up with Beaverbrook's offer to construct an archives building, an offer about which Flemming was not sufficiently excited. Tweedie conducted some shuttle diplomacy with the help of K.C. Irving, and the storm passed. "We have them jumping now," Beaverbrook said to Tweedie one evening, "and we'll keep them jumping. If they are good boys, we may build the archives, but not now." Tweedie bounced, Flemming jumped, and the gallery was saved.[10]

And then came the great lighting crisis. Wardell was again the bearer of bad news, telling Beaverbrook in early July of 1958 that a test of the newly installed lights, supervised by his Fredericton men and by Stewart's design team, left the top half of three walls "interlaced with shadows" — an effect that would obviously defeat the purpose of hanging paintings on the walls. Clearly the system would need a radical overhaul. "This is the penalty we pay for Stewart's lack of experience, and I bitterly regret my part in pressing him on you," Wardell said. The lighting consultant from Montreal with whom Stewart had contracted "was unable to make any contribution to the discussion," Wardell noted. Beaverbrook, his attention to detail always sharp, reminded Wardell that the subject of the lighting had come up when an earlier change in the design raised the ceilings. At the time, the Montreal consultant had told Stewart the changes would be fine. Beaverbrook was furious, asking Tweedie if Stewart was "now going to disturb the lining and damage the walls to carry out the alterations to the lighting which obviously must take place?" Tweedie tried to calm his patron. "The fact that Stewart made no immediate preparation to extend the lighting is not too serious — only stupid."[11]

Wardell and Tweedie met with Stewart and the Montreal consultant again on the night of July 17, joined by Claire Watson and by Constable, who had arrived from Boston. Constable immediately suggested some makeshift solutions, including raising the lights by six inches, switching from floodlights to spotlights, and installing some glass panels to diffuse the light — panels that had been eliminated to save money. The contractors worked through the following day and everyone gathered again late in the afternoon with the skylights covered. "We examined their work thoroughly and hung a painting" in one of the side galleries, Tweedie reported. "It showed up splendidly. Dr. Constable was satisfied. Miss Watson was delighted and Wardell and myself vastly relieved." The central gallery was still a problem, and Stewart would experiment there "with all possible speed." Tweedie told Beaverbrook he would withhold all payments until the work was done. "I want to assure you that Wardell and myself will live and breathe lights and gallery until we have won the battle," he vowed. Wardell, too, believed the crisis was all but over. "Lighting trouble now cured and all well," he cabled to London. Constable was "charmed with the gallery," he added. "I am sure it will be very greatly admired. And architect Stewart will make a great reputation. Heaven help the customer who wants him to design another gallery."[12]

Correcting the lighting in the central gallery proved to be beyond Stewart's abilities. Beaverbrook's friend C.D. Howe recommended he bring in Willard Thompson of Boston, whom Constable described as "one of the best lighting men in the United States." Thompson, Constable, Stewart, Tweedie, Wardell and Colin B. Mackay gathered at the gallery again on August 6. Thompson pronounced Stewart's design twenty-five years out of date and offered two alternatives: he could finish Stewart's work, with adjustments, for $25,000, or he could devise an entirely new plan for $50,000. According to Wardell's minutes of the meeting, Constable was disappointed that the improvements that seemed possible in July "had not come up to his expectation. . . . He felt that the gallery is exceptionally beautiful and that perfection will be expected by many members of the informed public." Yet he suggested the less expensive plan that would incorporate Stewart's lighting in the side galleries. But Tweedie, Wardell and

Mackay, all of whom knew Beaverbrook much better than Constable did, sensed that Beaverbrook's desire for perfection would, in this case, outweigh his considerable frugality. They all endorsed the more expensive Thompson plan.[13]

Within a week, Thompson had decided the work would cost not $50,000 but $65,000. However, the cost of tweaking Stewart's system had shot up as well, to $43,000, and Thompson would offer no guarantee on that option. "We have had a tragedy," Beaverbrook lamented to a friend. "The lighting system has failed us. We have to put in a new system altogether, so it is said." Thompson's new system was a success, but — most frustrating to a man increasingly aware of his own mortality — the delays forced Beaverbrook to postpone the official opening from October 1958 to sometime in 1959. "Our lighting is now entirely satisfactory and I only regret that I did not know as much about lighting problems a year ago as I do at present," he wrote to Alan Jarvis of the National Gallery early in the new year. "I visited many galleries in the United States, studying the lighting. I was particularly impressed by the Gallery at Williamsburg and also by the lighting in the National Gallery in Washington. The New York galleries are poor examples of lighting practice and the Boston Fine Arts is dreadful."[14] This last museum, Jarvis must have noted, was the one Constable had run.

Beaverbrook's search for a curator would prove equally quixotic. One of his first candidates was Russell Harper, a young art historian who had worked at the New Brunswick Museum in Saint John. Beaverbrook's first thought was to give Harper a role at the archives he planned to build, and the two men corresponded at length about tracking down documents and old books relating to New Brunswick history. Beaverbrook eventually hired him as acting curator with an understanding that he'd be considered for the permanent position the following September, but Harper was warned by George Millar — in a remarkably disingenuous letter that denied Beaverbrook's control over the entire project — that "those who are responsible for the appointment are not to be regarded as in any way committed to you, or obligated to you or to Lord Beaverbrook in that connection, and they are free to act quite independently."[15] Harper got a more accurate view of the press baron's level of influence after taking the job, when he found himself assigned several decidedly non-curatorial tasks, such as writing a long report on the progress of a rink that Beaverbrook was building in Newcastle.

Tweedie liked Harper, at least at first, though Wardell felt that Beaverbrook should be more ambitious and seek out someone with more experience. Constable recommended that John Steegman, from Montreal, be hired on a one-year contract; Wardell suggested Constable himself: "He would be a source of strength in the launching period."[16] In February 1959, Beaverbrook, Tweedie, Mackay and A.G. Bailey, the university librarian, met with a Dr. Breiger, an art historian from the University of Toronto, who provided a list of possible candidates.[17] When Tweedie wrote up the minutes, including Breiger's list, and sent it to Beaverbrook in London, he also included a separate list of nineteen applicants, including Harper and another young man Tweedie was championing, Sinclair Healy.

Healy was a young artist from Moncton and a Beaverbrook Scholar, though Beaverbrook felt he had been "improperly prepared" to study in England. He also applied some unusual criteria to Healy, asking Tweedie whether he was attractive and dressed well. Noting that Healy had a wife, he reminded Tweedie "that Dr. Mackay had a tremendous success at UNB on account of his being a bachelor. The female student body increased by some 500% — I think!" He suggested that Tweedie meet Mrs. Healy. "If she is personable and, indeed, attractive, with a capacity for mobilizing support for her husband, then that will strengthen Healy's application considerably." Healy himself decided that he wasn't a good fit. "I had ideas about running the gallery relative to it being an education thing as well as a gallery," he says now, whereas, he said, Beaverbrook wanted it to be more of "a social circumstance." Invited to write down his vision for the gallery, Healy realized he could either cater to the press baron's ideas or be straightforward about his own view of art and the public. "I do believe you have to approach it in ways that people understand," he said, in ways "that reach into all aspects of life." Therefore his vision statement included a warning that the paintings in the gallery would be quite new to most New Brunswickers. "Most have not had art in their education and now have little appreciation or understanding of art and consider it to be a mystic thing only for the select few," he wrote. They would need to visit the gallery repeatedly, so he suggested exhibitions that catered to "present interest levels," such as "bridges or building for engineers and architects, silver and tableware for housewives, travel posters, photographs, fine automobiles for their appeal to men, etc."[18] He guessed, correctly, that these ideas would take him out of the running. "Assessing it in retrospect, I made the proper decision for me," says Healy, who shortly afterwards moved to Vancouver to start a long career teaching art at the University of British Columbia. "I wouldn't change a thing." Told in 2007 of Beaverbrook's interest in his wife's appearance, Healy says, "She's *still* attractive."

Healy had unwittingly confronted one of the chief reasons why the press baron had so much difficulty finding a curator: his desire to impose his own will and vision on the gallery, including on the curator. The legislation that created the gallery said that it would be run by a board of governors, chaired by New Brunswick's lieutenant-governor and composed of other provincial notables, including the premier and the leader of the opposition; the curator, naturally, would report to the board. But the act also created the role of custodian and gave that person final authority over which paintings were brought into and taken out of the gallery. Beaverbrook's decision to give himself the position sent a clear signal that the curator would not have much leeway. John Steegman told him this was not the way most galleries operated. "In all museums, responsibility is divided between the Board and their Curator," he said, not even mentioning the anomaly of the custodian position. The powers of both the board and the curator had to be "defined and adhered to" so that the curator would know "the extent of his personal responsibility and authority." Steegman would later tell Beaverbrook that one reason he turned down the job himself "was, frankly, my feeling that the Curator would have very little say in the matter of acquisitions, and that the extent of his responsibility as an advisor would not be clearly defined; maybe I'm wrong there, but that was the impression I formed."[19] Steegman, as it turned out, wasn't wrong at all. He was remarkably perceptive about Beaverbrook.

The need for a permanent curator became more acute when Bob Tweedie began to sour on Harper. The acting curator had begun setting up a registry of paintings in the collection, known in the art world as accession records. One Beaverbrook biographer says it appears he had "no notion of the proper way to document the paintings that Beaverbrook shipped over." But London didn't help matters, rarely sending complete histories of the ownership. "It was almost like you were receiving hot merchandise," one gallery official was quoted as saying.[20] Harper never finished the job, though in February 1959, he did successfully organize the transportation of the paintings from the Bonar Law–Bennett library to the gallery "without casualties," as he put it. Tweedie told Beaverbrook that Harper was "moody, temperamental and continually talks of frustrations. He is certainly lacking in personality and on sober reflection I share fully your view that he could not lead the Gallery to the success that we all wish for it." Beaverbrook had offered Harper the job permanently, but he now told Tweedie not to let the offer stand too long in case Harper wanted to use it as "a basis on which to negotiate for employment elsewhere." Tweedie stepped up his lobbying against Harper. "I believe we would be in conflict with him were he appointed permanently. He seems to have a chip on his shoulder and appears happiest when he has found a crack in a wall or a splinter off a table. The Gallery must be buoyantly and joyously led — nothing else is good enough." The same day, Harper told Tweedie he'd accept the job at $8,000 a year — a considerable sum at the time — "but only if the terms of reference are well defined."[21] Harper, too, appeared to sense just how little independence Beaverbrook would give his gallery staff.

In the midst of the tug-of-war over his future at the gallery, Harper was confronted with a more practical challenge: what to do with Dali's massive *Santiago El Grande*. "It comes to us rolled in [an] enormous box weighing about 1000 pounds which Dr. Mackay insists must be placed in the vault with the result that the vault passage is partially blocked," he told Mrs. Ince. "Lord Beaverbrook has written to Lady Dunn saying that the box is not to be opened until

Sir Alec Martin arrives to open it. Consequently we cannot take a photograph." A frame for the painting would have to be built inside the gallery because the gallery did not have doors large enough to accommodate one assembled elsewhere. The Dali caused considerable consternation, and Beaverbrook's various advisors were pressed into service. "The problem, as I am sure you will realise, is not just the simple matter of constructing a frame," John Steegman wrote from Montreal. "The rolled-up canvas has to be very carefully unrolled and stretched on to the stretcher. This, especially for a canvas of this size, is a highly expert job, quite separate from the actual framing." Steegman could spare no one from his staff, nor could the National Gallery in Ottawa, but a gallery in Toronto might have someone. In the meantime, he suggested the canvas would be safer rolled up in its box. Beaverbrook decided to have a frame made in London and shipped to Fredericton in sections. "I am making enquiries at this moment," Mrs. Ince wrote in late April, "as to whether they can get through the door of the airplane from London to Montreal and then from Montreal to Fredericton."[22] They could, and the segments were dispatched to Fredericton, with Sir Alec Martin recruited to supervise the unrolling, stretching and framing of *Santiago*.

Harper chose this moment to demand that Beaverbrook hire him by mid-April or else he would leave by the end of May. Mrs. Ince told Tweedie that Beaverbrook would arrive in Fredericton toward the end of May and would speak to Harper personally. "In the meantime, Lord Beaverbrook says 'let things drift.' There is no answer to an ultimatum." As Beaverbrook had speculated, Harper had another job lined up, as an archaeologist at Fortress Louisbourg in Nova Scotia, and he made good on his threat to quit. "The fact that I have not been appointed to a position at the Art Gallery indicates a failure to feel that I am the proper person to take charge," he said. He was interested in the archives project, "but future developments seem shrouded in the mists of uncertainty." A few days later he wrote a personal letter to Mrs. Ince. "I make the break with many misgivings and regrets but I dislike intensely living in a turmoil and uncertainty and really felt that I have more to offer in the way of a contribution to things here than was being used. I am afraid that Lord Beaverbrook will feel hurt at my decision, possibly not, but at any rate am sure that I would have been unwise to do other than I have."²³ Beaverbrook thanked Harper for his service and immediately offered John Steegman a one-year contract. After Steegman turned it down, Beaverbrook contacted Edwy Cooke of the University of Toronto, one of the names on Breiger's list, and Cooke accepted.

All that remained now was to plan a ceremony grand enough to honour Beaverbrook's great gift suitably. "I am excited about the gallery opening," Tweedie enthused in a letter in March 1959. "We can make it the biggest, the most colourful and important event which has ever taken place in the province." If ever Tweedie would bounce for his patron, it would be now. With the board narrowing its choice of dates to sometime in September, he contacted the Lord Beaverbrook Hotel in March — six months in advance — to instruct them to keep the ballroom, dining room and guest rooms free of bookings. He was anxious to avoid a repetition of the previous summer, when Beaverbrook flew into a rage upon learning that the hotel was already booked for the dates on which he wanted to host a dinner for military regiments. He called the situation "monstrous," perhaps forgetting that though his name was on the building, he didn't own it. "I wonder why they make all those plans without asking me if I want anything," he fumed. "I hope that Mr. Tweedie will try to break through that stuff, so that I can have proper facilities."²⁴

Beaverbrook showed considerably more forbearance when Tweedie informed him in April 1959 that the hotel was prepared to bump a May 25 wedding reception out of the ballroom to make room for a small dinner on his eightieth birthday. He had decided to mark the occasion, not in grand style in London, but in Fredericton, no doubt so he could check up on his gallery. But, he cabled Tweedie, he "would not on any account disturb wedding party." He instructed him to stand down and arrange for facilities elsewhere. Beaverbrook's stature was such, however, that the hotel persuaded the family to put off the reception an extra day to accommodate him. The family, which was Jewish, Tweedie reported, "would be happy indeed to meet our wishes and defer their affair until May 26th. May 26th happened to be some sort of a Jewish holiday and the Rabbi here had to obtain special dispensation from the higher authorities in Montreal to hold the function on May 26th."[25]

Preparations raced forward and Tweedie was kept bouncing. Teachers and Beaverbrook Scholars who had travelled to England chipped in to pay for a plaque next to the gallery door. Their plan was to refer to their benefactor as "Max Aitken," something Tweedie found a bit too familiar. He suggested that it be changed to "William Maxwell Aitken," but Beaverbrook overruled him. "As tablet dedicated with affection Max Aitken happier choice," he cabled, and Tweedie saw his point. "I must say that I agree fully and completely with you. I thought it was a much warmer choice than William Maxwell." Having wrested from Maritime Electric an agreement to charge the gallery a lower rate, thanks to the new wiring that it would soon install, Tweedie was then instructed to persuade the utility to absorb the cost of installing the new wiring "because they never ought [to have] put in the present system." And it was Tweedie who informed the art gallery's board that Beaverbrook had agreed to their suggested opening date, reminding them that the powers they had in law had limits in reality. "As Lord Beaverbrook's plans unfold concerning the opening, you will, of course, be kept fully advised."[26] Tweedie's loyalty was rewarded: Beaverbrook asked Flemming in a letter, hand-delivered to the premier by Tweedie himself, for a suggestion about what Tweedie should be paid for his work as secretary to the gallery.[27] Flemming proposed a lump sum of $4,800, or $200 for each month of the two years he'd served. When added to Beaverbrook's annual $3,000 "gift," the salary represented a significant increase in Tweedie's indebtedness to the press baron.

A final drama had to play out before the gallery could open, an echo of Beaverbrook's role in the abdication crisis more than two decades earlier. Queen Elizabeth was to visit Fredericton in July, and Beaverbrook told Wardell that she was to be admitted to the gallery in advance of its official opening, but only she, no one else. "I am spending a great deal of time and money in making arrangements for an Opening which will bring to the capital many distinguished visitors from Foreign lands. But the labour is considerable and the expenditure might be described as substantial. I will certainly give it all up if the Gallery loses its virginity now. . . . I am bound to say that it would be a relief to be rid of the trouble. Strange how men pay to make trouble for themselves." In the event, the Queen's schedule in Fredericton did not include the gallery, and Beaverbrook was hurt that, in his role as chancellor of the university, he was not invited to meet her. "I take it all this arises from my support of the Duke of Windsor when he was Monarch," he grumbled to Wardell.[28]

The gallery opened at last on September 16, 1959, a bright, cool day of the kind for which Fredericton is famous. All of the city's hotels were booked solid. Queen Street, where the gallery stood across from the Legislature, was closed to traffic. University students led invited guests in the hundreds to chairs set up on the lawn in front of the building. Premiers, federal cabinet ministers, judges, and press barons were among the dignitaries. Sir James Dunn's widow, Lady Dunn, known to her friends as Christofor, was there, as was Sir John Rothenstein of the Tate Gallery. The Royal Highland Regiment military band played, and an RCMP guard of honour stood at the gallery's entrance. Beaverbrook came out the doors at three o'clock, followed by Constable, Cooke and members of the gallery's board. Beaverbrook had chosen Constable to deliver the only speech of the afternoon. "This is not the first great service that Lord Beaverbrook has done for the arts in Canada," he said, but "it's incomparably the most important." He urged the people of New Brunswick — many of them listening at home to a live radio broadcast of the ceremony — to make the gallery their own. "Make this gallery your gallery, let us say our gallery. Make it our playground, our delight, our source of inspiration, and learn to use what you have before you, and above all learn to enjoy it. . . . It makes me greatly daring to paraphrase one of the most moving sentences, I always feel, ever uttered by an Englishman and to say that this day, Lord Beaverbrook, you've lit such a candle in New Brunswick as by God's grace will never be put out."[29]

Beaverbrook rose, thanked him, and invited him to open the gallery. Constable cut a red ribbon draped across the doors, and the public streamed inside.

In addition to the Gainsboroughs, the Turners, the Dali and the Freud, there were countless other treasures on the walls to delight these first visitors: works by Sir Joshua Reynolds, Homer Watson, John Constable, William Hogarth, Thomas Lawrence, John Singer Sargent. There were paintings by Canadian artists whose stature would continue to grow in the decades to come, such as Emily Carr and Alex Colville. And there were pieces that would stir the kind of controversy that so delighted Beaverbrook. In 1955, he had bought from his artist friend Graham Sutherland several studies of Winston Churchill. Sutherland had made the studies as preparation for painting a portrait of Churchill commissioned — as a result of Beaverbrook's prodding — by the British Parliament to mark his eightieth birthday in 1954. But Churchill hated the result, calling it "malignant," and his wife Clementine had it cut up and burned, despite a last-ditch attempt by Beaverbrook to buy it for Fredericton.[30] Churchill felt "he was badly used," Beaverbrook would write.[31] Sutherland later argued that he was "at the mercy" of his sitter. "What he feels or shows at the time, I record." Just then, Churchill was convinced that members of his government were trying to force him out of the leadership, hence his "bull dog" appearance.[32] The studies, all that survived, were a novel addition to the gallery. Sutherland's portrait of Beaverbrook himself still hangs in Fredericton.

The gallery also held several paintings by another artist Beaverbrook had patronized, Walter Sickert. Sickert had been the only artist who had refused a commission from Beaverbrook's British War Memorials Committee — not on anti-war grounds, but because he disliked a member of the committee. Beaverbrook did not hold this against him and played the role of mediator in a dispute between Sickert and Sir James Dunn over a portrait of Beaverbrook that Dunn had commissioned.[33] Later, Beaverbrook decided that Sickert should be well represented in his collection, a choice that would generate publicity for the gallery in 2002, when an American crime novelist, Patricia Cornwell, concluded that Sickert was Jack the Ripper. Cornwell spent her own money to buy Sickert paintings and letters, comparing watermarks, signatures and even DNA. But her bold conclusion — "case closed" — was debunked by some Ripper experts, and she never responded to an invitation to visit Fredericton to analyze the gallery's collection of Sickert's letters to Beaverbrook.

The gallery closed at seven o'clock in the evening of its opening day, and select guests adjourned to the Empire Room at the Lord Beaverbrook Hotel, where Beaverbrook hosted a dinner. The menu featured Consommé Gainsborough, Fillets of Haddocks Hogarth, Chicken Sutherland, Légumes Krieghoff, Champagne Churchill, Exotique Dali, and demitasse. It was at this more intimate, less public event that Beaverbrook explained his own vision of the great legacy he had unveiled. "This Gallery will not satisfy my aim if it is thought of as the last home of a collection of pictures and works of art," he said. "It should rather be a place at which new talents are kindled and guided. A beginning and not an end. That is its purpose above all others. And with that it mind I hand it over to the people of my own province of New Brunswick and in a sense to the young people of Canada. Here is the past and the present. The future lies with them."[34]

A month earlier, Beaverbrook had drafted a different version of the speech. "When a man reaches my age, he can hardly expect to have many new opportunities for leaving his mark on the world. He is going to be remembered by what he has already done. That is usually the case. But perhaps in this respect I am more fortunate than others. In my old age, I had the idea of building this gallery and forming this collection. . . . So it may be that, in time to come, I shall be remembered not by my newspapers — each copy of a newspaper passes into oblivion in twenty-four hours — nor even by my work in politics. It brought me many disappointments as well as some successes. No, it may be that I shall be recalled chiefly as the builder and founder of an art gallery. The labour of age may prove more lasting than the strident achievements of youth or the aggressive toil of middle life. If this should be so, I shall be content. My name will be linked with a beautiful building, with a collection of fine paintings some of which will be imperishable relics of our time, and — most important of all in my eyes — with a fresh inspiration imparted to the art of Canada. The eyes of youth, falling upon these walls, may draw from them an impulse to create and emulate. What happier thought could come to a man of eighty than one which brings him into vital contact with the youngest generation of today and with the generations still to come?"[35]

Lord Beaverbrook chats with Kay McGuire and
Lucinda Flemer at the dinner following the opening
of the Beaverbrook Art Gallery, September 16, 1959.
Beaverbrook Art Gallery

The opening of the gallery was widely praised in the press, and not just by those newspapers that Beaverbrook controlled or influenced — though they were particularly rapturous. In London, the *Daily Express* called it "the day that enriches a nation" and published a large photo of the patron in his gallery, "alone in the treasury of canvas, colour and vision that now belongs to his fellow citizens."[36] Wardell, true to form, showed little restraint in penning a twenty-page article for the September issue of *The Atlantic Advocate*, praising Beaverbrook to the hilt: "it is his idea, his gallery and his pictures that he gives to New Brunswick."[37] Newspapers and magazines with more objectivity were also lavish. The Saint John *Evening Times-Globe*'s headline called the gallery an "incomparable gift,"[38] and even *Time* dubbed it "Beaver's Greatest Landmark." The story, accompanied by images of paintings including Freud's *Hotel Bedroom* and Gainsborough's *Peasant Girl*

Gathering Faggots, said, "Beaverbrook's biggest donation is not the museum but most of the 300-odd paintings hanging in it."[39] Decades later, lawyers would parse all of these phrases with great interest.

Shortly after the gallery opened, Beaverbrook granted an interview to the CBC program *Close-Up*. He was in a reflective and playful mood as he led the television crew through the gallery, reminiscing about his boyhood on the Miramichi and the great men he'd known, such as R.B. Bennett and David Lloyd George, both of whom, he said, had not received their due from history. He remarked briefly on some of the controversies that had touched his life, commenting almost casually that Edward VIII should never have abdicated and that Britain should have stayed out of the wars in Europe. He lamented the decline of the British Empire he loved and the growing movement for independence from what he called "benign" colonial rule. But mostly he wanted to talk about his gallery. When the interviewer asked, "Are you concerned about Red China?" Beaverbrook paused, chuckled, and said, "Let's go and see the pictures. See the red pictures, the red colours in the pictures."

The interviewer clearly knew his subject: he tailored his questions accordingly, prodding the great benefactor on works of art less conventional than those he had put in the gallery. But Beaverbrook was less garrulous on matters artistic than he was on the abdication crisis or the Second World War. "I think some of it is very attractive," he said of modern art. "I like Riopelle very much indeed." He restrained himself as well when asked about abstract art, a genre he had banned from his gallery. "I like various forms and it depends upon the picture," he said kindly, "not upon the kind of art that is presented by the picture." But the journalist was less interested in art than in money: what Beaverbrook had spent on the gallery, what various paintings had cost, and what his father — who never earned more than $1,300 a year as a minister — would have thought of the vast amounts spent on the gallery. "He would have understood, I think," Beaverbrook said, his voice suddenly hushed. "He was a man of great understanding." In a lighter moment, he added, "I am an interesting example of a money-mad man, because I enjoyed immensely making it, and I am enjoying immensely spending it. I enjoyed most making it because it's an easier job. Spending it is much more difficult than making it."

Later, on the banks of the Saint John River just behind the gallery, he told his interviewer, "I never cared for money. If you asked me what I'm worth, I don't know. I have no idea. I've never totalled up my fortune. But I do know how much I'll have if I live much longer. None." He laughed. "It'll all be spent. If I live long enough, I'll spend it."[40]

Beaverbrook was eighty years old. He had lived long enough to spend what was needed on his gallery. "Life is not worth living unless I get the gallery going," he'd written earlier in the year. Now, as the leaves on the trees along the river changed colour, it was open at last, full of beautiful paintings and grateful New Brunswickers.

After so much delay and frustration and so many obstacles, he must have savoured that triumph and the knowledge that all those difficulties with the gallery were surely, finally, behind him for good.

A crowd at the Beaverbrook Art Gallery. *White Dog in a Landscape*
by George Stubbs is at the top, with Gainsborough's *Peasant Girl
Gathering Faggots* directly below it. To its right are two works by
Sir Joshua Reynolds, *Mrs. Thrale and Her Daughter Hester
(Queeney)* and *Mrs. Billington as St. Cecilia.*

CHAPTER SIX

"Let them come and see the paintings where they belong"

The day after the official opening, Bob Tweedie resigned as secretary to the board of governors of the Beaverbrook Art Gallery. The previous evening, during the festivities at the gallery, he had encountered Beaverbrook. "He was cold and aloof, a condition that I regarded as rudeness," Tweedie recalled. He and his wife left the party soon afterwards, inviting Albert Trueman, the head of the Canada Council, and his wife back to their home. Thus Tweedie missed a good part of the grand event he had devoted so much time to organizing. "We spent a happy evening together sipping champagne of a somewhat lesser quality than the supply we had left behind," Tweedie recounted.[1] The next morning he sent his resignation letter to the small flat Beaverbrook had installed in the gallery for his use during his visits to Fredericton. Rather than forthrightly telling Beaverbrook how he felt about the way he'd been treated, Tweedie offered a rather elliptical explanation. "For various reasons, I find it necessary to lighten some of my tasks," he wrote. He offered to continue working with two other Beaverbrook programs, the scholarships and the pension fund set up for retired Presbyterian ministers, but said he would understand if his patron felt that it would be "more efficient and advantageous to lodge all your New Brunswick affairs in one set of hands." Tweedie's stated need to "lighten some of my tasks" was fleeting, however; when Christofor, Lady Dunn, called him an hour or two afterwards to discuss some gallery matter and he told her of his decision, she promptly offered him the job of secretary to the Sir James Dunn Foundation, which she administered. She agreed to match the half-time salary of $7,500 he was earning from the provincial government for his work at the New Brunswick Travel Bureau. He accepted.

Later that day, Beaverbrook summoned Tweedie to the gallery to ask why he was quitting. When Tweedie again talked of lightening his load, Beaverbrook didn't believe him and asked if it was because "I am arrogant, dictatorial and overbearing? I am, you know. I have always been in the driver's seat and that is the way I operate." Tweedie denied that was the reason, but an aide-memoire from later that year — part of Tweedie's correspondence file, though he refers to himself in the third person — describes his true feelings. "Beaverbrook attacked him violently and would not let him have holidays. Attacks were delivered in presence of others which humiliated him."[2]

In the great man's presence down in his private flat in the basement of the gallery, however, Tweedie could not bring himself to complain. Beaverbrook pushed him, saying there had to be "subsidiary reasons" for the resignation. "I declined to elaborate," Tweedie recounted. Beaverbrook said that he was setting up another trust fund, an apparent reference to the establishment of the Beaverbrook Canadian Foundation, that he wanted Tweedie to be the sole executor of it after his death, and that Tweedie's departure from the gallery would make things awkward. "I replied that I would be sorry to cause him inconvenience, but that no man was indispensable, and that I could easily be replaced." Beaverbrook wanted his Tweedie to bounce around, however, and told him he would "shove your letter of resignation aside and . . . come back to it later." Beaverbrook believed Tweedie had resigned to work for Christofor and the Sir James Dunn Foundation. Tweedie could have explained that his resignation had preceded the offer by a couple of hours but felt the truth placed "too much strain on his credulity. . . . I knew he would never accept my explanation." They eventually agreed that Tweedie would carry on as secretary of the gallery until a successor could be found.[3]

Beaverbrook's demands on Tweedie continued as before. He wanted him to continue lobbying Maritime Electric for more favourable power rates. He questioned the gallery's telephone bill, prompting Tweedie to note that two expensive calls to London were "probably ones placed by yourself." He wondered if Tweedie might get concessions for water and sewage charges from the city. He instructed Tweedie to take a tough line with Neil Stewart in another dispute over the architect's bill. He asked about part-time employees at the gallery and opined that Cooke was "overstaffed." Tweedie tried to extricate himself again in July 1960, but rather than insist that he be treated better, Tweedie apologized for not doing enough. "The past twelve years have given me a great deal to reflect upon and perhaps regret that I may not have responded to the constant challenge with as much tenacity as was required, but I have so valued the privilege of serving you that I would like to feel that my efforts were not all in vain."[4] Beaverbrook did not reply to what seems like a plea from Tweedie to be put out of his misery.

Michael Wardell told Beaverbrook that, though he wanted out, Tweedie was also, paradoxically, "bitterly offended" at seeing some of his powers and duties, including signing authority over gallery accounts, shifted to Helen Savage, a young woman Beaverbrook was grooming as secretary. Equally frustrating for Tweedie, Wardell said, was the fact that Beaverbrook had not spoken to him during his two most recent visits to Fredericton. Beaverbrook applied the soothing balm of money, asking the gallery board to pay Tweedie $1,000 to thank him for his services. "They regret your decision to resign your task on account of pressure of duties as secretary of the Sir James Dunn Foundation," he wrote, confirming Tweedie's fear that Beaverbrook had misconstrued his motives. The press baron added that the board wanted Tweedie to return as "Honorary Secretary," with duties that, he said, would be "agreeable, though not onerous." Tweedie seemed thrilled at the prospect of subjecting himself to more of Beaverbrook's treatment. "I intend to be the most *active* honorary secretary you ever saw," he wrote.[5]

Within two months Tweedie was in the hospital with a hemorrhaging ulcer. Beaverbrook sent best wishes for a speedy recovery and followed up with more instructions: his new Canadian Foundation was giving $25,000 for a rink in Newcastle and Tweedie was to oversee the grant. Tweedie's momentary and half-hearted assertion of his rights and his dignity was quickly forgotten; he soon lapsed back into the posture to which both he and Beaverbrook were accustomed. "I am very grateful for this consideration," he wrote when he received another thousand-dollar cheque late in 1961, "and will try very hard to warrant your good-will and friendship in the days and months ahead." When Helen Savage, his replacement as secretary, was preparing to leave the job in March of 1962, Tweedie offered to fill in until a replacement could be found.[6]

Obviously Beaverbrook was more attentive to the minutiae of gallery administration than he was to the feelings of his acolyte. In the time he had left — he was well into the ninth decade of his life now — he was determined to see the gallery run his way, to maintain his control to the very end, particularly over which paintings were shown and how much the gallery was spending. He micromanaged to a remarkable degree, sending letters to curator Edwy Cooke about when to turn off the lights or how to adjust the thermostats. Since his gallery lacked a Bible, he instructed his personal chef to buy all his groceries and other supplies at Sobey's, where a promotion offered customers a free Bible if they collected enough coupons.[7] He reined in Cooke when the curator suggested, upon the death of Canadian painter Paul-Emile Borduas, that the gallery purchase a second work by him. The gallery already had one Borduas, Beaverbrook replied, and that was enough. "I think all that type of painting is nonsense," Beaverbrook grumbled. "I think it will die." He remained vigilant about abstract art, admonishing Cooke several times that it was "intolerable." He carefully approved the publication of the gallery's first catalogue and was kept fully informed about potential flooding from the Saint John River. He insisted on monthly reports on the number of visitors and the volume of sales at the gift shop, specifying they be "as brief as possible, with no details attached just gross figures of sales and so on," then complaining scarcely a month later than he wanted "other information, any other information of interest. . . . I'm only satisfied if I get a full account of what's going on."[8]

In the spring of 1960, he informed Edwy Cooke that a portrait of Princess Margaret should hang in the gallery on May 6, her wedding day. He "suggested" — though Beaverbrook's suggestions were generally taken as commands — that the portrait be decorated with roses and put against the large window looking out on the river. Cooke proposed it instead hang in the British gallery, temporarily replacing five Sickerts, because next to the window, "it would be in competition with the view and the view with it." Cooke also noted that the light coming in would put the painting in shadow. And, he said, the gallery had no easel on which to display the portrait. Beaverbrook overruled him, saying Lady Dunn would send an easel from St. Andrews. Cooke did win on two points, persuading him that the purple velvet he wanted draping the canvas would "cheapen the painting," and that the Queen Elizabeth roses he had asked for were out of season, but Beaverbrook got his way on the placement of the portrait in front of the window.[9] Cooke overcame the lighting problem by having the curtains drawn.

When there was a major crisis Beaverbrook intervened directly. The first occurred just six days after the gallery opened, when Christofor sent him an angry letter written from Dayspring, the estate in the resort town of St. Andrews, New Brunswick, that had belonged to her husband. In it, she complained about the lack of publicity given to *Santiago El Grande*, her gift via the Sir James Dunn Foundation. She was also upset about where she'd been seated at the dinner following the gallery opening. (Tweedie's aide-memoire explained that she had been "confused and aggrieved when she found that the same table was used for rag-tag overflow.")[10] Beaverbrook might have shrugged off the letter and her vow to withdraw from the Maritime Art Exhibition she'd been organizing had she not declared, ominously, that three portraits by Walter Sickert she had given to the gallery — *Sir James Dunn, Viscount Castlerosse*, and *H.M. King Edward VIII* — had not been permanent gifts after all; they had been "lifetime gifts" to Beaverbrook himself. When this term was up, she expected them back.

Alarmed, Beaverbrook contacted his New Brunswick lawyer, Charles Hughes, and the two men quickly put together a case to refute Christofor's assertion that the paintings were not gifts. Beaverbrook "appeared to be very much disturbed about the situation and said that

LADY DUNN
DAYSPRING
ST. ANDREWS, N.B.
CANADA   22nd September 1959

3 p.m.

Dearest Max,

Since our telephone conversation I am more than ever convinced of the impression created to suppress any mention worthy of Santiago.   In my opinion whatever you may do now will be superfluous. The Glasgow Museum, The National Gallery at Washington and the Metropolitan Museum at New York, all realized the vital importance of advance publicity before they presented their Dali's to the public.   The almost studied neglect to do anything in this regard for Santiago - the acclaimed Masterpiece of Dali - is more than a grief to me, it is a crime.

When I stripped the walls here of the three Sickerts' I did so only for your personal gratification and I mentioned at the time that these were lifetime gifts to you personally, not to the Gallery. James was extremely proud of these paintings and I see no reason why I should be bereft of them all my life - it would be different if I were thirty years older.

I willingly fell in with the plan to place myself below the salt for the sake of protocol etcetera but I hardly expected such short shift as I did receive on the evening of the 16th.   I have never expected, nor would I appreciate, fanfare, trumpets or pipes, but at least in public I might be excused if I expected some warmth and courtesy.

Doubtless plans for the Maritime Exhibition have been settled and perhaps you have forgotten your intention, four days ago, to inform me of them. I wish to save you the trouble, since I have no purpose to serve in being present.

With love, as ever,

The Rt. Hon. Lord Beaverbrook, P.C.,
Fredericton. N.B.

Christofor's letter claiming ownership
of three paintings by Walter Sickert.

he would never agree that she could have them back," Hughes wrote, "and he wanted to do whatever was necessary to defeat any claim of Lady Dunn to the right to possession after his death." Beaverbrook quickly collected affidavits from two witnesses, one of them Sir Alec Martin, who said they heard Lady Dunn refer to the Sickerts as permanent gifts. He also had Wardell dig out a telegram from the previous August in which he had written that she wanted it recorded that the Sir James Dunn Foundation "presented" the paintings to the gallery. At the same time, Beaverbrook sent Christofor a grovelling letter, apologizing for the lack of publicity for the Dali — "I can only conclude that my one-time talent for propaganda has failed me in my old age" — and for the seating problem. Ignoring her threat about the Maritime Art Exhibition, he told her that a date for it had been set. "I cannot support your claim that the Sickerts were given to the Gallery for the space of my lifetime only," he continued, almost as an afterthought. "But I will at once examine my correspondence and send you forthwith a full account of my enquiry." He told her again that his gratitude to her "has no limits" and hoped that the "dark places may become bright spots again."[11] Christofor abandoned her claim to the paintings — at least for the time being.

Beaverbrook could be equally determined with other benefactors. Lucile Pillow, a wealthy St. Andrews cottage owner whom Beaverbrook had appointed to the gallery board and who had donated a collection of porcelain, would be sending some of her paintings to the gallery in the fall of 1960 for an exhibition. Wardell reported to Beaverbrook that Pillow was proposing a complicated — and costly — way of getting the paintings to Fredericton. Because her son-in-law, Murray Vaughan, had had what she called "a terrible time" arranging insurance for the works, he would probably travel with them on a private rail car. "Vaughan is obviously talking rubbish, to justify himself, perhaps, in his previous attitude, or to continue to obstruct, I do not know which," Wardell said. If Pillow planned on paying for the arrangement, that was fine, but Wardell told Beaverbrook it wasn't clear who would bear the cost, which Vaughan put at $6,000. Beaverbrook agreed he would not pay for a private rail car and told Wardell to stall her — unless, of course, she was willing to pay herself, in which case "we would love to have the pictures." There was more jockeying over dates for the exhibition. Pillow eventually appeared in Fredericton. "She is still sticking to the preposterous idea of a special coach with armed guard, Edwy Cooke and a member of the family in attendance," he told Beaverbrook. "All this is, of course, spoof invented by Vaughan. I feel sure that the insurance companies could not insist on any such folly. However, it does not matter to us as long as we do not have to pay."[12]

Beaverbrook was equally frugal when it came time to fire the young assistant curator of the gallery, Tom Forrestall. Forrestall worked mainly in the vault, completing accession records for the paintings in the gallery. He had been hired on the recommendation of Alex Colville, who was teaching at Mount Allison University and who called Forrestall "the most promising artist our school has produced in a decade." But Forrestall had epilepsy, and he had two seizures at the gallery early in 1960, one in front of a group of schoolchildren. That was enough for Cooke, Tweedie and Wardell to agree he should be dismissed. Wardell called him "a good boy, highly talented and honorable, with a young wife and a baby," and told Beaverbrook he would try to set him up as an artist to supplement his three months of severance pay. But Beaverbrook balked at the $780 severance. "We knew that this boy was in bad health when we took him on. We were persuaded to do so, but that is as far as we can go with Gallery funds," he wrote. "These are trust funds and cannot be dispersed save on the most rigid adherence to the terms of the Deed." Beaverbrook reluctantly agreed to pay the severance himself, then got into a debate with Wardell about which account the money should pass through. Wardell's compassion for Forrestall was genuine. "The poor fish has the faculty of attaching to himself sympathy to a remarkable degree," he wrote. "I even find myself moved by it. For that reason I would like to see the Gallery act generously towards him." Wardell set up Forrestall in an apartment where he could paint, an arrangement he sought to keep secret from people in Fredericton. "They must all believe that poor Tom has to be helped."[13] Forrestall, unaware of how much grumbling his severance had provoked, wrote Beaverbrook to thank him for his kindness. Beaverbrook kept a painting of the gallery by Forrestall for one of his homes in England.

Forrestall's departure meant that the work on the accession records was incomplete, and in October, Beaverbrook dispatched Mrs. Ince to Fredericton to get everything in order. Helen Parker, formerly Helen Savage, remembers Mrs. Ince removing labels from some of the paintings, an act that would assume great importance more than four decades later. "I remember Mr. Cooke being very noncommittal" about Mrs. Ince removing the labels, Parker says. "If I were there now and this was all happening, I'd be saying, 'What's she doing, Edwy? Why is she taking them off?' But he didn't say a word." At the time, she chalked this up to Cooke's awareness of his patron's quirks. "Lord Beaverbrook was changing his mind all the time," she says.

And he often did so without bothering to inform the board of governors, which was made up of the premier of the province and the leader of the opposition, as well as respected educational and religious leaders. When he wrote Cooke to tell him of an acquisition for the collection, his unilateral approach was, naturally, welcome. But in November of 1960, Beaverbrook informed Cooke that he had sold *The Synnot Children*, a valuable painting by Joseph Wright of Derby, to an Australian woman who was related to the family in the painting. "She has paid me for it and it is now her property," Beaverbrook said. Wardell chastised him. "This news will be greatly deplored by the people who have grown fond of the picture. You have the undoubted legal write [*sic*] to do what you like, under the Gallery Act; but I think a decision such as this should have been discussed with the Governors, at least as a gesture of respect to them. Some may be offended and bewildered. I am." Wardell was wrong: as custodian, Beaverbrook had the power to *approve* additions to, or removals from, the collection, but he did not have the authority to initiate them on his own. "This letter is too tough," Beaverbrook wrote at the bottom of Wardell's letter. "I prefer not to answer."[14]

The loss of *The Synnot Children* came at a time when acquisitions were beginning to decline in both quantity and quality. Beaverbrook and his foundation continued to send paintings, including a handful of treasures, but overall the several hundred paintings shipped between 1960 and Beaverbrook's death did not rival *The Fountain of Indolence, Hotel Bedroom, Peasant Girl Gathering Faggots,* or the other gems sent in advance of the official opening in 1959. And the gallery did not have the means to buy paintings on its own. Beaverbrook expected the gallery to survive on its endowment, paying staff, funding programs and buying paintings out of that limited pile of cash. When the money fell short, acquisitions were easier to sacrifice than salaries. "The Gallery must learn to live within its income," Beaverbrook wrote to Wardell in 1961. "It is not doing so at the present time. It has no money to buy pictures. It is depending at present on private gifts."[15] As a result, Beaverbrook was even more vigilant about how the gallery was spending money, brushing aside, for example, Wardell's suggestion that it required an air conditioner.

With the excitement and pressure of getting the gallery open now behind them, Wardell, Tweedie and Cooke were increasingly at odds over the more mundane day-to-day administration of the place, such as whether the gallery should be open on Christmas Day. Tweedie, aware of Fredericton sensibilities, said it should close, and Cooke agreed, but Wardell disagreed and insisted on getting Beaverbrook's approval — which he gave. A more serious clash took place when members of the Royal Commission on Transportation were in Fredericton in November 1959. As Wardell told the story to Beaverbrook, Tweedie had arranged for the gallery to stay open past five o'clock so the members could visit, but Cooke complained he hadn't been given enough notice. There was still a large crowd of ordinary visitors in the gallery at five o'clock, and Wardell announced to everyone that they could stay because the gallery was not closing. Then the lights went out, and the visitors began heading for the doors. Wardell followed them, explaining that there had been a mistake and they could stay. He met Cooke near the entrance. "Please turn on the lights," Wardell told him.

"I shall not. The gallery is closed," Cooke answered, according to Wardell's account.

"Mr. Tweedie gave you instructions," Wardell said.

"I do not accept them," Cooke answered.

"His instructions are given on behalf of the governors," Wardell insisted.

"These are not the instructions of the governors," Cooke said.

"They are," Wardell answered, "and Mr. Tweedie is the channel of communication to you."

"The gallery is closed," Cooke repeated.

The visitors left, but Wardell remained to greet the first group of commissioners and show them around. He then asked Cooke to close the gallery and sent a message to other members of the commission at their hotel apologizing that the gallery had closed before they arrived.[16]

The incident prompted Wardell to launch a campaign against Cooke. When Robert Stanfield, the premier of Nova Scotia, announced the following week that Lady Dunn would fund the construction of an art gallery in Halifax, Wardell told Beaverbrook, "Cooke might make a good curator for Lady Dunn. She might well take him along with Tweedie." In another letter two weeks later, Wardell opined that Cooke was "utterly unsuited to the job and should be replaced as an essential first step to the permanent success of the Gallery." Wardell's anger over the botched visit by the Royal Commission on Transportation may owe something to his growing relationship with the man who would eventually replace Beaverbrook as his wealthy patron: industrialist K.C. Irving. In 1957, Wardell had told Beaverbrook that Irving was planning to buy thirty per cent of the non-voting stock in his company, University Press, but was demanding fifty per cent of the voting shares, which would give him effective control of the company.[17] This was the first step toward Irving's later acquisition of the *Daily Gleaner*. In 1960, Irving was trying to get federal government approval to build a canal across the isthmus linking New Brunswick and Nova Scotia. Ottawa's decision would be influenced in part by the Royal Commission on Transportation — which likely explains the intensity of Wardell's desire to have the members visit the gallery in his company.

Cooke and Tweedie were less prone to complain about Wardell than he was about them, though Cooke did tell Mrs. Ince that Friends, a supposedly community-based organization of gallery supporters organized by Wardell, was "not functioning as effectively as it might" and was "more or less standing still." Individual members felt they lacked a voice, Cooke complained, because there had never been a full membership meeting to elect officers, draft bylaws or define the organization's policies with respect to the acquisition of art works for the gallery. The implication was that Wardell had turned it into his own private club. Cooke suggested to Mrs. Ince that Friends might be advised to promote "not only its own growth" but also to "provide greater benefits to the gallery itself."[18]

*

Perhaps fortunately for the feuding members of his Fredericton entourage, Beaverbrook was finally shifting his attention ever so slightly away from the gallery. One of his new causes was rapprochement with the Soviet Union, and to that end, he arranged for the university to offer an honorary degree to Nikita Khruschchev. The ceremony would certainly have added to his legend in Fredericton had an anti-Soviet speech by the Canadian prime minister, John Diefenbaker, not derailed Khrushchev's visit. Beaverbrook was also doing a lot of writing. He had recently published two biographies of fellow New Brunswickers who had achieved greatness — *Friends: Sixty Years of Intimate Personal Relations with Richard Bedford Bennett* in 1959 and *Courage: The Sir James Dunn Story* in 1961— and later that year he was hard at work on other books, including *The Decline and Fall of Lloyd George.* That autumn, after his annual visit to Fredericton, he returned to London to marshal his newspaper empire for a final crusade, this time against Britain's proposed entry into the European Common Market. His beloved Empire had already been eclipsed by the growing power of the United States, and integration with Europe, he was sure, would shatter it for all time. Even in this battle, though, his thoughts were with New Brunswick. He warned often that Britain would be cut off from the Dominions. "We and they have everything to unite us. We have the one God, the one loyalty to the Crown, the one language, the one law," he wrote. "Let the people demand that our ties with the Dominions be strengthened and not cut off. We must not abandon those great nations which sent their sons to die for us. We must stand by them and work together to advance the greatest achievement in civilisation and brotherhood that the world has ever known."[19] Britain did remain outside the Common Market for the time being, though because of objections from France, not Beaverbrook's propaganda campaign.

Beaverbrook's continuing interest in the conduct of the newspapers was an implicit criticism of his son Max, who was nominally in charge. In the flat in the gallery, Tweedie once witnessed Beaverbrook barking down the telephone line to London. He demanded to speak to Max, only to be told Max was in Southampton, where he kept his yacht. "Give him this message," Beaverbrook said. "In the midst of a crisis, Southampton is no place for the boss. Tell him also that it is a painful episode in the life of Lord Beaverbrook." This was the behaviour — the need to be "very much in control" — that Lady Violet Aitken would describe in 2006 as taking such a toll on her husband. Max finally protested in a long letter to his father in April 1963. "For some thirty years I have gratefully accepted your criticisms, usually I hope with good grace. But lately all we do or don't do is muddle and muddle." He and the senior executives, he wrote, were "weary from trying to patch up oversensitive and deeply loyal feelings hurt by constant criticism seldom if ever tempered by a little praise. . . . When you used to work at the office with your coat off you drove everyone hard but you also made them laugh and feel that they were on the `sunny side of the street.' That is still necessary and some of it must come from the master however far away he may be. Therefore I hope you will continue to hold us by the hand each and every day and beam an occasional smile our way." The extraordinary rebuke — Max's first and last to his father — seemed to have an effect, for the old man's criticisms were, from that point on, "made in a gayer tone."[20]

Beaverbrook was told in 1962 that he had cancer of the bladder, though a surgeon friend disputed the diagnosis and he didn't quite believe it himself. But by early 1963 he told a friend that he was "approaching the moment when I must bring out my Late Night Final," a reference to the very last edition of a day's newspaper. "I am not greatly concerned with the future in New Brunswick for obvious reasons," he wrote Wardell in April. "Frankly, Captain, I am a lame duck and that's that."[21] Yet he remained ever concerned with his gallery. Cooke reported that the skylights were leaking and nasty weather prevented temporary patching. "Should we have a heavy rain, we will be in for a lot of trouble."[22] When a company manufacturing a new type of window said it would guarantee the unit itself but not the installation, Beaverbrook insisted that Cooke persuade the firm to alter its policy. It refused, saying installation was the responsibility of the architect or engineer — neither of which Beaverbrook and Cooke had contemplated needing to hire.

In June Beaverbrook wrote to Cooke that he was disappointed in the results of the annual Maritime Art Exhibition, which had seen only eleven paintings sold. "If we cannot do anything, we should end it," he said. (The exhibition continued, though the gallery handed over the task of organizing it to the Maritime Art Association.) He also told Cooke he was getting fed up with all the requests to borrow paintings from the collection. "Let them come and see the paintings where they belong. We will become a lending library before long," he said. When Cooke received funding from the Canada Council that would pay for him to visit Western Canada and would match up to $1,500 spent on the purchase of paintings, Beaverbrook attached one condition: "he is not to buy an abstract." Beaverbrook complained to Cooke after the trip that he was "shocked" by his selections. "I wish to say that there is to be no hanging of abstracts in the Gallery during my lifetime, and I have made a deal with Lady Beaverbrook and Max Aitken that there will be no hanging of abstracts after my death. The prospects for abstractionism are pretty dull as far as our Gallery is concerned." A handwritten postscript says simply, "No abstracts. No abstracts. No abstracts." When teenage vandals destroyed a stone bench on the terrace of the gallery entrance that summer, Beaverbrook demanded answers. "Why didn't the nightwatchman hear them?" he asked Cooke. "What was the nightwatchman doing? Had we better check up on the nightwatchman and see if he is really nightwatching?" He also sent word that he wanted the two convicted vandals to receive severe sentences — and then be released early "on account of youth."[23]

New Brunswickers, unaware of his declining health, continued to write to Beaverbrook seeking his help. Some of the letters were poignant: Laurie-Anne Godin, a fifteen-year-old girl from Lower Neguac, an Acadian community northeast of Newcastle, had seen the skating rinks Beaverbrook had built there and in Chatham. "I like to skate but as we are very poor, my father can't buy me a pair of ice skates," she wrote. "I have been thinking that perhaps a pair of skates to you would seem such a small thing compared to these great donations. Would it be asking so much to beg you for a pair. My size is 8." Other exchanges were more comical and calculated: Elizabeth Hunt, a Saint John woman, had begun sending birthday cables "and so forth" on a regular basis, Mrs. Ince told Beaverbrook in a memo. "It rather looks, from this letter, as if she may not have been altogether disinterested." The letter suggested that Beaverbrook finance a motion picture to be shot in Canada — with young Miss Hunt in a starring role, of course. "This is my chance now Lord Beaverbrook while I am young," she wrote. Ince acknowledged that letter and wrote a second to Ms. Hunt later the same day. "There has just arrived a parcel containing something which I cannot identify for Lord Beaverbrook." Hunt wrote back to say it was dulse, an edible sea algae considered a tasty snack in some coastal communities. She asked Mrs. Ince to please see he received it "while it is eatable." Beaverbrook instructed Mrs. Ince, "Pay no attention to Miss Hunt, and don't send any dulce to me or acknowledge it either."[24]

Late in October Beaverbrook was still dealing with trivial matters — "We buy some paper bags. What are they for? What is the library purchase for? What is the fertilizer for? I would like all these things explained. I am not objecting at all, I want to know" — when there occurred a most remarkable moment in the history of his relationship with the province he called his home. *Maclean's*, one of Canada's most widely read magazines, dispatched British journalist and satirist Malcolm Muggeridge to New Brunswick to write about Beaverbrook's hold on the public's imagination. Muggeridge, who'd worked at Beaverbrook's *Evening Standard*, was best known for a 1957 article, "Does England Really Need a Queen?" which was published in an American magazine just as the Queen was making a state visit to the United States. It caused a controversy in England, where he briefly lost his job with the BBC and with Beaverbrook's newspapers. The *Maclean's* piece, "The Cult the Beaver Built," had a similar impact, albeit on a New Brunswick scale, when it appeared in early November 1963.

Muggeridge mocked the numerous statues and edifices dedicated to Beaverbrook around the province. "How extraordinary . . . to find a case in which someone still living has been memorialized to a degree which might have been considered excessive if accorded to Napoleon in Corsica, or to Shakespeare in Stratford-on-Avon." He mercilessly skewered Beaverbrook's purchasing of the private papers of Bonar Law, R.B. Bennett and Lloyd George, comparing it to Stalin's attempts to rewrite history in the Soviet Union, and he had a bit of sport with an exhibition of modern art due to open at the gallery shortly after his visit. He also spoofed Wardell, whom he'd known in England, saying his eye patch "lent a touch of distinction to a face which recalled the Duke of Windsor's before he teamed up with Mrs. Simpson, or almost any Conservative member of parliament with a reasonable expectation of becoming president of the Board of Trade, or at any rate First Lord of the Admiralty." Muggeridge wrote that it was "part of the Beaverbrook technique to involve unlikely persons in his own manias and enthusiasms, and then, at a carefully chosen moment, to, as it were, pull the rug from under them," and he suggested this was why Wardell, "having been induced to share Lord Beaverbrook's enthusiasm for the Empire . . . finds himself in Fredericton, trying to promote the *Gleaner* among a spare, stubborn and mostly penurious population, by descent largely French and Scottish, two of the most obstinate and recalcitrant races on earth. Does he sometimes, in the harsh winter months, think of the Great Empire Crusader sunning himself on the Côte d'Azur? If so, he never lets on. His newspaper is full of Lord Beaverbrook's praises, as is his magazine, *The Atlantic Advocate*, on whose cover New Brunswick's most famous citizen makes more frequent appearances than he does among Frederictonians in the flesh."

Muggeridge — who'd worked as a journalist in the Soviet Union, first as a communist sympathizer and then as an ardent critic of the system — returned to the Stalin parallel to close the article, remarking how strange he felt when he left the province to suddenly find himself no longer surrounded by statues or other memorials to Beaverbrook. He compared it to his feeling of relief upon leaving the USSR. It was, he admitted, a "preposterous" comparison, "yet the principle is the same, the passion of a human ego to occupy the wide open spaces of history, to ensure that the notion achieved or enforced in life shall endure after death. Stalin's effort was based on the expense of blood, Lord Beaverbrook's on the expense of money; the one hacked and killed his way into history, the other has tried to buy his way in — a more comical, and infinitely more innocuous procedure."[25]

This was something altogether new: a journalist who dared to suggest that Beaverbrook was motivated by something other than generosity and good will, and that the many monuments to his name were something other than the honest, earnest expression of local appreciation. "When Judas Iscariot hanged himself, mankind had fallen very low," Beaverbrook wrote to Wardell just days after the magazine was published. "Mankind continued to fall until Muggeridge came along. Then they reached bottom." His New Brunswick lawyer, Charles Hughes, suggested he sue for libel, but Beaverbrook acknowledged that he was too ill to travel to Canada to testify.[26] To another friend, he claimed to be unperturbed. "I make no objection to Muggeridge's attacks. On the contrary, I find them amusing. But it is all old stuff. I could have helped him with some fresh material. No one is asked to look after my reputation. That stands on the foundation of fifty years of hard work. Errors there have been. Many mistakes. Much service."[27]

Wardell lacked his patron's equanimity. He penned and rushed into print a lengthy rebuttal in *The Atlantic Advocate*, attacking the "incredible impudence" of *Maclean's* and suggesting Muggeridge "consult a psychiatrist." Choosing not to count the many buildings named for Beaverbrook or his late wife, Wardell asserted that there were only three memorials to Beaverbrook in New Brunswick and he "neither suggested, nor erected, nor paid for any of the three." This was a dubious assertion, given that he had arranged for Oscar Nemon to sculpt the Newcastle bust because it would cost the town considerably less than commissioning Vincent Apap, the creator of the Fredericton statue,[28] and given that, according to one biography, he topped up the fundraising effort for the Apap statue when it fell short of its target. Unwittingly proving Muggeridge's point about his own devotion to Beaverbrook, Wardell devoted several long paragraphs to correcting some of the article's minor factual errors and defending his proprietorship of the *Gleaner* — though he may have been somewhat optimistic when he wrote that Fredericton was "fast becoming the cultural centre of Canada."[29]

It was surely a coincidence that less than a month later, Beaverbrook informed Wardell that he was trying to "tidy up my will" and wanted to remove an intended bequest of $25,000 and hand the money to Wardell right away. The problem, Beaverbrook said — showing how conscious he was of the implications of his gifts — was that if he died within three years, Wardell would have to pay tax on the money at a rate of fifty-four per cent. Wardell thanked him but asked that he instead instruct his executors to apply the money against the $100,000 he still owed Beaverbrook because of the failure of his Fredericton ventures to turn a profit. Beaverbrook replied on December 19: "Christmas 1963 is not recognized by old time Presbyterians — that's me. But New Year is a gay festival. So I give up the $25,000 present I suggested and instead I cancel the note for $100,000." Wardell told Beaverbrook he was overwhelmed by the gift. The cancellation of the debt "radically alters my future," he wrote, and is "a very visible and touching proof of your feelings for me of affection and friendship. This knowledge I prize very much."[30]

*

Winter gave way to spring, and a gala dinner was organized in London for May 25, 1964, to mark Beaverbrook's eighty-fifth birthday. Four days before the party, he wrote to the gallery about the winner of the Maritime Art Exhibition, the event he had scorned a year earlier. A painting called *Connivance* by Helen Parsons won top prize — $400 supplied by Beaverbrook himself — and would become part of the gallery's collection. "I look forward to being in Fredericton again and seeing the original of the beautiful picture chosen by my good friends and helpers," he wrote.[31] But he knew by then that he would never see New Brunswick again. Still, he managed a triumph at his birthday dinner. It had been expected that he would be unable to speak and perhaps not be able to attend, so he'd attempted to record his speech earlier in the day, but to no avail. His voice was too weak and muffled. "Never mind," he said. "I'll be there anyway." That night he found his voice and delivered a moving valedictory, laced with charm and mischief. "It is time for me to become an apprentice once more," he said at the end. "I am not certain in which direction, but somewhere, sometime, soon . . ."[32]

He then retreated to Cherkley, spending his time checking on the expense claims of some *Express* journalists and working the phones. On June 7 he marked the first anniversary of his marriage to Christofor, which had made her the second Lady Beaverbrook. She and Wardell, visiting from Fredericton, joined him to sing a few First World War songs. But the end was near. "Lord Beaverbrook has been exhausted since his birthday," Mrs. Ince wrote to a well-wisher on June 8. "He undertook a very extensive program and carried it through with his usual spirits. But it was such that it would have left a much younger man limp."[33]

That evening, his daughter Janet joined him for dinner in front of the fire in his bedroom, and he talked about his love for her mother. "He spoke of nothing else, during which time he revealed his true feelings, so often suppressed behind an outward veneer of toughness and unpredictability. . . . Now at last, when the truth no longer made him feel vulnerable, he could speak from the heart. I think that in those last few hours, we were closer than we had ever been."[34]

The next morning Beaverbrook gave Max and George Millar a box of papers, and the two men took them outside and burned them. Janet was summoned back to Cherkley by the family doctor. When she arrived at noon, Beaverbrook was semiconscious. In the bedroom with him were Christofor, George Millar, and Max. Christofor sent Max to London to get the will and some other papers. "I held his hand until the end, fighting back my tears," Janet recalled. "He died peacefully that same afternoon."[35]

Christofor took control, telephoning selected friends and employees the next morning and inviting them to view the body, which lay in state at Cherkley for five days, "a most unusual procedure in England," his biographers noted. Some of the mourners who had not met the new Lady Beaverbrook mistook her for a housekeeper as she unlocked the doors of the drawing room and led them in to pay their respects.[36] "Tonight he is lying in his coffin, poor old darling, tucked up in white silk and looking about as unlike our beloved old vagabond as it is possible to imagine," Wardell wrote to Tweedie from Cherkley. "But the effect is peaceful."[37] Though he was an ocean away, Wardell ensured that the *Gleaner* treated the death with the solemnity normally reserved for a head of state. A black border framed the front page and a giant headline declared, "World Mourns Death of Lord Beaverbrook." Wardell may be forgiven for this bit of hyperbole, given that the "world," as he saw it, consisted mainly of Great Britain and New Brunswick.

Five days after Beaverbrook's death, a small funeral was held. Before it, there was an elaborate buffet lunch at Cherkley for a small group of twenty to thirty invited guests. When they returned to their cars to drive to the church, "there was no sign of a coffin or a hearse," and several drivers became confused, accelerating to stay within sight of the car ahead because they had no way otherwise of finding the chapel. "We all sped round this roundabout at tremendous speed and proceeded to the crematorium at forty miles an hour at least, dashing to Beaverbrook's funeral," one mourner recalled. "It was just so typical of Beaverbrook that the funeral would be like this." The same day, in Newcastle, New Brunswick, several churches held memorial services. At St. James and Saint John's United Church, bells that Beaverbrook had donated tolled for him, and Reverend S.R. Purchase committed to God "a good Samaritan to the neglected and the forgotten, a maker of politicians, a patron of the arts, a visionary in education, a non-conformist in religion, a rich man furnished with ability — may his name live for evermore."[38] The following week a large memorial service was held at St. Paul's Cathedral in London. Among the guests were Bob Tweedie and his wife, their travel from Fredericton paid for by Lady Beaverbrook.

Lady Beaverbrook, accompanied at rear by Edwy Cooke, curator
of the Beaverbrook Art Gallery, enters the gallery for a ceremony in
September 1964 to mark the death of Lord Beaverbrook.
Beaverbrook Papers, HIL-UNB

The final ritual took place in September. Christofor attended a
ceremony at the gallery and then travelled to Newcastle, carrying
an urn to be encased in the plinth below the great bronze bust in
the Square. This was the last element of Beaverbrook's carefully con-
structed scheme to avoid death duties in England. His will, which had
been probated on August 4 by the registrar at the Northumberland
County courthouse in Newcastle, listed as his address "MacTavish
Farm South Esk Miramichi," a parcel of land he had purchased but
never developed. "I declare," he had written, "that I was born in
Canada and that I am a Canadian citizen and have at all times during my life been domiciled within Canada in the Province of New
Brunswick and that I desire this Will to be construed and to take

Sir Max Aitken (far right) and his wife, Lady Violet Aitken,
join other dignitaries as Lord Beaverbrook's ashes are encased
in a plinth on the Square in Newcastle, September 25, 1964.

effect according to the laws of that Province." This seemingly obvious
fiction — along with the statement that "I wish to be buried in the
Province of New Brunswick" — allowed his executors to claim that no
estate tax should be paid in England. At first, British Inland Revenue
contested this assertion. But Beaverbrook had been meticulous: that
long-ago letter to Borden declaring his intent to return to Canada and
run for office, his work on behalf of Canada during the First World
War, his 1950 decision to turn over Cherkley to his son, and even the
Canadian registration of his yacht. And, not incidentally, the investment of his fortune — other than what he'd already turned over to
his foundations, which the British government could not touch — in

Canadian and American securities. The UK authorities, "not often confronted with a scheme for avoiding English tax that featured the interment of ashes in a public square as evidence of domicile," gave in.[39] His estate paid a pittance, £100,000, in British tax on his sale of his farm in Somerset to his son Max. Almost $13 million, meanwhile, passed to the Beaverbrook Canadian Foundation, which he had established in 1960. "All the elements of this final success story were Beaverbrookian," one biographer concluded: "money, ingenuity, semi-farce, mystery, and affection for the colonial backwater whence he came."[40]

On September 25, 1964, Christofor placed the urn in the plinth, and she and the Aitkens, who had also come to Newcastle, sang "Onward Christian Soldiers." An attack of gout had nearly forced Beaverbrook to miss the bust's unveiling in 1962. "This is my own tombstone," he'd remarked. "Why would I want to see it unveiled?"[41] Some members of Beaverbrook's family would later question, however, whether the urn really contained his ashes, given that Christofor had shown her attachment to her first husband's ashes by burying them in the grounds of Dayspring.[42]

It was not the first note of discord between Christofor and the family, nor would it be the last. Eventually their differences would tear at Beaverbrook's beloved gallery and feed the bitter dispute that erupted decades later.

Lady Beaverbrook with the bust of her husband unveiled
at the Beaverbrook Art Gallery in 1963.

CHAPTER SEVEN

"I will strive to climb the mountains"

The telephone call came at six-thirty in the morning. Donald Andrus, the assistant curator of the Beaverbrook Art Gallery, was still at home. He picked up the phone and the voice at the other end snapped him into a state of alertness. It was Marcia Anastasia Christoforides, Lady Beaverbrook. In her distinctive high-pitched voice, she informed Andrus that he was to go the gallery immediately and prepare the Graham Sutherland portrait of her late husband, Lord Beaverbrook, for delivery to Dayspring, her estate in the resort town of St. Andrews on the Bay of Fundy. "I hadn't heard anything about this at all," he recalls, "so I said I would need something in writing."

"There's no need for that," Christofor replied. "My brother is on his way now."

Andrus made a quick calculation: St. Andrews is about a hundred miles by car from Fredericton, which meant he had, at best, an hour or two to sort this out. He knew that in the world of art galleries, one wasn't permitted — regardless of one's connection to the institution or its primary benefactor — to simply decide to borrow a painting, even if one claimed to own it. His immediate superior, curator Stuart Smith, was one of several curators from across Canada chosen to oversee exhibitions at Expo 67 in Montreal that summer. He had left Andrus in charge, and this put the young art historian in an awkward position, convinced that Lady Beaverbrook's demand was unreasonable but unsure how, or whether, to stand up to her. "I was very leery about the whole thing," he says, recalling how he headed downtown to the gallery, unlocked the doors, disabled the alarm system and waited. He cannot recall today whether he tried to contact Bob Tweedie, who was then secretary to the gallery's board of governors, to the Beaverbrook foundations and to the Sir James Dunn Foundation. Given Tweedie's unquestioning loyalty to Lady Beaverbrook at the time — gallery staff considered any command of his to come directly from her — it is unlikely that Tweedie would have done anything other than instruct Andrus to acquiesce to her Ladyship's wishes.

Christofor's brother arrived, "not in great shape," recalls Andrus. The assistant curator explained that he needed some time to fill out a condition report, a standard requirement any time a work leaves a gallery, and to properly package the painting. That would not be necessary, Christofor's brother told him.

"I haven't made up a document for you to sign," Andrus protested.

"I'm not going to sign anything," was the reply.

Andrus could hardly believe his ears. This was not what he had thought he was getting into back in 1964 when, on the very day of Lord Beaverbrook's death, he had accepted the position at the gallery. There were few jobs at the time for art historians, and he felt fortunate to have the chance to work with what he says was "a pretty amazing collection . . . quite possibly the best collection of British art in the northeast part of the continent." He conducted gallery tours, helped organize exhibitions and arranged for evening screenings of films about art. "There was a lot to do," he says. "There always is." His dealings with Lady Beaverbrook, the co-custodian of the gallery along with Beaverbrook's son, Sir Max Aitken, had been minimal except for what he calls the occasional "crisis situation" when she would sweep in to quash an exhibition he'd been planning or otherwise interfere.

Andrus would regret for decades that on that summer morning in 1967, he did not stand up to Christofor or her brother. "This was the latest in a series of autocratic decisions by Lady Beaverbrook, and I guess by that time I was conditioned. So I wrapped it as well as I could, and it went into the trunk of the Oldsmobile." He would not see the Sutherland painting again — in fact, he would not know whether it had survived the trip to Dayspring, never mind been returned — until he attended an event at the gallery in 2003, when, to his immense relief, he spotted it on the wall. Of Christofor, he says simply, "She was never a force for the good of the gallery."

It was Beaverbrook's pet cause, Empire Free Trade, which first brought Christofor into his life. At the height of the *Daily Express* crusade in 1930, she wrote a long letter to one of the paper's editors, S.W. Alexander, with suggestions for the campaign. Impressed but misreading her signature, he replied to "Mr. Christoforides," asking for a meeting. By chance, Beaverbrook's friend and fellow expatriate New Brunswicker Sir James Dunn had asked Alexander for help finding another secretary for his staff, and when the editor met Christofor, "he was impressed by her youthful appearance and zest," Beaverbrook wrote. "Her complexion was a healthy combination of attractive colours with a texture as though recently exposed to sun tan. A long neck, high cheek bones and hair of a slightly golden hue gave her an exotic appearance. Her movements were free and she walked with dignity." Alexander sent her to meet Dunn. "Looking very smart and wearing her Empire Free Trade pin," she immediately charmed him, and he hired her on the spot despite her lack of secretarial training or experience. Early on, she made some mistakes that nearly cost her her job, but Dunn was forgiving and she became, Beaverbrook wrote, "his indispensable secretary, and then his inseparable companion."[1] She herself wrote, "from the moment we met I was under the spell of his vital spirit. I had never been curious about 'Life' before this time and from then on I knew James was my entire world. That is how it happened."[2]

Christofor's father was a tobacco magnate of Greek origin living in England. She became wealthy in her own right after she invested all her money, on Dunn's advice, in some shares that had bottomed out in the Depression. They recovered — one particular stock grew tenfold in value — and she sold them at an enormous profit. Then

Lord Beaverbrook and Sir James Dunn.

Archives and Special Collections, Harriet Irving Library, University of New Brunswick, PC 25 No. 10 (1)

she put all the money on a single horse, Maid of Essex, in a single race. It belonged to a business associate of Dunn and had been given odds of eight to one. The mare won, Christofor's fortune was made, and she never bet on a horse again. In 1941, she intervened at a key moment in Dunn's ultimately successful struggle to buy controlling interest of Algoma Steel, selling her jewellery and other assets to buy fifteen thousand shares in the company and keep his takeover hopes alive. In the midst of the battle, he suffered a debilitating heart attack. Christofor insisted that the best doctors care for him, and she sat at his bedside during the entire ordeal. "That James and Christofor had been attracted to each other for many years was abundantly clear to all of us in their intimate circle," Beaverbrook wrote. "But it was during this dramatic illness that their relationship deepened into love. . . . Now he knew above all argument that they were essential to each other. Even with his possessions, his acclaim, and his ambition, life without Christofor would be but an empty desert to be crossed alone without comfort or solace."³

Following Dunn's recovery, the couple travelled together to his private camp in the New Brunswick forest, where Christofor wrote an extraordinary letter to Dunn's wife, Irene. "I know James would never have been with us today if I had not kept an eternal vigil over him until he was out of danger," she wrote, warning Irene not to let the strains in their marriage affect his still fragile health. She feigned surrender: "If, as I have reason to believe, you are going to try to make a new start it would hardly be a fair beginning for me to be around," she said, agreeing to withdraw to Algoma's head office in Ontario. But it was clear she was raising the stakes. "If you feel you can give him the care and comfort he so sorely needs," she wrote, "you will be able to give him happiness also." Irene was not up to the implicit challenge, and, after a meeting with Christofor at the Ritz-Carleton Hotel in Montreal, she agreed to divorce her husband. He and Christofor were married on June 7, 1942.⁴

The new Lady Dunn spent $250,000 on renovating Dayspring, the spacious manor in St. Andrews, New Brunswick, purchased for her husband by Algoma. The town was in its heyday as a resort town for the wealthy, with Canadian and American tycoons idling away their summers on the tennis courts and the beaches, at picnics and performances by the orchestra of the majestic Algonquin Hotel. Dunn would join fellow captains of industry most mornings at the Cockburn Corner Drug Store to read the newspaper before returning to Dayspring, protected by the nine-foot fence he had installed around the property. It was one of his many eccentricities; he also refused to shave with an electric razor, convinced that flying bits of whisker would contaminate the air around him and cause cancer. He feared fire and refused to let the heat be turned on while flying on Algoma's private plane. He was fastidious about polishing his shoes and was constantly trying new diets.⁵

Dunn also collected paintings. Forced by financial ruin during the First World War to sell his collection, which included works by Gainsborough, Manet, Hogarth and others, he built a second one, patronizing artists including William Orpen and Walter Sickert. He commissioned Sickert to paint portraits of Christofor and of his friends, including Beaverbrook and their mutual friend Lord Castlerosse, who wrote for the *Express*. In 1947, Dunn and Christofor were introduced to Salvador Dali at a restaurant in New York. "The countenance, the bone formation of Caesar — Augustus Caesar," Dali exclaimed. "You are a Roman." Dunn protested that he was of Irish descent, but to no avail. Dali insisted he was descended from Caesar and proceeded to monopolize the conversation, asking at one point, "What's Algoma? A new vegetable?" This chance meeting led Dali to paint portraits of Dunn in the clothes and setting of a Roman emperor, *La Turbie*, and Christofor astride a horse with a falcon on her arm, *Equestrian Fantasy*. The two works would eventually flank Dali's *Santiago El Grande* in the Beaverbrook Art Gallery.[6]

Dunn died on the first day of 1956, after suffering pain and shortness of breath for most of December. His will left half his fortune to Christofor and divided the other half among his five children and one granddaughter.[7] Michael Wardell reported to Beaverbrook that Dunn's son Philip was not told about his father's poor health until three days before his death, meaning — thanks also to winter flight delays — that he arrived too late to say goodbye. "What a funny game Jimmy or Christofor or both played in suppressing the first attack," Wardell wrote. "Philip made it very clear he can't stand Christofor." Beaverbrook replied, "Of course you know what Lady Dunn is like, and her conduct in this case is not at all unusual. In fact, it is true to form."[8]

Despite this note of disapproval, Beaverbrook found himself consoling Christofor, who was so crushed by Dunn's death that she spoke of retiring to a convent. He invited her to Cherkley and to his villa in the south of France, and during his trips to New Brunswick he visited her at Dayspring. "I am expecting you to arrive in a very few hours and the thought of your kind strength so near at hand helps to assuage the strangely recurring anguish that sweeps over me towards the dying end of every month," she wrote at the end of September 1956. "I seem to sink beneath a rising tide of deep emotion, so dense, as to 'feel' like a tangible force. With every new beginning the flood recedes as desolation is replaced by a purpose and a comforting familiar tenderness — love — sheds its rays upon another course. . . . When you have gone, the battles in the valleys will be many, but you have bravely given me fresh courage. I will strive to climb the mountains."[9] Christofor sent Beaverbrook something else bound to impress him even more than her prose: paintings for his Fredericton gallery, both from her own collection and from the Sir James Dunn Foundation.

Beaverbrook did not surrender easily to her charms. Much like any of his other friends, "she had to be there when he wanted her company and disappear when he did not."[10] In March 1959, when Bob Tweedie told him he had offered to do some work for her in New Brunswick if "some exceptional matters" arose,[11] Beaverbrook advised against it. "It would be unfortunate for you and the project would end in tears," he wrote, more prophetically than he could have imagined. Six months later, on that fateful day after the gallery's opening, Tweedie did go to work for her while trying to sever his links to Beaverbrook, which left his loyalties in doubt. When Beaverbrook successfully resisted Christofor's threat to withdraw the Sickert portraits, Wardell sensed that Tweedie's allegiances were in play. "You left him in complete charge of the Gallery during your absence," Wardell told Beaverbrook, "and he might have handed the pictures over to Lady Dunn or made a written acceptance of her claim. . . . I have now told him that there is no longer an issue, that the pictures are the property of the Gallery."[12]

Sensing, perhaps, that Christofor was becoming his rival for Beaverbrook's attention, Wardell mocked her. When she announced late in 1959 that she would fund the construction of an art gallery in Nova Scotia, Wardell commented, "You lit the torch, others follow. But I cannot resist the impression that in Her Ladyship's mind there is a song that runs: 'Anything you do, I can do better.'"[13] He must have been relieved when Beaverbrook revealed that he was "entirely responsible for diverting Lady Dunn's attention," suggesting that he wanted her preoccupied not with his gallery but with her own.

"I consider it most desirable that she should have interesting duties there in association with such a worthy project." But she was not so easily distracted, and by the following autumn, she was supervising the rehanging of paintings in Fredericton.[14] When Wardell criticized Beaverbrook for selling *The Synnot Children*, Christofor lashed out in a letter to Tweedie against those who would "stir up complaints. . . . It would be better if the dissidents would concentrate on benefits bestowed."[15] There were more headaches for Wardell when she decided on short notice that the art exhibition she was sponsoring in Fredericton should be announced on her birthday. The announcement date was postponed in Canada but not in England, meaning that the London papers scooped the Canadian Press, which was honouring the later embargo date. The news agency was "disgusted," Wardell complained to Beaverbrook. "The result is that we shall get very poor publicity and the next time I set out to try and organize publicity with the news agencies here, I shall have difficulty in getting co-operation."[16]

In the contest for Beaverbrook's favour, Christofor played her hand expertly, giving him Dunn's papers and her own diaries so that he could write a glowing biography of her late husband, *Courage: The Sir James Dunn Story*, which Wardell's company published in 1961. Dunn's children from his first two marriages considered going to court to block its distribution, but Christofor was "overcome with pride and gratitude for this magnificent tribute to James." Beaverbrook then nominated her as chief governor of the gallery, which, Tweedie pointed out, the law did not allow him to do — the board, not the custodian, made that appointment — but Tweedie knew where the ultimate power resided. If the board were asked by Beaverbrook to select Christofor, he wrote, "I am sure that this matter could be speedily concluded." Tweedie, who already held the position of secretary to the Sir James Dunn Foundation, would later contact the newly installed Christofor to orchestrate his own return to the job of secretary of the gallery board. "I have offered to do what I could to look after the books, banking business, etc. until a Secretary is engaged," he wrote to her.[17]

Christofor's influence on Beaverbrook, now well into his eighties and increasingly feeble in body, continued to grow. They lived apart only during visits to New Brunswick, when Beaverbrook stayed in Fredericton and she went to Dayspring.[18] "She is evidently going to take a deep interest in the Gallery, and that is as it should be," Beaverbrook wrote to the curator, Edwy Cooke, in February 1962. Two weeks later, he wrote Cooke again. Christofor, he said, "bids me correct my letter. . . . She has been taking a great interest in the Gallery for a long time now." He told Cooke he was giving Christofor an effective veto over hiring decisions at the gallery,[19] and she soon became a constant presence in his gallery correspondence. "Lady Dunn agrees," he noted to Cooke when he suggested that K.C. Irving be consulted about repairs to the skylight. He also became increasingly insistent that Cooke "on no account" move Christofor's greatest gift to the gallery, *Santiago El Grande*. "It is not to be taken down no matter what demands for space there are for the Exhibition," he wrote in June 1963. "It stands where it is."[20]

By then Christofor was no longer Lady Dunn. She had become Lady Beaverbrook. On June 7, the anniversary of her marriage to Dunn, Beaverbrook's daughter Janet had encountered him in the driveway of Cherkley, hunched in the back of his car, "not looking very happy." "I'm going to keep a promise," he told her. "It was made a long time ago." He sped off with Christofor, his assistant, George Millar, and his son, Max, to the local registry office. By lunch, they had returned. Christofor, who usually retreated from encounters with Janet when she was at Cherkley, now remained at his side. "I married her this morning," Beaverbrook told Janet. "Go and give her a kiss and congratulate her."[21]

Wardell quickly transferred his obsequiousness to his patron's bride. When Beaverbrook was too ill to attend the Dunn International Exhibition she sponsored in the autumn of 1963, Wardell reported to him that Christofor was "radiant and full of life and energy" at the opening. "All went well and she made an outstanding personal success with her speech delivered to the 220 diners who included a sophisticated sprinkling of cynical art critics. They were delighted with her and no praise could be harder to earn." Edwy Cooke did not share Wardell's ardour, but the curator acquiesced as Beaverbrook passed on ever more detailed instructions from his new wife on which paintings should hang in the gallery and which she intended to borrow. "If she is willing to return the John picture of *Dorelia* belonging to the Gallery, we will be glad to display it for a time," Beaverbrook wrote on September 16, 1963, the fourth anniversary of the gallery's opening. "If she wants to borrow it again it is to be sent back to her forthwith, as we have so much from her that we are willing to do anything we can to please her."[22]

Christofor was now the one who kept Tweedie bouncing and the other Fredericton boys jumping. In England, she was a less benign presence. She had blocked Dunn's children from seeing their father, and now, in what would prove to be the final months of Beaverbrook's life, she gave his children the same treatment. Christofor "got rid of all the people around him . . . and she got rid of them absolutely deliberately," says his grandson Timothy, then a teenager. "My aunt [Janet] was absolutely devastated that she didn't get to play a part in his life at that time. . . . It's so bloody obvious that it's terrifying. . . . [Christofor] came up to Fredericton [the year before their marriage] when he was ill. And he had nobody. There was nobody there. She made herself very available and supported him in every sense of the word. When you're a man and you're physically ill, are you going to get dear old Wardell to come and sort you out? . . . So you have huge vulnerability as an individual and she happened to step into that breach. And my communication with my grandfather started to get cut off at that point. And she set about it in a pretty religious way." Timothy, who had been raised by Beaverbrook after his own father, Peter, had died, has never forgiven Christofor for a final cruelty in the spring of 1964, when he returned to England after his first year of university in Montreal. "I had lunch with my grandfather two weeks before he died and I was trying to tell him about McGill and what was happening and how excited I was by it. She cut me off in the middle of the lunch and kept me cut off. Stone dead. I've replayed that conversation many times in my head. I very much wanted to thank him for what he'd done for me and she cut it off. And I shall never forget that. She was a miserable bitch."[23]

Beaverbrook's will became a focus of Janet's and Timothy's resentment and suspicion. An earlier version had provided for his secretaries and staff, "but his new wife had swept it all away," Janet wrote.[24] The will set up a trust fund for Timothy and his brother Peter, but Timothy suspects that another will was destroyed and "my brother and myself were front and centre in it."[25] As for Christofor, the version probated in Newcastle said that "Lady Beaverbrook having ample resources of her own has asked me not to make any provisions for her in my Will other than that contained in sub-clause (A) of clause 6 of this my Will." That sub-clause gave her his portrait by Graham Sutherland, his bronze bust, his gold and silver, his musical boxes, and, other than a few other small bequests to others listed elsewhere, "all the rest of my personal effects in the Province of New Brunswick and in the United Kingdom" — another phrase that would prove important in the art dispute decades later.

*

Christofor had not yet brought Beaverbrook's ashes to Newcastle for burial in the Square when she made a second attempt to reclaim ownership of the three Sickert portraits she had threatened to pull from the gallery in 1959. Beaverbrook had refused to concede, but now she pressed her case again, just two months after his death. She had Bob Tweedie tell the new curator, Stuart Smith, that while the three Sickerts as well as *La Turbie*, Dali's portrait of Sir James Dunn, were recorded as gifts to the gallery, they were actually on loan. "Please rectify immediately," she demanded. Tweedie knew the truth: he had been told clearly by Wardell in 1959 that the gallery owned the paintings, and in response to a query from Margaret Ince in 1959 about whether *La Turbie* was a gift or a loan, Tweedie — or someone with access to his mail — had written "gift" in the margin of the letter. Yet five years later, in 1964, Tweedie endorsed Christofor's claim to all of them. "I have personal knowledge of the Sickerts," he wrote to Smith, "and am prepared to establish the fact that on more than one occasion Lady Dunn, as she was then, made it abundantly clear to me, as Secretary to the Board of Governors, the three Sickerts above referred to were on loan only for the lifetime of Lord Beaverbrook, and not beyond."[26]

Smith had been recruited as curator of the gallery during the final months of Beaverbrook's life — the press baron had died while the gallery was awaiting his approval of the hiring — so Smith was utterly unaware of the 1959 drama surrounding the three Sickerts. He did as Tweedie instructed and altered the ownership records for the four paintings. "Who would I have discussed it with?" Smith asked in 2006. "There was no one to discuss it with. . . . There was no recourse. There was no functioning board and this is how things proceeded, by Tweedie running up the street or sending the secretary up the street with a letter saying 'Lady Beaverbrook wants this.'"[27]

It quickly dawned on Smith that he had inherited an administrative nightmare from Edwy Cooke. Cooke at least had had the benefit of one clear line of authority: Beaverbrook himself. With the old man gone, the governance of the gallery descended into confusion and suspicion. "In a normal gallery operation," Smith recalled, "the director or chief curator is an administrator as well as [responsible for] the academic and art discipline. In this case the administration of the gallery was essentially reserved to Bob Tweedie." Perhaps as a result, governors showed little interest in board meetings, and it became difficult to get a quorum. Smith could not sign cheques, and he had no budget for the acquisition of new paintings. Instead, Tweedie called the shots, appearing at the gallery two or three times a week with instructions from one of the two co-custodians — occasionally Beaverbrook's son, Sir Max, but usually Lady Beaverbrook. "The sight of him meant trouble, or annoyance at least," Smith remembered. One day Tweedie instructed Smith to ship an entire filing cabinet, padlocked with an iron bar running through the drawer handles, to Mrs. Ince in London. He told a baffled Smith that it contained Lord Beaverbrook's "correspondence and dealings with the collection," and that, to Smith's astonishment, it must leave the gallery. Donald Andrus, Smith's assistant curator, says Tweedie "was very effective and he worked very hard but he was completely possessed by Lady Beaverbrook. And the

August 10, 1964.

Dear Mr. Tweedie:

On receipt of your instructions, I have today altered our records to indicate that the paintings listed below were on loan from Lady Beaverbrook personally.

SICKERT, W.R.

The Prince of Wales, Edward VIII
Lord Castlerosse
Sir James Dunn

With regard to the two portraits, the painting entitled "ORCHESTRAL REHEARSAL" is already listed as on loan from the "Sir James Dunn Foundation" (item 6, or 7 list).

The portrait of Sir James Dunn, "LA TIPOSE", was added to the rough list of Gallery Property as a result of the letter from Lord Beaverbrook's office. Our records have now been altered to indicate it is a loan from the Sir James Dunn Foundation.

Yours faithfully,

Stuart A. Smith,
Curator,
Beaverbrook Art Gallery
Fredericton, N.B.

Mr. R. A. Tweedie,
Secretary,
Board of Governors,
Beaverbrook Art Gallery

SAS/cc

Stuart Smith's letter confirming his alteration
of ownership records for three paintings by Walter Sickert.
Beaverbrook U.K. Foundation, exhibit 24-3594

terrible thing was we didn't completely trust him, because anything we said would get back to Lady Beaverbrook."

None of the prominent New Brunswickers on the gallery board — not the lieutenant-governor, John McNair, nor the premier, nor the leader of the opposition — appear to have questioned this increasingly dysfunctional state of affairs. The deference that the Fredericton elite had shown to Beaverbrook had been inherited by Christofor, who was eccentric at best and "difficult, contrary, arbitrary" at worst, according to Smith.[28] Her co-custodian, Sir Max, so disliked his father's widow that he avoided the gallery rather than provide leadership to the institution. "He always reminded me of a kid being dragged off to his grandmother's," recalls Helen Parker. "You know, 'you have to go two times a year' or something." The dislike was mutual, with Christofor convinced that Sir Max routinely violated his father's wishes.[29] "The Berlin Wall was a temporary structure compared to the wall between those two," Smith said. He recalled a rare visit to the gallery by Sir Max during which he confided to Smith his real reason for renouncing his father's title. "I will not be Lord Beaverbrook to her Lady Beaverbrook," he said.

And so Christofor enjoyed the freedom — through Tweedie — to turn the gallery into her plaything. Stories spread around Fredericton of her appearing at the gallery with a scrubbing brush to "clean" the paintings.[30] Helen Parker remembers Christofor accidentally tearing a one-inch gash through the canvas of *La Turbie* as she carried it up the gallery's back staircase after having borrowed it for Dayspring — a mishap that Parker says Christofor insisted be kept quiet; the gallery's records make no mention of a tear in the painting in the 1960s. Other incidents were less serious, even comical. She once kept the audience waiting for the opening of the Maritime Art Exhibition she sponsored because she disapproved of Smith's tie and would not allow the event to proceed until he went home for a replacement. McNair, the lieutenant-governor, once remarked that she'd missed another opening because she'd had "broom trouble."[31] And in December 1966, Smith recalled, she phoned one night to demand the cancellation of a children's performance of Christmas carols the next day "because, as she said, those dreadful children will come in and muddy the floors and they're probably just coming to use the bathroom anyway." Smith decided not to cancel the event. "They came and muddied the floors and sang and it was quite wonderful, because those rooms, while they weren't very good for paintings, had marvellous acoustics."

On May 25, 1965, the eighty-sixth anniversary of Beaverbrook's birth, Christofor contacted Donald Andrus with a bizarre new directive. That night, in Lewiston, Maine, Sonny Liston and Muhammad Ali were meeting for a rematch of their world heavyweight boxing bout. Wardell by this time was running the Playhouse on Queen Street in Fredericton, another gift from Beaverbrook to the province, and had sold tickets to a closed-circuit television broadcast of the Liston-Ali fight to be shown on the theatre's large screen. Christofor explained to Andrus that both of her husbands had been boxing aficionados, and she instructed him to carry two paintings from the gallery — the Dali of Sir James Dunn and a Zinkeisen portrait of Beaverbrook — over to the Playhouse and arrange them on easels, one on each side of the screen, so her two late husbands could "watch" the fight. Christofor's whimsy put the two paintings in danger. Wardell had sold liquor to the audience, and when Ali knocked out Liston halfway through the first round, people in the theatre, who had spent a lot of money on their tickets, felt cheated and became unruly. Fortunately, the two paintings survived and were safely returned to the gallery.

No one took Christofor to task for treating the two portraits to such a lively night on the town, but Wardell's setting up of a bar at the Playhouse touched off a nasty row that underscored how chaotic things had become without Beaverbrook pulling everyone's strings. Though Beaverbrook had, along with the Sir James Dunn Foundation, provided the money to build the Playhouse, he had shown little interest in it, preferring that it become Christofor's pet project.[32] Before his death, he had, however, put in place a typically Byzantine governance structure: Tweedie was secretary to the board, which, like the gallery board, was composed of members of Fredericton's ruling class. It delegated to Wardell the job of running the facility. Christofor and Sir Max became co-custodians, meanwhile, upon Beaverbrook's death. Wardell and Tweedie were soon feuding over control of the theatre's fundraising account, while Christofor and Sir Max sought

to wash their hands of the facility.[33] In the aftermath of the Liston-
Ali fight, Premier Louis Robichaud, a member of the board, accused
Wardell of violating the "well-defined restrictive conditions" of the
special liquor permit the government had given him for the evening.
Robichaud and two of his cabinet ministers who were on the board
declared the body impotent and refused to sit unless the agreement
delegating management to Wardell was revoked.

Sir Max had no objection, and he and Christofor withdrew as
co-custodians. Wardell agreed to retire, but when the board fired
Alexander Gray, the director of the playhouse, for supposedly encouraging audience members to drink the night of the fight, Wardell
roared back to life. He told a public meeting of the Patrons of the
Playhouse, an organization he controlled, that the premier was at
fault. Beaverbrook had funded the construction on the condition that
the province would grant a liquor licence. "I bitterly blame myself
that I assured him over and over again that we could be sure . . .
that there could be no breach of faith on the part of Mr. Robichaud.
I was wrong." True to form, Wardell used the *Gleaner* to advance
his arguments, setting aside almost a full page for a transcript of
his remarks.[34] Christofor, for once a voice of reason, told him she
and Sir Max wanted to cooperate with Robichaud and would defer
their resignations. "I suggest AGAIN that you leave the matter with
the Premier and not continue to rush in to print with your flaming
torch and noble intentions for the honour and glory of WHOM?"
she wrote from Dayspring. "Stop agitating the boat — you are not
helping Gray. . . . I do hope you will calm down and be realistic-
ally rational." Remarkably, Wardell had provoked a rare consensus
between Christofor and Sir Max, who cabled her, "I agree [with]
your letter to Mike but I doubt if anything will stop him."[35] The
dispute finally died down, the Playhouse board agreed to pay Gray a
settlement, and in 1966, after tempers had cooled, Christofor withdrew as co-custodian of the Playhouse and ended the Sir James Dunn
Foundation's support.

Wardell's long service to the Beaverbrook name drew to a close
around the same time, though his feud with Premier Robichaud would
continue in the service of his new master, Saint John industrialist K.C.

Irving. Irving opposed Robichaud's ambitious social and taxation reforms, and Wardell used the *Gleaner* to attack the premier and his
program. In one memorable editorial Wardell accused Robichaud of
winning power "by falsehood" and of having "monstrously abused"
his "rightful critics" — a category in which Wardell surely included
himself.[36] Despite Wardell's whipping up of anti-French bigotry in
the subsequent battle over the reforms — Robichaud was repeatedly
caricatured in the *Gleaner* as Louis XIV — the Liberals won re-elec-
tion in 1967. Two years later, an ally of Robichaud, Liberal senator
Charles McElman, revealed in Ottawa that, six months earlier, Irving
had secretly purchased the *Gleaner* from Wardell. The revelation
prompted a Senate investigation of media ownership, with a particular focus on Irving's now complete control of all the English-language
daily newspapers in New Brunswick; Wardell vigorously defended
his new patron. Eventually, Wardell retired to Wales, destined to be
remembered as much for his pandering to bigotry and his role in the
Robichaud-Irving feud as for his ties to Beaverbrook.

*

By late 1966 the Playhouse was free of Christofor, but the gallery
was not. In 1967 she demanded, and obtained, the firing of Donald
Andrus, the assistant curator, after he dared to criticize the annual
Maritime Art Exhibition that she sponsored. Beaverbrook himself,
less than a year before his death, had questioned the merits of the
event and had mused about ending it.[37] By 1967, few professional artists were submitting works to the competition, and it was dominated
by amateurs; Smith would call it "the most awful exhibit the world
has ever seen." Andrus says it was "considered quite terrible" among
artists and was "a hugely depressing event for us" because Christofor
and other board members faithfully attended every year while not
showing up for more legitimate exhibitions he organized. Andrus
spoke to a friend of his at the *Gleaner*, who prepared a story for the
paper. "Why don't we call it 'the annual disaster at the Beaverbrook
Art Gallery,'" Andrus suggested to his friend, "since it coincides with
the [Saint John River] flooding every year." That phrase found its

way into the *Gleaner* headline, and Andrus was fired. The firing in turn prompted the blacklisting of the gallery by the association that represented Canadian museum directors: no one would come to Fredericton to fill Andrus's job. "Amateur art has no defensible place in a serious public gallery," Toronto art dealer Dorothy Cameron said in a telegram to Tweedie. "Firing your dedicated curator Don Andrus for stating this truth constitutes an outrage against every professional artist in this country."[38]

The boycott continued until 1969, when Andrus returned on a short-term contract to install a travelling exhibition and reorganize the permanent collection. Smith was exasperated at the never-ending turmoil. "There was no sense that the gallery was the focus of the artistic life of the province," he said. "We did not have an acquisition policy. We were not growing as a collection. . . . There was no sense of outreach to the community, there was no sense of the gallery functioning in an educational way. . . . All of those marks of how a gallery functions in the community were simply not there and it was a desperate struggle to get anything done."

And Christofor loomed over everything. In 1967 she was given a legal opinion that the phrase "all the rest of my personal effects" in that subclause of Beaverbrook's will included the paintings he owned when he died — paintings that were hanging in the gallery and that the Beaverbrook Canadian Foundation had believed it owned. "Smith is disturbed about the situation and is worried that any moment she may recall these paintings from the gallery," the president of the University of New Brunswick, Colin B. Mackay, reported in a letter, "and we shall lose works of art which obviously were meant by Lord Beaverbrook to be part of his collection."[39] Among the dozens of paintings were the three Sickerts that Christofor had claimed in 1959 and again in 1964, when Smith had altered their ownership records at Tweedie's request.

Two years later, Smith's and Mackay's fears were borne out. When Christofor saw the catalogue for the 1969 Summer Exhibition, she was outraged. The Sickerts were listed as the property of the gallery, as were several works by Sir Winston Churchill. Nor were the Dali portraits of her and Sir James Dunn listed as belonging to the Sir

James Dunn Foundation. "I am so sorry you have been caused concern," Tweedie wrote to her, "but I can assure you that the records are crystal clear and your interests protected 100 per cent."[40] The catalogue, it was explained, was designed for tourists and was not an official statement of ownership, and there were plates affixed to the frames with the correct information. Christofor was unmoved. "Lady Beaverbrook is far from satisfied and expects full-scale corrections," her secretary, Joyce Burman, wrote to him. "In her opinion few people bother to go up and examine the plates at the bottoms of paintings when they have a catalogue."[41]

The provincial law governing the gallery stipulated that the chairman of the board was to be New Brunswick's lieutenant-governor, and Wallace Bird, the man who held both positions in 1969, asked Tweedie to look at the records. He reported that seventy-nine paintings belonged to Christofor or the Dunn foundation. Bird, a businessman with a more active interest in the gallery than his predecessor, John McNair, realized that the institution was facing yet another crisis and, with nowhere else to turn, wrote to Sir Max in London. The paintings claimed by Christofor, along with eighty-two others owned by the Beaverbrook foundations, "comprise the life blood of the gallery," Bird wrote. "If any time these paintings and others which have been associated with the Gallery for the past ten years were lost to the Gallery, this would be a grievous blow."[42] Sir Max's lack of interest in the gallery had not changed, but now he stepped in to render a final service to his father's New Brunswick legacy and put an end to Christofor's games. "He was possibly the only person who could handle her," Lady Aitken remembered in 2006. "I think she was quite fond of him in her own way."[43] Sir Max asked Jack Main, an official at the Montreal Trust Company and a director of the Beaverbrook Canadian Foundation, to get in touch with the gallery and solve the Christofor problem. Meanwhile, the problem deepened: in January 1970 she told Tweedie she wanted all of the paintings belonging to her and the Sir James Dunn Foundation locked in the vault "until such time as there is full cooperation in running the gallery."[44]

Tweedie was facing his own pressures. He had resigned as secretary to the Beaverbrook Canadian Foundation in 1966, signalling the final shift of his loyalties from his patron's heirs to his widow. Christofor in turn took care of him much as Beaverbrook had, sending him $2,000 to pay for surgery on another ulcer and inviting him to Cherkley to recuperate.[45] Tweedie's loyalty to her became the impetus for several clashes with the new curator of the gallery, Ian Lumsden, who was hired in 1969 to replace Stuart Smith when Smith left to finish his doctorate. Tweedie chastised Lumsden for not checking with Wallace Bird, the board chairman, before rejecting Christofor's request that the gallery lend paintings to Sir James Dunn Academy, a high school in St. Andrews.[46] Bird and Lumsden were not easily intimidated by Tweedie, however, and his power began to ebb. "We know Mr. Tweedie is a man of great experience and is very capable," Bird wrote to Christofor in March 1970. "We are concerned about his health. The problem that confronts us is how to meld together his ability and experience with that of a young ambitious curator."[47]

Melding proved impossible. One day early in 1970, Helen Savage, Tweedie's secretary, relayed instructions to Lumsden that he was to change some accession records. "On what authority?" Lumsden asked. "Lady Beaverbrook's," he was told. Lumsden went to Bird to tell him he found the request odd, and Bird evidently concurred. Exactly what happened next remains unclear. At a board meeting on May 12, 1970, while Tweedie was away at his son's wedding in Quebec, his position "came under considerable discussion." Lumsden asked Savage for the keys to Tweedie's filing cabinet. She told him she didn't have them. "He was very upset," she recalls. "I think he thought I was lying. I wasn't and was very happy not to be." The governors decided to hire a locksmith to open the filing cabinet and allow them to examine the documents inside.[48] "I can truthfully say I had no idea what was in those files," she says. "To this day I still don't know what they found."

Tweedie pondered suing the gallery over the incident but agreed to leave in return for a severance payment. "I have now decided that insofar as I am concerned I would prefer one lump sum payment — no matter what percentage must go to income tax," he told Bird in a handwritten note. "I want no continuing reminder of my Gallery association through yearly payments." His subsequent official letter of resignation, also to Bird, concealed his bitterness. "Please accept my resignation as Secretary to the Board of Governors of the Gallery, and also as a Governor of that institution. This resignation to be effective at the next meeting of the Board," it said. "As you know, for health and other reasons, I have been anxious to be relieved of all Gallery duties at the earliest convenient moment." Tweedie thanked Bird for his "support and encouragement."[49]

And so Tweedie joined Wardell in cutting his ties to Beaverbrook and the gallery that had so dominated his life. Loyal and discreet until the end, he said nothing about his unhappy departure or indeed about any of the nastier business at the gallery in his 1986 memoir, *On with the Dance*. He declared his affection for Beaverbrook and even for Wardell, and his description of Christofor was particularly kind. "She is an extraordinary woman, capable to the point of near perfection, frequently quick on the trigger, but always fair, generous and understanding. I hope someone will write her life. It has been one of hard work, accomplishment and generosity."[50]

A few months later Christofor made her own exit. On September 7, 1970, Sir Max met with her in England, and later that day he reported to Jack Main that she had agreed to sell all seventy-eight disputed paintings to the Beaverbrook Canadian Foundation, including the three Sickerts, which she claimed she owned, and the two Dalis, which she said belonged to the Sir James Dunn Foundation. By early November they settled on a lump sum of $250,000, which Sir Max quickly confirmed with her in writing. She replied the next day. "I very much enjoy our visits together," she added, "although they are so few and far between." There was, inevitably, a last-minute wrinkle when Christofor's secretary wrote to Jack Main to say one of the Sickert portraits, *Sir James Dunn*, had not in fact been owned by Christofor but had been given to the gallery years earlier by the Sir James Dunn Foundation. "Her concern arises out of the fact that it would be an abuse of our tax laws if Lady Beaverbrook got paid something for a picture which was owned by the Dunn Foundation," Main wrote to Sir Max. Main checked with the gallery in Fredericton and discovered that Christofor was right. The painting had been given to the gallery in 1964, but Tweedie had later changed the records to

5th November 1970

CHERKLEY,
LEATHERHEAD,
SURREY.

Dearest Max —

I received your two letters of the 4th this morning at 6.50 a.m. and thank you very much for both.

The paintings you have offered $250,000 for in order to retain them in the Beaverbrook Gallery, I accept on behalf of myself and the Sir James Dunn Foundation.

I enclose copy of my letter to Kenneth Thomson which I think will conclude the matter concerning his offer for Merrymaking.

I am sorry to have bothered you with the Sporting Life problem but it has, and it will bother me, a lonely old woman remember!

I very much enjoy our visits together, although they are so few and far between. I will let you know when I am able to decide on my departure.

Loving thoughts as ever

Christofor

Sir Max Aitken, Bt.,DFC.,DSO.,
DAILY EXPRESS,
Fleet Street,
London, E.C. 4.

Christofor's letter agreeing to sell her paintings and those of the Sir James Dunn Foundation to the Beaverbrook Canadian Foundation.

Beaverbrook U.K. Foundation, exhibit 27-4030

show the painting belonged to Christofor. Main had her acknowledge gallery ownership in writing, deleted the painting from the list being sold, and went ahead with the lump-sum purchase of the seventy-seven other paintings for $250,000. "I thought it best not to haggle, on the theory that what we want to do is get the matter completed without further ado," Main wrote to Sir Max.[51]

There was a great sense of relief in Fredericton, and Sir Max, for most of the decade a nonentity at the gallery, was suddenly its saviour. "It is wonderful news that you have resolved the ownership problems of the paintings now within the gallery," Bird wrote to him. "I wish to thank you on behalf of all our people of the Province of New Brunswick for your great support." Three decades later, the gallery would provide an entirely different and much less benign interpretation of Sir Max's actions. At the time, however, he appeared nothing less than heroic, for just two months after resolving the ownership dispute for good — or so it seemed — he eliminated an even bigger headache. In February 1971 he sent a telex to Christofor to inform her that the legislation governing the gallery was due to be amended. "This therefore is a suitable opportunity for you to consider whether you wish to continue as a joint custodian and also whether the Sir James Dunn Foundation still wishes to have the power to nominate custodians into perpetuity."[52] Christofor's reply was laced with resignation and melancholy: "I expected this final request to withdraw from all your father's concerns." A week later she agreed to do so. After a tumultuous decade, Christofor's power and influence over the Beaverbrook Art Gallery was gone.

She remained a presence in New Brunswick, however. With her sister, she spent her winters at Dayspring, in St. Andrews, where she continued to support local causes such as the health centre, the high school, the fire hall and the arena. She was often seen in town in her grey limousine, and her mail was kept in a separate bag at the local post office, where she would send her driver every morning to collect it. Dalhousie University in Halifax was another beneficiary of her fortune: she'd been appointed chancellor in 1968, a selection designed both to honour her generosity and to encourage her to maintain it. She did — among her gifts was $2 million to restore the law school after a fire — which is why administrators were reluctant to replace her, even though she never set foot on campus again after her installation. In 1990, Dalhousie's president, Henry Hicks, finally eased her out by persuading her to accept the designation of chancellor emeritus, an echo of the way Beaverbrook had been placated at the University of New Brunswick in 1953. Her successor at Dalhousie, entrepreneur Reuben Cohen, repeated in his memoirs a barb he had heard about Christofor: she was proof that the British monarchy was more powerful than God because "it was able to make a Lady out of her twice, while God was not able to do it once."[53]

In the summers, Christofor lived at Cherkley to avoid the crowds that filled St. Andrews. Beaverbrook had given the house to Sir Max as a gift in 1950, and he later put it into a trust, allowing Christofor to live there after his father's death. Relations remained cool. "I went to Cherkley once to show somebody the house," Beaverbrook's grandson Timothy remembers, "and there she was, leading a very strange life, behind the curtains in one of the top windows, hiding."[54] Sir Max and his family lived in the much smaller garden house on the Cherkley estate, a quarter of a mile from the main house and out of sight behind a small hill. The relationship "was personally warm, which was right and proper, but I wouldn't say they were close," says Sir Max's son Maxwell. "She wasn't a matriarchal figure. . . . I didn't visit her frequently. By this time I was in my teens. My interests were elsewhere, really. I was living in London, I was married in 1974 and my life had moved on. But she was generous. When we got married, she came to the wedding. She gave us very nice wedding presents and what have you, and entertained us for lunch."[55]

Though Christofor never bet on a horse again after that single wager in the 1930s, she owned many thoroughbreds — all of which she gave seven-letter names — and in the 1970s and 1980s several of them won high-profile races in England, giving her a reputation, as the *Times* put it, as "one of the very few private individuals who could, single-handed, command enough capital to challenge, for the good of British racing and breeding, the domination by Arab owners of the thoroughbred bloodstock market. This was a spirited duel which she very much relished."[56] One British racing writer described her as "pretty knowledgeable about horses. . . . She was never concerned if they won, only that they were fine." She loved her dogs as well; once she bought all 227 seats on a DC-8 flying to Canada so that Alexander, a brown pinscher, and Casanova, a white poodle, could roam free in the cabin rather than endure the flight in small cages in the cargo hold.[57]

After her sister's death in 1990, and with her own health in decline, Christofor stopped coming to Dayspring, though St. Andrews had not heard the last of her. The following year, she filed objections with the town council to the planned expansion of the provincially owned Algonquin Hotel near the estate. Hotel guests would be able to see into the Dayspring property over the nine-foot fence James Dunn had installed, she feared, and the historic area of the community where the wealthy had maintained their summer mansions would be threatened. When the council ignored her request and approved the expansion, she pulled her funding from the Sir James Dunn Arena and demanded that the name be changed. The controversy divided the town, with some older residents arguing that her wishes should have been respected and municipal leaders suggesting that the funding for the arena was due to expire soon in any event.

Christofor died at Cherkley on October 28, 1994, at the age of eighty-four. She had lived as a recluse in her final years, using only her bedroom, her sitting room and a dining room among the thirty-odd rooms. Her staff of three was unable to maintain the entire house properly. Except for the small section visible from her window, the gardens had been allowed to deteriorate as well. This was a final thumbing of her nose at Beaverbrook's family. The trust Sir Max had set up for Cherkley had expired in the 1980s, and ownership had reverted to the U.K. Foundation, making Christofor a tenant of a charity controlled by her late husband's descendants. A condition of the lease was that she keep Cherkley in good repair at her expense, and she'd been urged to do so. But when members of the Aitken family entered the house after her death, "it was really terrible," Lady Violet Aitken recalled. "It was falling apart."[58] Water had seeped in behind the plaster over the stone, and it had begun to fall off. The problem had spread to balustrading at the top of the house, and algae was growing. When it rained, water came down through a dome in the roof into the main hall. Wallpaper was peeling off the walls and there was dampness and mould everywhere.[59]

"The condition of the house was very poor," says Maxwell, who by the time of Christofor's death had inherited both the title Lord Beaverbrook and chairmanship of the U.K. Foundation. He and the foundation's other trustees demanded that Christofor's estate pay to repair the damage. "The trustees of the foundation have a duty to look after the interests of the foundation, and the interests of the foundation were that the late tenant's estate should contribute to the restoration of the condition of the house," he says.[60] Although the eventual settlement was subject to a confidentiality agreement, testimony at the 2006 arbitration hearing suggested that Christofor's executors paid the foundation £500,000, or more than $1 million Canadian — far less than the amount eventually required to restore Cherkley to its earlier splendour.[61]

Christofor's will bequeathed the Sutherland portrait of Beaverbrook to the gallery in Fredericton and set aside money for a centre for dogs and horses and other animals in the Maritimes. It also stipulated that when her two favourite horses, Boldboy and Totowah, died, they were to be buried "with every care and attention . . . and the grave to be covered with a suitable stone or marble memorial slab with appropriate wording." An Air Canada supervisor in London who had arranged her trips to Canada received $50,000. The bulk of her $28-million Dayspring estate was liquidated at four auctions in Saint John, with proceeds going to a foundation she had established in her own name.[62] The items included Sir James Dunn's handmade leather boots, several signed first editions of Ian Fleming's James Bond novels, a mahogany table attributed to Thomas Nisbet, a renowned Saint John furniture maker, and a print and a sketch by Dali, which prompted the Dali Museum in Figueres, Spain, to send a representative to the auction.

The more valuable items went to buyers from outside the province, some of them bidding by phone. Some New Brunswickers, however, managed to leave with small pieces of Dunn's and Christofor's remarkable life. One government employee from Fredericton who travelled to Saint John for one auction managed to pick up a small framed photograph of Beaverbrook. When he returned home and took the frame apart to examine it, he found another photograph of Sir James Dunn tucked in behind.[63] Most poignantly, Dunn's daughter Anne appeared at the auction. Christofor had frozen his children out of his life and had spurned their requests for a few sentimental items from his home after his death. Anne was left to bid against strangers to own a handful of mementos of her father.

No doubt Christofor had believed she was protecting Dunn, just as she had been certain she was protecting Beaverbrook and his legacy. One day during the 1980s she had appeared at the gallery in Fredericton unannounced to look at the paintings. Afterwards, she wrote to Ian Lumsden, the director, to tell him the Dali portraits of her and her first husband, *Equestrian Fantasy* and *La Turbie*, were on loan from the Sir James Dunn Foundation. "He had to write back," a gallery official would recount, "and explain to her, 'Well, they were the subject of your agreement with Sir Max, and you basically sold them . . . to the [Beaverbrook] Canadian Foundation.' And there was no further inquiry."[64]

Christofor's extraordinary devotion to her two husbands had loosened her grip on reality and turned her into a caricature of the eccentric dowager. She went to her grave certain that she had protected the legacies of those two great men whose pictures she preserved in a single frame. But her whims and her tantrums had done just the opposite. In 2004, they would reappear like ghosts to torment the Beaverbrook Art Gallery yet again.

Sir Max Aitken, Chancellor of the University of New Brunswick.

CHAPTER EIGHT

"He's not at the centre of anything"

To meet Timothy Aitken in the late winter of 2007 is to feel ushered into the presence of the original Lord Beaverbrook reincarnate. Small, puckish and full of energy, he bursts into the third-floor headquarters of his company, Allied Healthcare, located in the fashionable Knightsbridge area of London near embassies, boutiques and the landmark Harrod's Department Store. Barking a "Hi," he flashes past the receptionist and the office-within-an-office of the Beaverbrook U.K. Foundation, which he permits to rent space from Allied. At sixty-three, Timothy's hair is turning white, which, combined with his lively eyes, animated face and blunt manner, reinforces the connection with his legendary progenitor. The only quality lacking is the false modesty. "I am far and away the most successful member of this family in this generation," he states matter-of-factly, drawing on a cigar as he fumbles with a pastry he had picked up for lunch.

"I suppose I feel more strongly about it than anyone else," he says about the dispute with the Beaverbrook Art Gallery, "because in a sense, the only thing I believe I can give back to my grandfather — who after all brought me up and paid for my education — is keeping his memory alive. I also certainly in my early days did not appreciate the impact he personally had on me. . . . Eight public companies later, and significant turnarounds in three of them, you're looking at a man who's been driven from his childhood. The person who established that was undoubtedly my grandfather and not anybody else."

That bond prompts him to criticize decisions other members of his family have made — decisions that, it becomes clear, amount in his mind to a betrayal of what the great man had built, decisions that he once dreamed of undoing. "I had a ringside seat to the final destruction of Beaverbrook Newspapers, which was a total scandal," he says, his voice rising, not for the first or last time this afternoon. "We're talking about the property alone, the physical buildings, being worth six or seven hundred million, and this business was sold [in 1977] for seventy million. It was total, ridiculous nonsense. . . . I mean, this was a joke. But it happened at the bottom of the stock market, [Sir] Max Aitken had had a stroke, and there was no leadership, and what leadership there was was pathetic. And my cousin was too young to really do anything about it. So that irritated the shit out of me, honestly."[1]

The cousin of whom he speaks, Maxwell, who works from the U.K. Foundation's rented office-within-an-office and who now holds the title Lord Beaverbrook, acknowledges that Timothy inherited more of their grandfather's fighting spirit than he did. "Tim is a very forceful personality," says Maxwell, who served as a minister in the Thatcher government in the late 1980s. "A career in politics is grounding for perhaps a more conciliatory style, and I regard myself as more conciliatory and Tim as being fundamentally more aggressive." Timothy feels a duty to guard the Beaverbrook legacy, Maxwell adds, on a profound, even visceral level. "My father came between me and my grandfather," he says. "There was a generation. Tim didn't have that because his father was dead."[2] It seems at first an inconsequential paradox that the grandson who was unable to inherit his grandfather's title is more outwardly passionate about defending his legacy. But it may explain what appears at times to be an uneasy relationship between the two cousins.

Timothy was only three years old when his father Peter, Beaverbrook's second son, died in 1947. Peter had become estranged from his father. "Neither would give way," his sister Janet wrote, "and that was how it would remain to the end." The end came when Peter was trying to sail from Stockholm to Copenhagen. He ran into problems and the boat's stem struck him repeatedly in the chest, breaking four ribs, while he was trying to push it off some rocks. One rib pierced a lung and he died in a hospital after making it back to Stockholm. "Perhaps father's grief about Peter was silent," Janet wrote. "I don't know. He never spoke about Peter's death, either then or later."[3] Beaverbrook expressed his sorrow in a different way: he became legal guardian to Peter's two sons, Peter and Timothy, and they moved into Cherkley when Timothy was eight years old; their mother left England for the United States. Beaverbrook took charge of their upbringing and their education in more ways than one. "I was brought up on stories of moments in history when something happened that made a difference," Timothy says, giving the impression that he could talk for hours about his grandfather's influence. "Thing is, when you're fourteen, you couldn't care less. . . . It's only when you get older that you realize what it is that makes a difference in history: people. Individuals. Not the goddamned party or the amorphous things that people write up today, the trends, socialism, this or that. It's people that make a difference."[4]

Beaverbrook turned out to be a better grandfather than father. He sent Timothy and Peter on holidays, including to his villa in the south of France, he arranged for Timothy's tonsil operation, and he intervened when the two boys — Catholics like their mother — were told by the bishop that the church would not allow them to take part in prayers at King's Mead, the Anglican preparatory school they were attending. "I am not, as you know, entirely happy about the way their characters are developing," the headmaster, Peter Barrett, wrote to the parish priest, seeking, in vain, to have the edict changed. Beaverbrook adopted a youthful manner with the boys: when Timothy signed off one letter with "see you later Alligator," his grandfather's next letter opened, "My dear Timothy, in a while, crocodile." Other members of the family understood his keen interest in the pair. Sir Max's wife, Lady Aitken, would send Beaverbrook detailed letters about their visits with her children. Timothy and Peter, she wrote in 1958, "are tough and enterprising without being wild, and their manners really are excellent now. . . . They are sweet to Maxwell and [his sister]

Laura, and Maxwell's great delight is trying to follow them on his tricycle. A procession can be seen which would make you laugh — Tim and Peter on their bicycles flashing by, a good deal after comes Maxwell, his legs working like pistons." Perhaps the best measure of how important Peter's children were to Beaverbrook is that on September 16, 1959, the day on which he oversaw the official opening of the Fredericton art gallery that had consumed him for years, Beaverbrook found a few minutes to write Timothy a letter thanking him for a postcard he had sent from Scotland.[5]

Beaverbrook's itinerant ways meant that his underlings were charged, in addition to their many other duties, with tracking and summarizing the academic progress of Timothy and Peter. One, Robert Pitman, was asked to find them a tutor. "They are a very mischievous pair and need to be controlled in the interest of fabric and furniture," Beaverbrook wrote. George Millar forwarded their school reports from King's Mead and later from Repton, another boarding school, as well as from tutors. One report noted that Timothy "did not lack ability, but was appallingly careless and overconfident" in his work. Another described him as talented but, "with greater concentration," capable of much better. Beaverbrook himself admonished Peter to improve his French because, he wrote with only slight exaggeration, "half the population of New Brunswick are French-speaking Canadians."[6]

It was not a shock, given his grandfather's influence, that Timothy would be inspired to follow in his footsteps. In 1963, while he was waiting to attend McGill University that fall, his uncle, Sir Max, arranged a six-month job for him at the Beaverbrook-owned *Evening Standard*. "Don't forget to send me cuttings of all that you write," his grandfather wrote.[7] After graduating from McGill, Timothy freelanced in India before returning to England for good in 1969, convinced that it would fall to him to draw the sword from the stone and save the Beaverbrook legacy. "I came back to find what I already knew to be the case . . . a completely dysfunctional family, a family where there was no communication at all. And I made a decision when I came back from India to set about bringing this family together. . . . I didn't have any particular idea about how we were going to do anything that was interesting, but it very much struck me that if this family with numerous talents got together and applied themselves, who knew where it might lead?"[8]

There was, however, an insurmountable obstacle to Timothy's ambition: Sir Max, his uncle, remained the nominal head of the family, and he could not be displaced even if he was not, in Timothy's view, up to the role of patriarch. "Max Aitken was not a businessperson. He didn't like the newspaper. I don't think he enjoyed running the newspaper at all. . . . I think his problem was he was the 'son of,' and measuring up to the father is always a big problem." Beaverbrook's biographers Anne Chisholm and Michael Davie concur: Sir Max, they say, "found it difficult to adjust from the excitement of the air force to the responsibilities of the newspaper business — particularly as his father constantly, and often publicly, criticized his performance."[9] He had his successes, however, such as winning for the *Express* the exclusive right to serialize the Duke of Windsor's memoirs in 1947. "This is the first of these ticklish jobs he has done for us," editor John Gordon told Beaverbrook, "and I cannot speak too highly of him."[10] In an interview eight weeks before his death, in an apparent act of contrition, Beaverbrook said, "I'm very proud of my son. He's a fine fellow. He's a nicer man than ever I was, a much, much nicer man." Still, the son recognized the challenge of stepping out from his father's shadow. On the day Beaverbrook died, he began the process of renouncing the title, declaring, "As long as I live there will be only one Lord Beaverbrook."[11]

It was an indecisive Sir Max who — to Timothy's dismay — presided over the decline of Beaverbrook Newspapers. The company had failed to diversify, so riding out a rough patch was difficult. And the first years of the 1970s were rough indeed: newsprint costs soared, the company's losses and debts mounted, and the circulation of the flagship *Daily Express* had plummeted to two million copies, half of its spectacular peak of four million in the final years of Lord Beaverbrook's life. His strategy of pouring profits back into the newspapers and paying large salaries that attracted top talent had been successful when times were good, but now it flooded the company in red ink. Union wages were high, the aging printing presses needed replacing, and the paper itself, once the liveliest in London, seemed

Sir Max Aitken and his father, Lord Beaverbrook,
at the Old Manse, Newcastle, New Brunswick.
Provincial Archives of New Brunswick , Miramichi Historical Society Photographs: P204-323

stodgy as competitors became more racy and visually exciting. By the
start of 1977, two crises had converged. Sir Max had suffered a mild
stroke, and Lloyd's Bank had told the company it would not extend
its overdraft when payment came due in April.[12]

Young Maxwell Aitken, just twenty-six years old, thus found
himself vaulted into a senior position as Beaverbrook Newspapers
fought to survive. Sir Max had been on his third and final marriage
when he finally produced a male heir in 1951, and Maxwell's famous grandfather had delighted in stuffing the boy with chocolates
at Cherkley.[13] Though he would not form the same bond with the
old man as Timothy, Maxwell also learned to revere his grandfather.

"Maxwell is thrilled with your letter which he carries about in his pocket," his mother wrote to Beaverbrook in 1958. "Tells everyone 'I just had a letter from Grandpa today.'"[14] Maxwell was only twelve when Beaverbrook died, "so we didn't have an adult relationship as such," he says. "I remember him as being a formidable figure and then a frail figure in the year before he died."[15]

Beaverbrook's poor treatment of Sir Max is well documented, and Maxwell does not deny it. "Anyone who is single-minded in what he was doing — family was a diversion that he didn't always tend to enough," he says. "But what are forgotten are the more caring moments. My grandfather in the war never went to bed until he'd heard that my father had landed in safely from night fighting missions." Maxwell told the *Sunday Times* in 1974 that his own upbringing had been strict. "One wasn't showered with everything one wanted," he said. "One was always conscious money didn't grow on trees."[16] But, he says in 2007, "I was not subjected to the same sort of difficult relationship that my father had with his father."[17] That is an account Timothy disputes. "Max Aitken was a loner. His relationship with his children was appalling. . . . Maybe not with his eldest daughter, but with his son. Appalling. The way he treated Maxwell was just ghastly."[18] Though destined to work on Fleet Street, Maxwell, as a young man, had no interest in politics, his grandfather's other passion. "I think one is well aware of the achievements of the people in one's family," he said in 1974, "but I've never thought one should try and exceed them."[19]

As several suitors lined up to buy Beaverbrook Newspapers in 1977, Maxwell was nominated to both the company's board of directors and a three-man team charged with exploring a sale to Associated Newspapers, owners of the rival *Daily Mail*. Maxwell's desire to hold on to his birthright was not clear. He had told the *Times* three years earlier that newspapers were in his blood. "Any executive in my position at my age would certainly want the top job. It's certainly my ambition. I love the industry." At one point he flew to Canada to persuade the Beaverbrook Canadian Foundation to put some money into saving the company, only to be told that this was beyond what a charitable foundation was allowed to do. And in the midst of the negotiations with Associated, claiming to act on Sir Max's authority, he sought to oust the company's chief executive, Jocelyn Stevens. But Stevens resisted and went to see Sir Max, who told him he could stay. Stevens agreed on the condition that two other executives who had joined Maxwell in the coup attempt be sacked. Maxwell, of course, could hardly be shown the door, so Stevens proposed that he be promoted to a job as his immediate deputy, where he could keep an eye on him. Evidently Sir Max's bond with Stevens was stronger than that his bond with his own son.[20]

Another suitor, however, found Maxwell considerably less ambitious and rather diffident about the prospect of inheriting the press baron's mantle. Rupert Murdoch, who met with him as he lobbied the directors to consider his offer, formed the impression that Maxwell would prefer to wash his hands of the family enterprise. "He wanted the money, he wanted to have the money for a comfortable life — those were his words," Murdoch said. Maxwell himself explained at the time, "I felt the proprietorial hierarchies of Fleet Street weren't going to go on forever. . . . One's whole life wasn't necessarily going to be devoted to running the *Daily Express*, the *Sunday Express* and the *Evening Standard*."[21]

Sir Max was doing little to disprove his own reputation for indecisiveness. He rejected proposed agreements with both Associated and Sir James Goldsmith, another potential investor. During a rebound in his health, he spoke of fighting on. "Now that I'm recovering, I want to bring some morale back to the situation," he told the *Sunday Times*. "I know what it is like to be without energy, and it is only with energy that we will survive. If you ask me if I'm going to sell the *Daily Express*, the answer is no. The *Sunday Express*? No. The *Evening Standard*? No. Beaverbrook Newspapers? No." On June 30, however, after considering no fewer than four offers, Sir Max reluctantly decided that it was in the best interests of the newspapers, the shareholders and the employees to sell to Trafalgar House Investments. The sale would give the Beaverbrook U.K. Foundation, the single largest shareholder, three million pounds, while Sir Max, the second largest investor, would receive one million for his shares.[22]

The board of the foundation had to approve the sale of its shares, however, and when the trustees met that afternoon, the three members of Sir Max's own family — his wife, his son Maxwell, and his daughter Laura — argued against the deal, which suggests that Maxwell may not have been as eager to cash in as Rupert Murdoch had believed. "It was a sale with only one person in the auction room, which was wrong," Maxwell would explain. The company's fortunes had improved slightly, and the three family trustees favoured holding out a while longer to see if a healthier *Express* might attract a better bid. But a majority of trustees sided with Sir Max, and over the objections of Maxwell, Laura, and Lady Violet Aitken, the foundation sold its shares to Trafalgar. The Aitken connection with Fleet Street, which Timothy had so cherished, was gone. Maxwell's employment contract would be bought out within the month. "This is a hard decision to take and it is particularly hard on young Maxwell," Sir Max told the company's directors.[23]

"It was controversial within the family, no doubt about it," Maxwell says now, providing no further explanation for the different accounts of his own wishes. Instead he paints the choice as inevitable. "The underlying reality was that my father was unwell. He'd suffered a series of strokes. He wasn't old — he was sixty-seven at the time — so there was this insurmountable problem of what would happen to the chairmanship. . . . . It had come rather too early for a succession. . . . I wasn't old enough to do so and therefore there wasn't a natural solution to the whole thing. If I'd been in my mid-thirties we might well have done a family buyout of the public shareholders or something like that, but it wasn't something that could be achieved at the time." Of his own feelings, he says, "it was like when any family business is sold. There are sadnesses because relationships with many, many people in the company tend to become less close, or don't really exist anymore. Sadnesses that plans for the future no longer are appropriate. And in a sense a way of life for the family in terms of being a focal point is no longer there."[24]

*

Leaving the building after the tumultuous meeting of the Beaverbrook Foundation trustees, Sir Max Aitken was asked by a waiting journalist what his father would have made of the decision. "I think he would have sold up long before," he answered.[25] Perhaps — but Beaverbrook might also have been more outraged by another sale, another casualty of his empire's decline.

In 1976, as the financial pressures began to mount, Sir Max had written to Peter Wilson at Sotheby's about the paintings at the Beaverbrook Art Gallery in Fredericton. "We are reviewing our assets in Canada and it is possible that we might bring back the English foundation's pictures to this country and sell them," he explained. He asked for a valuation of the paintings, adding, "the reason for the sale would be to purchase Beaverbrook Newspapers shares."[26]

Sotheby's estimated that the entire collection would sell for between £525,000 and £759,000. Alarmingly, it noted, three of the more valuable paintings were deteriorating: two by George Stubbs, *Hunters Out at Grass* and *White Dog in a Landscape*, were reported "in very poor condition."[27] This was hardly a revelation: Stuart Smith had said as early as 1964 that the two Stubbs works were in "critical" condition, and Sir Max had offered in 1967 to have them restored at the Canadian Foundation's expense.[28] The surprise was Beaverbrook's treasured *Peasant Girl Gathering Faggots*, by Thomas Gainsborough, which Sotheby's said in its report would likely fetch a mere £30,000 to £50,000 "in view of condition." The chairman of Sotheby's, Peter Wilson, advised Sir Max that given the state of the two Stubbs paintings, "it may be a good idea to get them over here and have them restored without spending too much money." He made no such recommendation about the Gainsborough, at least not in documents filed in the 2006 arbitration.[29]

What happened next — whether the foundation misled the gallery into handing over the paintings by suggesting they would later be returned — would be disputed. The U.K. Foundation's secretary, Anne Westover, wrote to Ian Lumsden in October, telling him that the two Stubbses and the Gainsborough "are to be returned to us for restoration." The letter does not mention the possibility of selling the works, though it does mention an earlier meeting at which Lumsden and the

FROM: Chairman - Sir Max Aitken, Bt DSO DFC

PRIVATE & PERSONAL

11th March 1976

We are reviewing our assets in Canada and it is possible that we might bring back the English Foundation's pictures to this country and sell them.

This would not damage the total collection on display because there are so many others which cannot find a place on the walls.

I enclose a list of paintings which we could bring back and I would much like your advice as to their sale value.

Or, would it be better to sell in New York or Zurich?

The reason for the sale, would be to purchase Beaverbrook Newspapers' shares.

I would much appreciate your advice.

With all good wishes.

Peter C. Wilson Esq.,
Sotheby & Co.,
34 New Bond Street,
London W.1.

Sir Max Aitken's letter to Sotheby's suggesting
the sale of Beaverbrook Art Gallery paintings.

Beaverbrook U.K. Foundation, exhibit 30-4490

foundation discussed sending the paintings to England, and at which the possibility of selling them might have been raised.[30] Five days later Lumsden suggested in a letter to Richard Bird, the chairman of the gallery board, that Sir Max's "guilt" over the "repatriation" of the Gainsborough might compel him to buy a set of drawings then on the market to fill the "gaping hole" left in the collection[31] — proof, the foundation would argue decades later, that both men knew a sale was at least possible and chose not to object. (Lumsden and Bird would not grant interviews for this book.) The customs form Lumsden eventually filled out for the Gainsborough referred to it as a "loan being returned to owner," further evidence that he knew what the foundation intended. In January 1977, after the three paintings had arrived in England, Wilson wrote from Sotheby's to tell Sir Max that the two Stubbses had deteriorated too much to even risk restoration "if you are contemplating selling them." This remark suggests that, if selling the works was not a foregone conclusion, it was a possibility.[32]

Though Wilson wrote in that same letter that the Gainsborough had "suffered" because of earlier poor attempts at restoration, he did not mention any risk to the painting, and he suggested it might sell for £30,000 at auction; curiously, someone wrote "No" in the margin of the page next to that paragraph.[33] By April it was clear that the *Peasant Girl* would be the main attraction at an auction that Sotheby's was arranging for July. Paul Thomson, the director of English pictures at the auction house, remained pessimistic about the two works by Stubbs, but he was becoming more upbeat about the *Peasant Girl*, raising his estimate of its potential sale price to £40,000 to £60,000 with a reserve price of £35,000. Again, there was no indication that the *Peasant Girl* was too damaged to risk restoration — a risk that, the foundation and its lawyers would assert in their 2006 legal arguments, was the main reason for removing it from Fredericton and selling it quickly. Maxwell repeated that assertion: "With the Gainsborough," he said, "the advice from Sotheby's was it was probably better to sell it rather than to risk a major restoration of the picture," he said.[34] On the contrary, while Thomson wrote that April that "very little can be done" to the two Stubbses and he would "not recommend touching them before sale," he offered no such warning about the

Gainsborough. It was, he wrote, "a beautiful painting and I think we may be able to suggest a very slightly higher reserve nearer the time, when I know how much interest there is in it."[35]

The foundation's trustees approved the sale on May 5, just five days before the Sotheby's auction catalogue had to go to press. The gallery was told in a letter on May 9 that "due to the financial situation here" the paintings would be sold. "It may be necessary to withdraw further paintings in the future," said the letter to Richard Bird. "The Trustees have asked me to convey to the Beaverbrook Art Gallery their sad regret at having to make this decision." Ian Lumsden made a last-ditch attempt to save the three paintings as the auction neared, asking the Canadian government's museums program to use its National Emergency Purchase Fund to bid on them. The Friends of the Beaverbrook Art Gallery organization was prepared to contribute all the money in its bank account, $35,000, towards the purchase. The paintings, Lumsden wrote to federal officials, "have always constituted the backbone of our collection of British paintings," and their departure from the gallery "has evoked considerable consternation. . . . Undoubtedly you appreciate the gravity of the loss of works of this magnitude, not only to the Atlantic region but to Canada as a whole."[36] But Lumsden may have been optimistic about how quickly the federal bureaucracy in Ottawa could move: he wrote his letter on June 21; the auction was scheduled for just two weeks later.

In the intervening days, Beaverbrook Newspapers was sold to Trafalgar House, seemingly defeating the entire point of selling the paintings: to generate money so the foundation could buy up shares and save the company. But the contract with Sotheby's stipulated that a seller could not withdraw a painting after the printing of the auction catalogue. There was no turning back. And Timothy Aitken says that saving the company wasn't the real motive in any event: the foundation's major source of revenue, upon which it relied to fund its charity work in the United Kingdom, was its shares in Beaverbrook Newspapers, but those shares had plunged to just thirteen pence, sapping the foundation's ability to fund its charitable work. The shares "were paying no dividend," Timothy says. "The foundation had no income. [The paintings] were sold in order to meet the things the foundation was doing then . . . to honour the commitments that had been made."[37] Maxwell disagrees with his cousin's version of events. "A lot of things were in the melting pot at the time. . . . Actually the foundation didn't need any money because . . . it received a lot of money from the sale of the newspaper shares. So the two I don't think in hindsight are really connected."[38]

Paul Thomson's pessimism about the paintings by Stubbs and his optimism about the Gainsborough proved prescient. Bids for *Hunters Out at Grass* just barely reached the reserve price of £15,000, and *White Dog in a Landscape* failed to fetch its reserve price of £8,000 and did not sell. *Peasant Girl Gathering Faggots*, however, went for £92,000, far above Thomson's predicted price. The buyer was the venerable London art dealer Thomas Agnew and Sons. Geoffrey Agnew, the co-owner, had told Beaverbrook when he bought the painting in 1956, "If I could not own the picture, I am delighted that you should." Now Agnew has his wish.[39] Now the *Peasant Girl* with the humble and deferential face, adored above all others by the founder of that remarkable gallery in Fredericton, had left the House of Beaverbrook, never to return.

*

Sir Max Aitken's health continued to decline after the sale of the newspapers. By 1981 he was in a wheelchair and too ill to travel. He decided that he could not continue to serve as chancellor of the University of New Brunswick, the ceremonial post that the school had passed to him, like an inheritance, after Beaverbrook had died. His wife, Lady Violet Aitken, travelled to Fredericton to give the news to university officials. While in the city, she was invited to a meeting with the premier, Richard Hatfield, who knew the value of the relationship with the Aitkens. In his second-floor office in the imposing Centennial Building near the art gallery, Hatfield asked Lady Aitken to step in as chancellor. "I nearly fell off my chair," she recalled. She told Hatfield she would have to check with Max back in England, and "on one of his good days" she told him about the invitation. "He seemed very pleased, and he said, 'You go ahead.'" Lady Violet Aitken held the post for a decade, served as co-custodian of the gallery as well, and in some years visited Fredericton three or four times.[40]

"Poor, dear Max," his sister Janet wrote in her memoirs. "I wanted him to die peacefully, without pain, and hoped with all my heart that he felt no awareness or frustration at living on the edge of consciousness, unable to move or speak." He died in 1985, and his ashes were scattered in the Solent Sea, between the British mainland and the Isle of Wight, where he loved to sail his yacht.[41]

Sir Max's death meant that the title he had chosen to renounce, Lord Beaverbrook, passed automatically to his son, Maxwell, who now faced the same decision. Timothy, ever mindful of his grandfather's legacy, felt Maxwell was no worthier than Sir Max and told him so. "I agreed with what his father did, which was to say, 'There should be only one Lord Beaverbrook.' How do you possibly take a title like that?" Timothy asks. "The man was a family wrapped up in one person. He wrote bestsellers, biographies. . . . He made gazillions and didn't pay any attention to it. He was absolutely at the centre of government in two world wars. He created a newspaper which, when he died in 1964, had four and a half million readers, the biggest newspaper in the world. . . . The reality is he was an extraordinary man." Just before he died, Beaverbrook had told Timothy — perhaps wanting to console the grandson who would never have a claim to the title — that the worst mistake of his life had been accepting it in 1916. "And I was absolutely gobsmacked," Timothy says. "I said, 'Why?' He said, 'Because it took me away from the Commons and the centre of power.'"[42] Monarchs had once routinely selected their prime ministers from the House of Lords, but in the more democratically minded twentieth century, a seat in the unelected Lords amounted to a ban on leading a government, an ambition Beaverbrook is said to have harboured.

Maxwell decided not to take Timothy's advice. "We had a family discussion and his view was one in about a dozen, which is fine," Maxwell says. "I think he would probably say his view today is different, but that's up to him."[43]

In fact, Timothy has not changed his opinion at all. "I think it was ridiculous, my cousin taking the title," he says. But it is not a sore spot between them, he insists. "No, he knows my views." Besides, he points out, Tony Blair's reforms of the upper chamber had rendered the peerage all but irrelevant in the twenty-first century. "What's it good for these days?" Timothy asks. "Restaurant tables? That's about all it is good for. He doesn't sit in the House of Lords. He's not at the centre of anything. I mean, come on."[44]

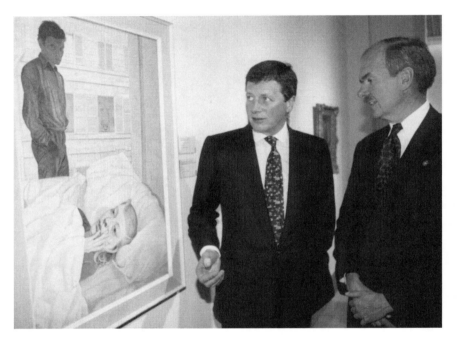

Lord Beaverbrook and Ian Lumsden
with *Hotel Bedroom*, by Lucian Freud, May 1998.

Beaverbrook Art Gallery

CHAPTER NINE

"Families are absolutely a necessary evil"

Timothy Aitken's disagreement with his cousin Maxwell over the title would prove to be a minor affair compared to his public falling out with another Aitken, a more distant cousin named Jonathan. The spat with Maxwell was, in the end, merely about a name. The row with Jonathan shattered Timothy's dream of rebuilding the Beaverbrook empire.

Jonathan Aitken was the son of Beaverbrook's nephew William and grandson of his brother Magnus. William Aitken had been summoned to England by his uncle to work for the *Evening Standard*; he served as a fighter pilot in the Second World War, was elected as a British MP in a safe Conservative constituency and was knighted in 1963, a year before his death. Jonathan had little contact with his famous great-uncle until 1960, when, as a student at Oxford, he wrote him a letter and was summoned to Cherkley. He soon became a frequent guest and correspondent of the old man, raving about a tour he took of New Brunswick and sending him a copy of *The Oxford Tory*, a student publication he edited, which included a review of Beaverbrook's book *The Decline and Fall of Lloyd George*. Beaverbrook evidently approved of his great-nephew's ambitions in journalism. "You will live to do a very great deal of mischief — and you will enjoy it," he wrote. Jonathan replied, "If in my lifetime I manage to stir up half as much mischief as you have in yours, I will feel more than satisfied."[1]

Beaverbrook was eventually proven right about the mischief, though not about Jonathan's enjoyment of it.

After Oxford, Jonathan went to work on Fleet Street, first for the family-owned *Evening Standard* and then for the *Daily Telegraph*, where he gained notoriety after being charged with, and acquitted of, violating Britain's Official Secrets Act by writing a story about British arms sales to Nigeria. He left journalism to run the Middle East operations of the investment firm Slater Walker, and he was elected an MP in 1974. He and another partner started an investment company with Peter and Timothy, who had been working in a variety of corporate management jobs. Using some of the trust fund that Beaverbrook had set up for Peter and Timothy, the four partners expanded the company quickly. They gobbled up a small bank in 1981, took the name Aitken Hume, and bought into a new breakfast television station, TV-am. In 1983, Britain's broadcast regulators objected because Jonathan, a Member of Parliament, also held the position of managing director of the station, so he stepped aside and Timothy took over. In his first week, Timothy fired two high-profile on-air personalities, Anna Ford and Angela Rippon, when they refused to accept salary cuts. This caused a stir in two ways: it established Timothy's reputation in London financial circles as a hard-nosed, decisive businessman, and it signalled that the Aitken family was determined to rebound from the humbling sale of Beaverbrook Newspapers six years earlier.[2]

Then it all fell apart. Timothy moved out of the top job at TV-am so he could return to running Aitken Hume, only to be ousted in a 1985 boardroom coup orchestrated by Jonathan. Jonathan's partisans would claim Timothy's abrasive personality was bad for business. "He could be fairly offensive personally to quite a lot of people," one businessman said. "He can rub people the wrong way," said another. "Even friends are aware that his irritability factor is perhaps higher than the average," a newspaper article reported. A 1984 book about the drama at TV-am had described Jonathan's view of Timothy as "that of an owner with an irascible Alsatian. It is true that he devours the occasional small child, but he certainly keeps the burglars away."[3] Shortly after the book's publication, Jonathan had hosted a fortieth birthday party for Timothy that included a cake bearing a miniature figure of an Alsatian. The two cousins had a good laugh; twelve months later, in the words of one London journalist, "Jonathan would be looking for a way to have the Alsatian put down."[4]

Another version of the story emerged: Timothy had sought to lead Aitken Hume into a merger with Fleet Holdings, the owner of the *Express* newspapers, which had been spun off from Trafalgar House. The deal, never consummated, would have seen Timothy regain control of the newspaper group his grandfather had built. But newspaper reports said Jonathan felt betrayed when he learned the merger would have included no role for him because of the perception problem inherent in a politician's helping to run a newspaper company.[5] Whatever motivated Jonathan, the Beaverbrook family was furious with him for ousting Timothy — his aunt, Lady Violet Aitken, reportedly sent a strongly worded letter to Jonathan's mother — and they put their shares in Aitken Hume up for sale in protest. It was rich fodder for the London newspapers, which delighted in publishing headlines that recycled variations on "the decline of" or "the fall of" the House of Beaverbrook. "Jonathan Aitken stuck a knife right between my shoulder blades in a particularly nasty way," Timothy says now, his bitterness evident more than two decades later. "I've never really talked about it. He got his comeuppance in due course without my participating in it. A very appropriate comeuppance, in my view. . . . He paid lip service to the family dream that I had. He just didn't participate in it."[6]

Jonathan's comeuppance began three years after Timothy's ouster, in 1988, when he was forced to resign his directorship of TV-am. A newspaper revealed that Saudi Arabian investors, backed by the kingdom's ruling family, had gained control of Beaverbrook Investments, the company through which he and Timothy owned 14.9 per cent of the broadcaster — a fact Jonathan had kept secret from TV-am's board. "There has been no wrongdoing or lawbreaking," he said when it became public, "but an error of judgment was made."[7] The Saudi investors, acquaintances of Jonathan's from the days when he ran Slater Walker's Middle East offices, had had no direct control of Beaverbrook Investments at first. But a subsequent shake-up had given them more than fifty per cent of the company, exceeding the percent-

age allowed by European regulations. Jonathan would explain that
he was scrambling to sell the Saudi stake when the story broke in the
papers, forcing him to resign from the board. But his comeuppance
also damaged Timothy, who had — despite the falling out — retained
his seat on the TV-am board and was serving as chairman at the time.
Though he had soured on the Saudis long before this revelation, he
had been part of the original deal, and he felt compelled to resign
as well. "Tim's dreams of a new Beaverbrook dynasty now lie shattered," the *Sunday Times* commented.[8] "The rest is history," Timothy
says now. "I packed my bags and went to the United States and got on
with life. I was finished. Finished."[9]

*

The crushing of Timothy's ambitions coincided with Maxwell's move
to centre stage as he settled into his role as Lord Beaverbrook, public
player and head of the family. Jonathan, suave and good-looking, had
once been considered a rising star in the Conservative party, but his
ascent had been blocked by Prime Minister Margaret Thatcher, who
reportedly left him out of her cabinet because he had broken off a
relationship with her daughter. Instead, as part of a 1986 shake-up of
her front bench in the House of Lords, Thatcher appointed Maxwell,
then thirty-four, and two other young peers as whips. The idea was
to inject youthful energy into the business of the Upper House. "We
were known as 'Thatcher's babes,'" says Maxwell, who also became
deputy government spokesman on trade, industry and the Treasury.
Though the reviews of his performance were often unkind — one
reporter described him as the "waif-like grandson of the old mon-
ster" — he enjoyed his role as insider. "It's fascinating and it's not
something I would have missed for the world. It was an opportunity
that I am delighted I grasped fully. And it was a time of tremendous
change in this country. The power of the unions was being tamed.
The Thatcherite economic reforms were beginning to become recognized as beneficial. And being on the inside of all that, and being
perhaps able to contribute to it in some small way, was an experience
of a lifetime."[10]

The excitement and the attention cut both ways. In 1988, the same year Timothy began his self-imposed exile to America, Maxwell was named deputy treasurer of the Conservative party, a position that put him at the centre of several party fundraising controversies. A BBC documentary suggested links between donations to the party and favours dispensed by the government, and after he had been promoted to party treasurer there were revelations of secret donations by foreign business tycoons. Meanwhile, the organization slid into debt, prompting Maxwell to introduce an array of modern, American-style fundraising techniques to the tradition-bound Tories. By the time Thatcher's replacement as prime minister, John Major, went to the polls in 1992, seemingly facing certain defeat, Maxwell had helped raise £38 million. By any measure, he was a success. "The party was solvent going into the election and solvent coming out the other end of the election," he says, "and we won the election." But his experience turned him into an advocate of public subsidization of political parties, which he believes would lessen the influence of big donors. "The quality of democracy that you get is what you're prepared to pay for," he says. "The quality of democracy is improved when the parties are not beholden to sectarian interest in order to pay the rent, i.e. the Tories with big business and Labour with the trade unions."[11]

Maxwell was unable to revel in his contribution to Major's April 1992 election triumph: he left the treasurer's job shortly after the campaign because, it was revealed in September, he was facing personal bankruptcy, a cruel irony given his success in raising funds for the Tories. His own financial troubles made for great newspaper copy, with much talk of how he was forced to fire domestic staff at his seventeenth-century home, Denchworth Manor, in Oxfordshire, and sell some of his collection of classic cars, which reportedly included four Ferraris.[12] Maxwell had put together a consortium to invest in a sawmill and forestry operation in Guyana, only to learn that the trees would have to be harvested in a "sustainable" and thus more expensive way for the wood to get a coveted green rating and command top prices on the world market. Maxwell sought a buyout, but the deal required him to invest more of his money in return for shares that he could not sell for a year and that plunged in value.[13] "It was simply bad judgment, with perhaps a bit of greed thrown in," he said later. "I watched assets go down and I couldn't even sell them."[14] In August the Royal Bank of Scotland called in a £500,000 debt, forcing his hand. It was a humiliating public reminder that Maxwell had not inherited anything close to his grandfather's vast fortune: Beaverbrook, preferring to devote his wealth to his foundations, had left his own son, Sir Max Aitken, no money, and Sir Max in turn had left Maxwell a mere £250,000.

A further embarrassment came in October, when his bankruptcy became official and he was stripped, as required, of his right to sit in the House of Lords. Maxwell said at the time that the move would only speed his financial recovery. "If I am to rebuild my business career I can't spend my time sitting in the House of Lords," he told the *Sunday Times*. "I am a deal-maker. That is what I intend to do. I still have energy and vision and I intend to use it."[15] He eventually did rebound and reclaimed his seat in 1996, only to lose it again in 1999 when Tony Blair's Labour government reformed the Upper House by eliminating the sitting rights of all but ninety-two hereditary Lords. It was an unremarkable end to Maxwell's brief career as a public figure. Timothy's assessment of his cousin comes in the form of a backhanded compliment to his success as a parent of four children, including his son Max, a future Lord Beaverbrook himself. "I will give Maxwell huge credit," Timothy says. "His kids are stunning. He may have failed in certain aspects of his life, but he's been hugely successful with his private family."[16]

Timothy might well have added that at least Maxwell was no Jonathan. In 1964, Jonathan had written to Beaverbrook after a visit to his villa in the south of France, "To be related, if distantly, to a man who has achieved so much in life and in the world gives me enormous pride. . . . My hope is that I shall be able to honor it through my life and through the lives of my sons."[17] By 1995 Jonathan had seen to it that those hopes were dashed in spectacular fashion. The same Saudi connections that had cost him and Timothy their roles at TV-am would now destroy his promising political career.

In 1992, with Margaret Thatcher no longer in office to block his ambitions and John Major in power, Jonathan had been appointed minister of state for defence procurement; in 1994 he became chief secretary to the Treasury, a full cabinet position. He was soon mentioned as a potential Conservative leader and prime minister.[18] But on April 10, 1995, the *Guardian* newspaper and Granada Television revealed Jonathan's connections with Middle Eastern arms traders, including new information that an Arab associate had paid for his stay at the Ritz Hotel in Paris in September 1993, contrary to ministerial conflict-of-interest rules. He promptly resigned from cabinet and announced he would sue for libel. "I have done nothing wrong," he declared at a news conference during which he delivered a blistering condemnation of the media. "If it falls to me to start a fight to cut out the cancer of bent and twisted journalism in our country with the simple sword of truth and the trusty shield of British fair play, so be it. I am ready for the fight — the fight against falsehood and those who peddle it. My fight begins today."[19]

It was a profound miscalculation. Jonathan's case was based on his insistence that he was in Paris to meet his Swiss-born wife Lolicia and their daughter Victoria, who was on her way to start school in Geneva. Lolicia, he insisted, had paid his bill. But when his lawsuit finally went to trial in June 1997, the *Guardian* produced airline tickets and car-rental receipts showing that Lolicia and Victoria had flown from London directly to Geneva, with no visit to Paris. The collapse was swift and dramatic: Victoria had been scheduled to testify about the fictional Paris visit the next day, but the new evidence led the judge to adjourn the case immediately. Jonathan announced that night that his marriage was over, and the following morning his lawyers formally abandoned the lawsuit and agreed that he would pay the entire £1.8 million cost of the case, including the *Guardian*'s legal bills. "He lied and lied and lied," blared the newspaper's main headline.[20] Jonathan was soon stripped of the Privy Council membership which had come with his elevation to cabinet. This meant he could no longer be known as the Right Honourable Jonathan Aitken.

The mystery of the hotel bill was finally solved in 1999, when it was reported, again by the *Guardian*, that a friend of Jonathan's who worked for a Saudi prince was to be paid secret commissions by three British defence contractors while Jonathan, as defence procurement minister, was promoting their products. They had met that fateful night at the Paris Ritz to prepare for a meeting with the prince in Geneva to continue negotiating one of the commission agreements. In both cities, the *Guardian* reported, the prince paid the hotel bills.[21] Jonathan had already pleaded guilty to perjury when these revelations came out; while awaiting his sentence, he declared bankruptcy and had to hand over his cufflinks and his Rolex watch when men with clipboards arrived to take possession of the contents of his home in a fashionable neighbourhood near Westminster. He was sentenced to eighteen months in jail and served six, during which he taught himself Greek and found God. When he mused in 2004 about returning to politics, the Conservative party told him they didn't want him, and he drifted towards the United Kingdom Independence Party, a marginal party devoted to pulling out of the European Union.

Like many another politician, Jonathan had been destroyed not by his initial transgression but by his attempt to cover it up. "He finished up in the right place," says Timothy. "His judgment is appalling. . . . I saw him just before he was taken off to jail. I was there for one reason and one reason only: I wanted to know the answer to a question, because I was an insider on some of the things he'd been up to. And I said, 'Given the Saatchi Brothers had offered to set up a [settlement] between the *Guardian* and yourself — everyone would have walked away from the whole mess — why did you not do it?' He said, 'Because I thought I would win.' I said, 'Win what?' He said, 'At least a million pounds.' I said, 'But you knew that it was a lie.' He said, 'Yes, but I thought I would win.'"[22]

The discussion of Jonathan, Maxwell and his own relationships with them puts Timothy in a reflective mood. "Families are funny things, you know. They can be very dramatically good news in terms of encouraging one another, or they can turn into spiteful affairs. And it's amazing what jealousy does. I never understood. Mostly what I've managed to do has been by a mixture of determination, a good education and good luck. But you make your own luck by standing in the traffic. It doesn't just fall from trees." Toward the end of the interview, while ruminating again on Lady Beaverbrook and on Sir Max, he adds, "families are absolutely a necessary evil."[23]

*

The history of the other House of Beaverbrook — the art gallery Beaverbrook built in Fredericton — was considerably less tumultuous. Ian Lumsden's appointment as interim curator at the time of Christofor's exit was made permanent in 1970, and the gallery board agreed to define the job more clearly.[24] Lumsden began corresponding with Sir Max's secretary, Anne Westover, to clarify the ownership of all the paintings in the gallery, and Margaret Ince was brought into the discussion to clear up a handful of discrepancies so that the curator could draw up authoritative lists for the foundation's auditors. At the same time, under Wallace Bird's chairmanship, the board itself became more active. More than a decade after its opening, the gallery was finally moving toward something that resembled conventionally structured governance. Still, it was a decade behind where it might otherwise have been in terms of maturity and credibility. This meant that granting agencies like the Canada Council often dismissed funding requests from the gallery. "They couldn't get anything because they hadn't done anything," one former official says, "and they hadn't done anything because they couldn't get anything."

The Beaverbrook Canadian Foundation, along with the U.K. Foundation, continued to support the gallery, covering its annual operating deficit, which was sometimes as large as $250,000, and also donating funds for special projects. Marguerite Vaughan, the daughter of Beaverbrook's friend Lucile Pillow, became another patron and donor after she was appointed to the board in 1971, often providing the required private-sector matching funds for federal grants. She and her husband also endowed the Hosmer Pillow Vaughan Gallery to house the family's collection of fine and decorative art. The gift allowed for the first major expansion of the building, with the Beaverbrook Canadian Foundation joining in to fund the Sir Max Aitken Gallery to house the British collection of paintings.[25]

In the wake of the expansion, which opened to the public in 1983, the board began thinking more critically about the gallery's financial future. The Beaverbrook and Vaughan foundations covered its operating deficit every year, but David Vaughan, who took over as chair of his family's foundation, suggested that the gallery should aspire to be more independent. That advice prompted the board to launch a major fundraising drive, Cherish the Gift, to raise $7 million for the gallery. Judy Budovitch, a member of the board, was put in charge of the campaign. She says the Aitkens did not object; in fact, Lady Violet Aitken lent her support to the effort. "They saw the reality of it," Budovitch says. "The institution was growing and they couldn't fund it in its entirety. I think they wanted some freedom from it too . . . and that was fair enough. They'd given us enough."

Budovitch, a lawyer originally from Cape Breton, had become involved with the gallery as a volunteer in 1980, when, as a young mother, she felt the gallery would be an ideal venue for art classes for children. She then got involved with the Friends organization, hoping to make the gallery more present in the Fredericton community, and she was later appointed to the board. "My whole thing was, 'Why aren't there more people here?'" she says. That same question — the gallery's relevance to New Brunswick — was a theme of a 1988 report to the board by Ian Lumsden on the institution's future. He wrote that while it might be "more convenient and to its greater glory" to focus narrowly on its claim to fame, the British collection, there were no other community-minded galleries in the province playing an educational role, and so this duty fell to the Beaverbrook. Conversely, to adopt an exclusively local or regional approach and neglect the jewels of the collections would be to sacrifice the gallery's cachet. "Without this distinction, the Beaverbrook Art Gallery becomes a much less attractive venue for the contemporary artist and emasculates itself as a teaching resource." While Lumsden clearly would have loved a large acquisitions budget that would allow him to add to the British collection, "the fact that many of the important British works are held either by the Beaverbrook Canadian Foundation or the Beaverbrook [U.K.] Foundation and their future with the Gallery is not guaranteed brings into question the advisability of trying to strengthen a collection comprised of numerous works only on loan to the Gallery."[26]

The local relevance of the gallery was the focus of its next expansion. Harrison McCain, the global frozen french-fry magnate based in the New Brunswick village of Florenceville, and his wife Marion

McCain, an art lover, had launched a biennial Atlantic Art Exhibition in 1987 to showcase artists from the region. "That was an area that the Beaverbrook wasn't addressing as well as it could have," says Budovitch, who became chair of the board in 1991. When Marion McCain was dying of cancer, Harrison offered to contribute a million dollars towards the construction of a new Atlantic Gallery named in her honour. It opened in 1995, after her death. Coupled with the federal government's creation of the Senator Richard Hatfield Memorial Fund, an acquisition endowment to honour the late New Brunswick premier who had been Budovitch's predecessor as board chair, the expansion symbolized the gallery's newfound maturity and active role in the community. "We started to become an accountable, appropriate, business-oriented board," Budovitch says. "They were very good years."

And colourful ones, particularly for board members, who were jolted by a new presence on their board: Timothy Aitken himself. Maxwell had asked him to step in as chairman of the Beaverbrook Canadian Foundation and save it from its own poor investment decisions, which had forced the U.K. Foundation to support the gallery because its Canadian counterpart had no revenue coming in. "I inherited a situation with the Beaverbrook Canadian Foundation which was dire in the early nineties," Timothy says. "Dire financially." The Canadian Foundation had purchased stock in Ventech Corporation, with which Maxwell was involved, "and the stock had collapsed," Timothy says. Ventech "had this investment in this company called Abbey Health Care Group, which was going bust." Timothy took over Abbey, turned it around, then persuaded the foundation to invest directly in Abbey rather than in Ventech. "And put simply, an investment made in November of '91 yielded over fifteen times on your money by the summer of '94 or the beginning of '95," Timothy says. In just six years, the foundation's assets increased in value from $11 million to $20 million.[27] "So the foundation benefited hugely from my efforts."[28] Maxwell does not tout his cousin's role to the same degree. "All portfolios have their ups and their downs," he says, "and Timothy took it over when it was not doing particularly well, but it has done very well since."[29]

Timothy's new role as chairman of the Beaverbrook Canadian Foundation led him to New Brunswick, the object of much of the foundation's charity. Oddly for a man so devoted to his grandfather's memory, he had never visited the province. "I had no desire to go there particularly either," he says. "I mean Montreal is one thing. New Brunswick is another. I love Montreal. . . . I saw New Brunswick as a widening in the road." But the foundation's causes in the province would now experience his trademark "Alsatian" approach. Theatre New Brunswick, a touring company based at the Playhouse in Fredericton, had been subsidized by the foundation since its inception. Timothy found that its extensive touring schedule in small-town New Brunswick made no business sense (a view TNB would resist for another decade) and he scaled back and eventually eliminated the foundation's grant. "I, after a series of meetings, was not prepared to put bad money after bad money," he says. "They had in some ways brought it upon themselves. . . . That was the first time I really put one of the things the foundation had been actively, historically supporting under the financial grill, as it were. The gallery very quickly followed in its footsteps."[30] The Canadian Foundation appointed Timothy as one of its nominees to the gallery board, and, exercising its power to appoint the custodian, named him to that post as well. At first, board members found Timothy's swashbuckling style charming and invigorating. "I thought he was more like his grandfather than anyone else I'd met," says Judy Budovitch. "He was feisty. He was far more of a character [than Maxwell or Lady Aitken]. The others were far more restrained, far more polite. . . . When Tim came on the scene, things were a lot more colourful."

As custodian, Timothy had the right to name two other governors to the gallery board, and one of his selections, Montreal lawyer Vincent Prager, became, effectively, his agent when he could not attend meetings himself. Timothy had become friends with Prager at McGill University in the 1960s, and three decades later asked him to be "the eyes and ears of the foundation on the board." Prager's frequent trips to New Brunswick eventually made him the owner of perhaps the ultimate piece of Beaverbrook memorabilia in the province: Dayspring, the mansion in St. Andrews that James Dunn had shared with Christofor. One July day in 1995, when a board meeting wrapped up early, Judy Budovitch, who'd been urging Prager to buy a cottage or some land in New Brunswick, put him in touch with an acquaintance who was selling a home in the coastal resort town.

Prager had thought about acquiring property outside Quebec because of a looming referendum that might see the province separate from Canada, so he drove down to take a look. "There was not one single redeeming virtue to that house," he recalls with a laugh. He decided to take a look around town with Budovitch's friend and they ended up at the gate of Dayspring, which was for sale. Because Prager had a connection as a member of the gallery board, the caretaker agreed to show him the house without an appointment and told him the price was $550,000. "I couldn't believe it," Prager says. "I didn't say anything, but I thought, 'They're giving this place away.'" He contacted Mike Doyle, the executor of the estate. "I really don't think I want this," he told Doyle, "but now I've got it in my system and I've got to get it out of my system." He made an offer, and a week later, the house was his. The following summer, Prager organized tours, finally satisfying the curiosity of New Brunswickers who had never seen the inside of the fabled Dayspring. He charged twenty dollars per person and donated the money to the gallery — a novel fundraiser and, one might argue, a small compensation for all the turmoil Christofor had provoked thirty years earlier.

They were indeed, as Judy Budovitch said, good years for the gallery. Appropriately, one of the few public controversies at the time concerned the merits of a painting. The massive canvas *In My Father's House*, by Canadian artist Attila Lukacs, was acquired by curator Curtis Collins, who liked to play Led Zeppelin in his gallery office. Budovitch judged the work's realistic neo-Nazi, homoerotic imagery too provocative for its first exposure to the public, the day of a family-oriented open house to mark a post-renovation reopening in May 1998. "We have to find some way of giving people a heads up about it," Budovitch said when she arrived at the gallery that day. She decided that easels bearing posters of past exhibitions should be mounted in strategic positions in front of the penises and anuses of the skinheads depicted in the painting. That made Collins "testy," she says. "He said, 'Only if you put easels in front of other paintings as well,' and we said, 'Fine.'" In the *Daily Gleaner*, a newspaper hardly known to embrace the avant-garde, an arts columnist sided with Collins, praising the gallery for accepting that art must be "disturbing and provocative. . . . It seems that the Beaverbrook Art Gallery has grown up, and it's wearing the artistic equivalent of a nose ring and a tattoo."[31] Vincent Prager also welcomed the Lukacs, saying "maybe Fredericton needs a bit of stirring up." But the U.K. Foundation would later claim that the work's realistic "neo-Nazi and erotic images" would have met with the disapproval of Beaverbrook himself[32] — a claim that was probably true, despite the press baron's philandering and his support for appeasing Hitler until the moment the war began. The foundation's argument, made in the heat of the ownership dispute, also ignored the fact that many of the gallery's masterpieces, including *The Fountain of Indolence* and *Santiago El Grande*, had not been universally praised by contemporary critics. And Beaverbrook would certainly have conceded that *In My Father's House* was anything but abstract.

The evening after the easel-punctuated open house, dignitaries gathered at the gallery for the opening of an exhibition that seemed almost custom designed to rebut the Lukacs controversy and flatter Timothy Aitken's nostalgia for his grandfather. For years, Ian Lumsden had been planning *Sargent to Freud*, a major retrospective of forty-five modern British paintings and fifteen drawings in the collection. The exhibition seemed to be a return to the gallery's roots. Many of the works were part of the original collection amassed by Beaverbrook, including Freud's *Hotel Bedroom*, Augustus John's *Dorelia*, John Singer Sargent's *Pressing the Grapes: Florentine Wine Cellar*, Sickert's *H.M. King Edward VIII* and Sutherland's *Lord Beaverbrook*. The show would tour galleries in Canada, the United States and England through 2000, and it was accompanied by a lavish catalogue featuring large colour reproductions of the paintings.

So significant was the exhibition that Maxwell travelled to Fredericton from London to attend the official opening. He spoke, naturally, of his grandfather and his paintings. Though the passage of time had meant that the gallery and the family had been inevitably "drawing apart," he said, "these pictures in the gallery have helped hold us together."[33] To that end, he noted that the U.K. Foundation was in the midst of a major project to renovate Cherkley Court and turn it into a public research centre — and he hoped it would be possible for some of the foundation's paintings in Fredericton to rotate through Cherkley in a way that might raise the gallery's profile in Britain.

The idea rattled Judy Budovitch. "I thought, 'Well, now they have a place for the paintings in England.'" At the private dinner that followed, she spoke discreetly to Ian Lumsden. "If the paintings start going over to England," she told the director, "I wonder, really, if they'll come back."[34] Far from holding the family and the gallery together, as Maxwell had said, the paintings were about to drive them apart.

Timothy Aitken with Graham Sutherland's
portrait of his grandfather, Lord Beaverbrook,
at the Beaverbrook Art Gallery, 1995.

CHAPTER TEN

"You really don't want to deal with my cousin"

David Hay had had an exceedingly long and busy week, and he was looking forward to relaxing by turning his thoughts to another task — presiding over the opening of an art exhibition on the weekend. Monday had been his first day on the job as the chief executive officer of New Brunswick's publicly-owned, debt-laden energy utility, NB Power. The task facing Hay was enormous: the utility had expensively overhauled one of its power generating stations to burn a fuel called Orimulsion, produced by a state-run fuel company in Venezuela. But the Venezuelans had backed out, saying they were free to do so because there was no contract in place. NB Power insisted there was a binding agreement and filed a lawsuit worth $2 billion. The New Brunswick government, seeking to distance itself from the fiasco, made sweeping changes to the corporation and recruited Hay, a highly regarded lawyer, businessman and consultant, to take over as CEO and lead the cleanup. The first order of business was to determine whether there was any hope of winning the lawsuit or whether it would be better to salvage a settlement and recover some of the $2 billion lost to taxpayers. Hay's first week on the job had been a dizzying series of meetings and legal briefings.

Finally, on Friday, March 12, 2004, Hay put on his other hat as chairman of the board of governors of the Beaverbrook Art Gallery

— and promptly found himself the only New Brunswicker to be ensnared in *both* of the province's sensational legal disputes.

Hay received a two-page letter that Timothy Aitken, who was sailing in the Caribbean, had dictated by phone to his secretary in London, who then faxed it to Vincent Prager in Montreal. Prager in turn sent it on to Hay. "You have received considerable amounts of money from the Canadian Foundation," Timothy wrote to the gallery board via Hay, "even during those years when income for the Gallery was not readily available and the English Foundation made up the shortfall. . . . It now seems that you choose to spend some of that money, along with other donations, on an expensive attempt to refute facts which auditors have systematically agreed to over the last forty years. What are you really trying to accomplish? To upset and anger your biggest and most consistent donors? To drive such a wedge in personal terms that you place the very future of the Gallery in doubt? As I said earlier, actions that are provocative if not hostile do not instil either confidence or support among the very Trustees upon whose support the Gallery has and may continue to depend."

Perhaps Timothy was acknowledging that his relationship with his cousin Maxwell was known to be uneasy when he underscored to Hay that he was "in constant touch" with Lord Beaverbrook and they were "of one mind as to what the *positive* outcome should be. Should you choose to imperil that outcome for whatever personal reasons you and some other directors have developed, then not only will you be subject to the financial consequences of those actions, but so will the Gallery and the rest of the Board. Accordingly, I would request that you personally distribute this letter to each and every director without delay."[1]

Hay interpreted the letter as a threat, and he thought back to something Maxwell had told him a month earlier in Toronto. The two men, along with the gallery's new director, Bernard Riordon, had met to discuss a proposal from the Beaverbrook U.K. Foundation that it and the gallery formalize the status of 133 paintings in the gallery's collection that belonged to the foundation. The arrangement would guarantee that the paintings would remain in the gallery for at least ten years, with two exceptions: J.M.W. Turner's *The Fountain of Indolence* and Lucian Freud's *Hotel Bedroom* would be removed and sold. Maxwell "really began to get quite pressing on the issue," Hay would recall, "and he said, 'Look, you really don't want to deal with my cousin.' I think we understood the implications of what he was saying. . . . I somewhat had the feeling that he was trying to give me a genuine warning. Not that this was a game, but that he was just saying, 'I'm reasonable, I'd like to do this with you, I'd like to get this cleared up as soon as possible. And you know, you don't want to deal with my cousin.' It was all very cordial."

No longer. Hay got in touch with other members of the gallery board to tell them about the letter. The next evening, a Saturday, Hay presided as planned over the official opening of the biennial McCain Atlantic Art Exhibition and, from the podium, thanked the various governors for their commitment to the gallery. It was an inside joke laden with gallows humour: no one else at the opening knew that, earlier that day, faced with what appeared to be a threat of lawsuits against them as individuals, fifteen of the eighteen governors had agreed to resign en masse. "The resignation thing was garbage," Timothy says, pointing out that the legislation that created the gallery board explicitly protects its members from any lawsuits stemming from gallery business.[2] The mass resignation did, however, serve another purpose: it stopped the clock on the escalating dispute, taking away the gallery's ability to sign anything and forcing the New Brunswick government to get involved. It also thrust the whole nasty affair into the public eye.

Judy Budovitch says she had seen it coming. Timothy's bold approach as the custodian and member of the board, so refreshing at first, had increasingly seemed to her to be an attempt to micromanage the gallery. He would complain about a particular exhibition or lament that there was too much emphasis on regional art and not enough on the traditional. Timothy says he found the gallery moribund, unable or unwilling to even arrange for brochures to be available at the new Sheraton Hotel five minutes away. "It was perfectly obvious to me that the gallery couldn't promote itself worth a damn, that it was very much an insiders' club," he says. The director, Ian Lumsden, knew art and deserved credit for organizing a successful exhibition of the

Beaverbrook collection in London, Timothy says, but in Fredericton, he found Lumsden complacent after almost three decades in charge, first as curator and then as director. "It was a sinecure, for God's sake . . . I think he found it all pretty trite. This was a guy who grew up in the big city and somehow finished up in the provinces. He intellectually was well advanced over contemporaries there."[3] Prager agreed with Timothy's complaints, particularly about declining attendance and about what he considered a large portion of the British collection being stored in the vault rather than hung on the walls. Often, he says, the problem was "what was being shown in lieu of those pictures, and it got worse and worse in my view."

Budovitch had arranged a meeting with the curatorial staff "to try to come to an understanding of what a fair rotation and fair balance was in terms of our mission, which was . . . regional art, Canadian art, and then British art," she would later testify. "You can't do everything in one year. You do some things one year, and you balance it with something else the next year. . . . We can't fit all of them in. I mean, it is nice to say, but we are now an institution with thousands of works, not four hundred or five hundred. . . . But there is a good percentage of the original works, what we call the permanent works and the British works, always on display." Budovitch remembered that the explanation "was very difficult for Vincent Prager to accept, and I have to say that eventually I wondered if it was a genuine concern for legitimate display or appropriate balance in our display, or if there was another agenda. That's just how I felt. I said, 'Well, I'm not sure that we could ever satisfy this, and if it isn't really about the exhibition, per se, then is it about something else?'"[4]

The Aitkens would deny any agenda other than a concern for the foundation's paintings that had been building for years and that had been crystallized by new British regulations governing charities. As of 2000, these regulations required that charities like the foundation include in their annual reports statements on "the major risks to which the charity is exposed" and "systems designed to mitigate those risks." The foundation asked Lumsden to provide a valuation of the collection, and he replied by sending a list of the foundation's paintings along with their values for insurance purposes — a total of $7.6

million Canadian. Just two years later, the foundation, in the words of its lawyers, "further considered its obligations" and hired Sotheby's to update the valuation.[5] The result came as a shock: the collection, Sotheby s said, was actually worth £35 million for insurance purposes, or almost $90 million Canadian. Turner's *The Fountain of Indolence* alone was valued at between $16.7 million and $25 million; Freud's *Hotel Bedroom* was worth between $5.2 million and $8.4 million.[6] The foundation trustees "were pleased and surprised at the huge value attached to the pictures," Maxwell said,[7] but they realized that, because of the "very large discrepancy," the collection suddenly comprised the majority of the foundation's assets.[8] "Instead of being a cash fund with a bit of art on the side, in fact, we had become a major art collection with a bit of cash on the side."[9]

The foundation immediately bought extra insurance to cover the increased value of the collection as it pondered its next move. The additional insurance expense, Maxwell would later explain, meant that the collection was actually costing the foundation money rather than generating revenue to fund its U.K. activities, such as supporting the Battle of Britain Memorial Fund, the Hospital for Sick Children in London and the National Society for Cancer Relief.[10] A longer-term solution was needed. Maxwell reasoned that the gallery would cooperate; after all, despite the passage of time and the loosening of the connection to the family that he had noted in 1998, its director and board had always shown great respect, even deference, to the Aitkens.

But Maxwell would not be dealing with known quantities in Fredericton. After more than three decades in charge, years in which he repeatedly acknowledged the foundation's ownership of the paintings, Ian Lumsden left the gallery in 2001. An interview he gave to the Ottawa *Citizen* had turned into a public relations nightmare. Galleries throughout the Western world were grappling with how to identify and possibly return works looted from Jewish families by the Nazis, but Lumsden told the *Citizen* that the looting might actually have served "the greater good of mankind." He explained, "if some of these works had been left in homes in Amsterdam and God knows where, they'd have been bombed and the works might have been destroyed. That would be much more heinous than actually having these things surface in major collections like the National Gallery in Washington or the British Museum or where have you. I don't think it's as negative as people feel. At least by having the Nazis remove them, they've protected them from that kind of fate. And that's an argument that's quite legitimate."[11]

Lumsden publicly apologized and took a paid sick leave from his job, never to return. The terms of his departure remain subject to a confidentiality agreement. In his 2007 interview for this book, Timothy Aitken speculated that the real reason for Lumsden's dismissal was that some board members were already laying the groundwork for their attempt to grab ownership of the paintings from the foundation, and Lumsden was deemed too compliant towards the Aitkens. It was true that Lumsden had promised Vincent Prager he would display more paintings from the permanent collection, as Prager and Timothy were demanding. But there is a problem with Timothy's conspiracy theory: he claims Lumsden's ouster was a surprise to him — "I didn't even hear about it until it was over. I never got drawn into it one way or the other," he says[12] — but the minutes of a January 10, 2001 board meeting explicitly contradict him. They record that Timothy, attending via conference call, "expressed his concern and pointed to his great disappointment that any comments coming from the Beaverbrook Art Gallery would in any way reflect a positive aspect of German conduct during World War II. He was most disturbed by the association of his family's name with the comments of the Director." The minutes show that Timothy even seconded a motion that the board appoint a committee to look at the gallery's options.[13] If Lumsden was removed for ulterior motives, Timothy had allowed it to happen.

Timothy maintains that there were other indications that the board was planning something long before 2004. Years earlier at a dinner at Judy Budovitch's home, he says, he was repeating his complaints that the permanent collection was not getting enough time on the walls. "I said, 'Continue down this path where you don't listen to your biggest donors and your biggest contributors and you're going to find yourself in a situation where they're going to start looking aggressively at showing pictures elsewhere.' To which she said, 'We've already thought of that and we're preparing for it.' Which I've never forgotten."[14] The gallery's attempts to recruit a successor to Lumsden also fed Timothy's theory. Prager urged the hiring of a leading arts-sector headhunter he knew in Montreal, but the board opted for a Halifax recruiter whose recommended candidate was, Prager says, "a buddy" of several board members. That "buddy" turned down the job, and the board relented and called in Prager's suggested headhunter. Timothy is convinced that the board wanted to install a director who would support the art grab. "They always knew they were going down this sort of route," he says. "I have never for a second doubted that they planned the whole thing."[15] This theory fails to account for the fact that it was the foundation's proposal, not the gallery's actions, that triggered the dispute.

*

The Montreal headhunter produced two names for the gallery board. One was Bernard Riordon, who was just months away from his planned retirement after thirty years spent running the Art Gallery of Nova Scotia, which he had built from scratch into a respected institution. Now he was planning to move back home to a farm he owned in Pokeshaw, a tiny Irish-Canadian enclave in the mostly francophone northeast of New Brunswick, and convert an old schoolhouse on the property into an Irish pub. Instead, the Beaverbrook Art Gallery came calling. "It seemed like a nice transition, coming from Halifax with a very busy career for thirty years," he says. And Riordon, with a solid reputation for savvy marketing and fundraising techniques, loved the challenge of injecting new energy into a gallery that had seen its attendance decline. "The question was how do we engage the public, how do we celebrate our artists," he says. "I was using a whole lot of buzzwords." For the board, Riordon offered much-needed stability and entrepreneurship. "He was organized, he was efficient, he was from New Brunswick, and his intention was to stay here," Budovitch says. "He has the energy of ten people, and he wasn't looking for a retirement job. He wanted to put the cherry on the cake of his career."

Riordon must have seemed an excellent choice to Maxwell, too.

When they first met in London in early 2003 to discuss the gallery's future, Riordon — like everyone else at the gallery over the years — did not question the foundation's ownership of 133 paintings at the gallery. In fact, he showed great admiration for Maxwell's grandfather, vowing to highlight the contribution of the original benefactor by re-establishing an annual Lord Beaverbrook Day at the gallery and hanging his portrait by Sutherland in a prominent position near the entrance. But Riordon's ambitions went far beyond that, and those ambitions required serious money. At Maxwell's request, he prepared a discussion paper on how he planned to enrich the gallery and raise its profile. "When we met, I described the gallery as a 'sleeping giant,'" Riordon said in the package he sent to Maxwell in May 2003, "and I truly believe that it can and will be one of the finest medium size art museums in the world." The new director foresaw a larger acquisitions budget, a more robust touring of the permanent collection, and a global tour of *Santiago El Grande*. To pay for this, he planned to seek government funding aggressively, to create honorary directorships that would be bestowed on major donors, and to put a price tag on naming various rooms in the gallery — from $1 million to have one's name adorn either of the two permanent collection galleries to a mere $25,000 to be immortalized in the small audiovisual room. He wanted the gallery's endowment to grow by at least $10 million.[16] "I'm going to make the mummies dance," Riordon told Timothy at their first meeting. "Fasten your seatbelt."[17]

Riordon was clearly a man with whom the U.K. Foundation could do business. Maxwell and his fellow trustees — all of them family members, including his mother Lady Violet Aitken and his cousin Timothy — formulated what they considered a reasonable proposal: the foundation would take back the Turner and the Freud, to which Sotheby's had assigned a combined value of $30 million, and sell them. The windfall would be used to cover the increased insurance costs for the balance of the collection, to continue funding the foundation's causes in England, and to provide the gallery with $5 million for its endowment fund. With a stroke of a pen, Riordon would be halfway to his fundraising objective, with the possibility that matching funds from governments and the private sector could put him over the top. Meanwhile, the gallery would acknowledge that the foundation owned the other 131 works, and the foundation would guarantee they would not be removed from the gallery for at least another decade.[18]

Maxwell arranged to meet again with the director in September 2003, in Montreal. "He said 'I'm going to go talk to Riordon about it,'" Timothy recalls. "And I said, 'Yeah, but be careful, because I'm not sure these people are at all what you and your mother think they are,' particularly his mother, who'd been very upset at my rather strong opinions about certain things. And he did go very cautiously and work out a deal with Riordon."[19] Not quite a deal: Riordon liked the proposal but was hesitant about returning the Freud, the only example of the artist's work in a public gallery in Canada, and he asked if the foundation might consider taking other works of equivalent value. Maxwell's memory is that Riordon identified the Turner as "not central to the gallery, not part of its Canadian collection,"[20] though Riordon remembers saying only that he was not personally an admirer of Turner's work. In any event, Maxwell would recall that Riordon was "quite excited . . . and saw the merit of the package I was proposing to him."[21]

"When a donor wants to recall a loan, that's their prerogative," says Riordon, pointing out that at the time he believed the foundation held clear title to the works. "It seemed at the time this was a win-win situation for the gallery, with the understanding these works were on loan. That's what I'd been told." The donation and the possibility of promoting the gallery in England by showing paintings at Cherkley fit perfectly with Riordon's ambitions. "If that meant sacrificing a painting, well, that was unfortunate," he says. When he returned to Fredericton, however, the board was not nearly as enthusiastic. "We were shocked" by the idea of losing the Turner and the Freud, says Judy Budovitch. "Bernie was shocked, too, but he liked the idea of the five million dollars." David Hay calls Riordon "a wonderful guy. He's a great fundraiser, and he always had great thoughts about growth for the gallery. I think the thought that we could raise a significant sum of money to enhance the development of the gallery was intriguing to him. It was completely consistent with what he thought was the right thing and what people generally thought was the right thing. It was only a question of the method. . . . Many people on the board had been involved with the gallery for a number of years. Bernie was a relative newcomer. So Bernie at that point didn't pretend to have the depth of understanding as to how the collection was held. And so Bernie wouldn't have understood in the initial parts of this discussion what the implications were of what was being asked by Maxwell."

Each side would later blame the other for a three-month delay between the meeting and the dispatching of three documents by Maxwell to the board on January 14, 2004. The key item was the text of the agreement he had proposed in September, now ready to be signed. It said that the 133 paintings "are and at all material times have been owned by" the foundation, and that the Turner and the Freud were to be returned while the others would be placed on loan for at least ten years, with the gallery covering the cost of insuring them. It also required that the gallery ensure "that each work in the collection is publicly displayed for a period appropriate to its artistic and cultural significance," and it allowed the foundation to sell any painting in the collection, provided it replaced it with another. A separate letter set out the conditions of the $5 million gift, including that the gallery allow the foundation to nominate two additional representatives to the board. A cover letter informed the board that a similar loan agreement would soon be coming from the Beaverbrook Canadian Foundation concerning its paintings. Finally, the entire agreement was to remain secret.[22]

Seeing the proposal cast in the hard language of a legal agreement concentrated the minds of the board members. As a group, they were quite unlike the deferential governors who had acquiesced to the wishes of the original Lord Beaverbrook and his heirs over the decades. Hay in particular possessed a sharp intellect and an awareness of the importance of good corporate governance. "Don't get me wrong," he says. "We wanted five million dollars. We would have been happy to take that. . . . It was just, 'What would we need, as directors, to sign this document?'" Hay had already contacted Stephen Smart of the Toronto law firm Osler, Hoskin and Harcourt, where he had once worked. Smart had literally written the book on the law pertaining to art collections in Canada, and Hay suggested to other members of the board executive that they forward the proposed text to Smart. "I have advised Bernie to maintain a good relationship with Lord Beaverbrook while explaining to him that this is a fundamental matter which if rushed may not work as smoothly as he would like," Hay wrote in an e-mail to the other executive members a few days after the documents arrived. "This is certainly a difficult turn of events," Judy Budovitch replied, "but not unexpected. I am in favour of having your friend in Toronto look at this. I have a very hard time with an arrangement that basically makes us their storeroom at our cost."[23]

Something else bothered Hay. He didn't entirely accept Maxwell's contention that the foundation's move had been prompted by the sudden increase in the cost of insuring the paintings. "That's what purportedly — *purportedly* — they were looking at. . . . Understanding the situation with Cherkley, I always felt it was more likely the requirement for cash for the Cherkley refurbishment was a more pressing issue than the valuation."

Cherkley Court would become the grandest prop in the drama that was about to unfold. It would be referred to repeatedly and erroneously, even by Hay, as "the UK home of Lord Beaverbrook." The notion that it remained "the family mansion," another common phrase in the media accounts of the dispute, would feed the perception that Maxwell was acting out of greed, trying to remove paintings from Fredericton to enhance his own fiefdom. In fact, because it was a registered historic property belonging to a charitable foundation, British law made it illegal for Maxwell or any other trustee of the foundation to benefit from its refurbishment, including by living there.[24] Cherkley was instead being converted into a venue for meetings, conferences, weddings and other events, a renovation that — like almost all others — would end up costing more than anticipated, thanks to unexpected work, such as the removal of asbestos. "It is like a board game," said Michael Marshall, an employee of the U.K. Foundation, who oversaw the project, "because you just don't know what is going to happen and what you are going to find, particularly in a house like that which had so much deterioration

Cherkley Court during its restoration, 2004.
Beaverbrook U.K. Foundation

and so little care taken of it for so long."[25] The total cost surged to more than £5 million, or in excess of $11 million Canadian.[26] Because Cherkley belonged to the foundation, money spent on it was considered a charitable expense, and the foundation diverted money from its other causes in England — the same causes it had cited in explaining its need to sell the Turner and the Freud to fund the renovation. Donations to non-Cherkley causes dropped dramatically, in fact, from £224,000 in 1997 to £69,000 in 2005.[27] But the project was never contingent on the sale of the Turner and the Freud, Maxwell insists. "The Foundation had already completed much of this work before it even requested the return of the two paintings in late 2003," the foundation lawyers would assert, leaving the impression that there was no link between the two.

But there was a link. In a 2004 radio interview, Timothy said the Turner and the Freud would be sold "in order actually to make the house which was Beaverbrook's house in Surrey, Cherkley, come forward faster because funds would be available to do it."[28] And he said in 2007 that the renovation had been done at the expense of the foundation's other causes: "Cherkley was sucking it up."[29] Maxwell concedes as much. "If we sell two pictures, we will have more money to spend on charitable activity," he says. "If you've got a charitable project of your own, you probably reduce supporting other people's charitable projects. . . . It's what we chose to do." He "absolutely" hopes to restore donations to those other causes once the Turner and the Freud are sold. He adds, "And we might well allocate some funds to parts of the Cherkley project that aren't essential but that would be a good thing to do, like a visitors' centre. So I'm not going to say we'll never spend any money from the sale of pictures on Cherkley."[30]

Maxwell flew to Toronto in February 2004 for his meeting with Riordon and Hay, who told him the gallery needed more time to conduct due diligence. Given the gallery's quasi-legal status in provincial law as a public art gallery, Hay explained, it would not be proper for the governors to hand over two valuable paintings without thorough research into their ownership. "Maxwell was a little uncomfortable with that," Hay says, "because their assumption had always been, 'Well, we own them,' and I guess I was of the view that, 'If you own them, why are you asking us to sign a document confirming that you own them?'" Hay suggested the foundation's lawyer send the gallery's lawyer whatever ownership documents it had in London. It was at that point that Maxwell warned them that they ought to move quickly, before Timothy got involved. "My cousin asked me to conduct the discussions," Maxwell says, "and you know Tim takes a more immediate and robust line. Very often in life you play the good-guy, bad-guy. And when the gallery did prevaricate and Tim became involved, the temperature rose. So I think what I recommended to Riordon was borne out as positive advice."[31]

Two weeks after the Toronto meeting, the gallery asked Maxwell for more time and told him the board had hired a lawyer for advice on how to "satisfy its statutory obligations" in signing the agreement.[32] Maxwell extended the deadline to March 15 but warned that the proposed agreement would be withdrawn on that date and the foundation trustees would "review their policy for their picture collection."[33] At the same time, the art gallery board moved to exclude Timothy, Vincent Prager and Hugh Cowans, the third appointee of the Beaverbrook Canadian Foundation, from its discussions, believing the three men would be in a conflict of interest. On March 2, while on vacation in Barbados, Prager sent Hay an e-mail demanding — despite his exclusion — "a detailed update as to what is going on regarding the proposed agreement with the U.K. Beaverbrook Foundation." Stephen Smart replied to Prager, repeating that the board felt he was in a conflict.[34] Smart's e-mail apparently triggered Timothy's angry letter of March 12.

Before joining the other resigning gallery board members, Hay responded to Timothy, revealing for the first time that the gallery's research had uncovered "an apparent inconsistency" in the ownership documents. This "inconsistency" suggested that paintings might have been handed over decades ago "in a manner that was inconsistent with law" — though this remark appeared to relate not to the 133 paintings being claimed by the U.K. Foundation, but to the seventy-seven works bought by the Canadian Foundation from Lady Beaverbrook in 1970, a transaction that had no bearing on Maxwell's proposal. A member of the gallery board, Doug Stanley, had conducted a quick search of Beaverbrook's gallery-related correspondence, housed at the Harriet Irving Library at the University of New Brunswick, and had found letters referring to Beaverbrook's "buying pictures for your new museum" or "paintings for your gallery." This prompted Stanley to recommend a more thorough search. Hay's revelation that the gallery might dare to challenge the foundation's ownership outraged Timothy, who found it absurd that money that the foundations had given to the gallery would now be used to sue those very foundations. He sent a second angry letter to Hay, complaining of the "lengthy, repetitive legalese" in Hay's explanation and repeating that the gallery governors "should know the financial consequences" of their position.[35]

Inevitably, the resignation of the fifteen board members became public, and journalists from across Canada and England pounced on this irresistible story: the heirs of a Fleet Street press baron locked in a battle with an art gallery he'd built over the ownership of priceless works of art. In London, the *Sunday Times* called it a £40-million "art grab" and referred to Cherkley as the "family estate," while the *Daily Telegraph* said the family had been accused of "plundering" Beaverbrook's art treasures. With the Aitkens not easily available for comment and the former board members refusing to talk, journalists sought out anyone they could find who was willing to be interviewed, among them Stuart Smith, a former curator, who described Beaverbrook as "a loathsome little man" and scorned his descendants. "If you had bought something for fifty thousand dollars and it was worth $3.5 million, you might want it back, too, especially if the founding families are in financial trouble," he told the Canadian Press. "They see much-needed money in the gallery," Smith wrote in an opinion piece for Toronto's *National Post*, "and they want it." Another article quoted anonymous members of "New Brunswick's art community" who feared the family was "looting" the gallery,[36] and several stories implied a connection to Maxwell's 1992 bankruptcy. Elizabeth Weir, the forceful leader and lone elected member of New Brunswick's New Democratic Party, declared memorably, "The Brits are coming. Lock up the family silver."

Vincent Prager effectively became the spokesman for both foundations, granting repeated interviews in which he tried to explain that Maxwell and Timothy could not benefit personally from the sale of the paintings and that there was a paper trail of documents dating back more than forty years in which the gallery had repeatedly confirmed the foundation's ownership. "No one in the last forty years had questioned that these pictures were owned by the foundation," he told the CBC. "Not one. Never."[37] But it was to no avail. The caricature of down-on-their-luck British aristocrats raiding the province's gallery became fixed in the public imagination. Timothy didn't help matters when he began granting intemperate interviews, giving New Brunswickers a glimpse of the aggressive personality well-known in London. He told one reporter that the former governors were "a bunch of hacks"[38] and suggested to another that people in the province lacked the sophistication to behave reasonably. "This is rapidly becoming not about Canada but about the province of New Brunswick and the way people in a small, tight-knit community, maybe, are reacting to something without ever finding out what the real facts are," he told the CBC. "If this was happening in New York or Toronto or Montreal, it would be a whole different story."[39]

Timothy would eventually say he regretted "not speaking with more tact and respect" about the governors in media interviews and not behaving more "diplomatically" in his two letters to David Hay.[40]

In an interview for this book, however, he referred sarcastically to the "great song and dance" made about his letters and rejected the notion that his comments helped rally support for the gallery. "No, I don't regret one word I said." He insisted the media in New Brunswick were biased against him and his family from the start. "I think that was pre-ordained and there wasn't much you could do about it. . . . Public opinion was going to be what it was."[41]

Positions began to harden; it would soon be impossible to put the genie back in the bottle. In the midst of the fallout, Harrison McCain, the french-fry tycoon, board member and gallery benefactor, died at his home in Florenceville. He was respected by everyone, including Timothy, and he was one of the few New Brunswickers who might have had the stature to engineer a compromise, but his skills were now lost to the gallery he loved. The New Brunswick government, anxious to have both sides step back from the brink, appointed a new board of governors, a mix of several of the incumbents who had quit and some high-powered newcomers, such as businessman Richard Currie, the chair of BCE, and Roy Heenan of the Montreal law firm Heenan Blaikie. On April 16, 2004, Maxwell and Timothy flew to Fredericton to meet with them, an encounter that did not go well. Vincent Prager suggested that if the gallery felt the ownership of some particular paintings was not clear, the board should sign the agreement "and we can add and subtract from the list over the next couple of years." But the board would have none of that. The atmosphere worsened, Prager says, when Maxwell noticed a small black device the gallery had installed on the table to record the meeting. According to Judy Budovitch, Timothy appointed himself chair of the meeting. "It wasn't a meeting like any other we had ever had," she said. "We were told we were procrastinating, we were ungrateful, that we were leading the gallery in the wrong direction. . . . He wasn't terribly interested in listening to us, and then he made some terribly disparaging remarks, I think something like 'very little New Brunswickers.'" He eventually stormed out in anger.[42] To reporters outside, Maxwell and Timothy suggested that the meeting had gone well and they were confident the whole affair could be resolved — but they instituted a new, final deadline of April 30 for good measure.[43]

Timothy says a planned meeting between him and a group of the "most influential" board members was scheduled for Montreal. "What we were supposed to do was stop the car crash," he says, but the meeting never took place: "they canned it."[44] Instead, the new chair of the board, Daniel O'Brien, wrote to Timothy on April 26 to say the gallery's research had established that most of the paintings in the U.K. Foundation's proposal were not on loan but were actually gifts to the gallery. O'Brien, the president of St. Thomas University in Fredericton, wrote that there was "no evidence to support the foundations' claims that title in those works resides in the foundations"[45] — a phrase that astonished Timothy and Maxwell, given the gallery's repeated acknowledgements of foundation ownership for more than four decades. "Where I come from," Timothy told the CBC, "if people believed there was an issue as to ownership, they had an obligation to talk about that, at the very least. The silence was deafening."[46] Judy Budovitch says the gallery's lawyers had discovered evidence that those repeated acknowledgements of ownership, most of them signed by Ian Lumsden, were based on gallery records prepared by Beaverbrook's secretary, Mrs. Ince, in 1960 — but, the lawyers had found, the basis for *those* records was murky. And the paperwork from the 1950s, when the paintings had been sent to Fredericton, wasn't clear. "We were not going to take anything that belonged to anyone else," says Bernard Riordon, "but we weren't going to give away anything that Lord Beaverbrook had given to the people of New Brunswick."

In his letter, O'Brien told Timothy that the gallery was willing sign a loan agreement covering twenty-nine paintings sold by the Sir James Dunn Foundation to the Beaverbrook Canadian Foundation in 1970, part of the group of seventy-eight for which the Canadian Foundation was making a separate claim. But, he said, unless the U.K. Foundation could provide more evidence of its ownership of the 133 works in its proposal, the committee was "not in a position to recommend that the Board treat the art works . . . as anything but the property of the Gallery." Just as Timothy had accused the gallery of hiring Stephen Smart behind his back, the gallery would now accuse the foundations of being similarly underhanded: the U.K. Foundation filed a lawsuit against the gallery in London on May 5 while the two sides were still trying to agree on a mediator.[47] The gallery responded nine days later by suing both foundations in New Brunswick and contesting the jurisdiction of the British courts. "The gallery was forced into the position it took," Riordon says, "and the board became the guardians of Lord Beaverbrook's legacy."

*

Timothy had warned David Hay back in March that he and Maxwell were "of one mind" about the dispute, but its evolution into two parallel legal battles revealed yet again the distinct personalities of the two cousins. In July, the U.K. Foundation and the gallery signed an agreement to have a Canadian arbitrator, working under the authority of New Brunswick's arbitration legislation, settle their feud over the 133 paintings, a decision attributed to Maxwell's more conciliatory disposition. Because the two foundations, and indeed the two cousins, were interchangeable in the minds of many New Brunswickers, Timothy was forced to send out a press release clarifying that the Canadian Foundation he chaired would fight on in the courts for its seventy-eight paintings — despite his position as a trustee of the U.K. Foundation that had agreed to arbitration. "There was a discussion [among the U.K. trustees] and that discussion led to arbitration. I am one trustee on a board of six or seven," he explained at the time. "One goes with the wishes of the majority. That's something they felt was appropriate for them and that's fine." But, he said, the Canadian Foundation was prepared for a longer, tougher court battle. "The issues that are coming out and the manner in which people at the gallery are behaving is so outrageous that the only way to settle it is in law, with the financial consequences to the loser."[48]

Timothy would eventually aim another lawsuit at the gallery, demanding that it repay the $10 million he calculated the Canadian Foundation had given it over the years. He would also reject the gallery's claim, made in an affidavit, that he deliberately avoided being served with legal papers at his office in New York City.[49] "I have two offices, okay? One in New York, one in London. Those offices are known to at least the acting chairman of the gallery's committee. He knew perfectly well I was in London. They went through a completely spurious and bizarre process of trying to serve a writ in New York while I was sitting in London. Did they bother to find out where I was? No. Did they bother to actually just say, 'Well, we'll serve it at his office when he's there?' No. They wanted to make a public debate out of serving a writ. That's the base level to which this case has gone. . . . All it does is guarantee the determination, on this side of the fence, with which the matter will be pursued."[50]

Along with his press release clarifying that his foundation would not go to arbitration, Timothy also sent out a large package containing charts and archival documents to detail its case. It was a well-organized, persuasive presentation that explained the 1970 purchase of paintings orchestrated by Sir Max Aitken, and it included several documents in which the gallery had explicitly acknowledged the foundation's ownership. A careful reading would cause the average lay person to doubt the gallery's case and view Timothy as the reasonable party after all. This savvy bit of public relations was quickly undermined, however, by his next gambit: cutting off his foundation's funding of other worthwhile causes in New Brunswick, including the Beaverbrook scholarships at the university in Fredericton, the New Brunswick Youth Orchestra and the maintenance of the Old Manse, his grandfather's former home in Miramichi. "Simply put, our assets are under attack and all our resources must be used to defend them," Timothy wrote in an open letter to the beneficiaries. "We do not know what the final cost will be but we fear it could run into millions, both for the foundation and the gallery. That's why we have been forced to take the painful decision to suspend distribution of funds for philanthropic and charitable purposes. We'd like to think this is a temporary state of affairs but the harsh reality is it may not be." He also rebutted the growing and seemingly unstoppable view that he and Maxwell were trying to line their own pockets. "You and your organizations, as beneficiaries of the foundation, know otherwise," he wrote. "Collectively, you have received millions of dollars over the past four decades as a direct result of the efforts of the very Beaverbrook heirs who are now being belittled and maligned."[51]

Visitors view works by Graham Sutherland at the
Art in Dispute exhibition, July, 2005.

Karen Ruet, *Telegraph-Journal*

Financially, Timothy's move may have been justified, but it was another publicity misstep that seemed to confirm what many New Brunwickers believed about him. And that perception was not insignificant. Left on its own, the gallery would not have been able to pay for two simultaneous battles for two groups of disputed paintings on two legal fronts. But so profound was the public's reaction to what was happening — and so strong was their conviction that, given Timothy's behaviour, the gallery must be in the right — that the New Brunswick government considered it politically safe in December 2004 to lend the gallery $1 million to keep its claim alive, a loan Timothy tried in vain to block in court. "I am not happy with what they have engaged in," said the culture minister, Percy Mockler. Brad Green, the justice minister whose constituency included the gallery, said, "Some of the comments made [by the Aitkens] serve no purpose whatsoever and really only contribute to mounting public opinion in favour of the gallery."[52] If ever there was evidence belying the notions that art galleries are a diversion only for the elite and that ordinary people would not care about a couple of disputed paintings, this was it.

This, and the ever-swelling number of visitors to the gallery. In the first two months after the dispute became public, attendance increased twenty per cent over the same period a year earlier.[53] Many of the visitors, the gallery staff noted, asked to see Turner's *The Fountain of Indolence*, Freud's *Hotel Bedroom*, and other paintings they had been hearing about. This gave Rachel Brodie-Venart, the gallery's young collections manager, an idea, which Riordon seized upon immediately as a stroke of marketing genius. As the various lawsuits worked their way slowly through the courts, the pair made plans for an exhibition called *Art in Dispute* that would show all 211 works that the two foundations were claiming. "To put them up all at once really makes a very powerful point about how much artwork we're talking about and the quality of artwork we're talking about," Brodie-Venart said on the eve of the opening as she supervised the hanging in ceiling-to-floor Victorian style. Copies of letters written by Beaverbrook that appeared to bolster the gallery's case filled the small gaps on the walls. Vincent Prager, who'd joined Timothy in loudly demanding more exposure for the works, sounded resigned to having been outfoxed. "It's good that the pictures are finally on display for the people to see," he said, "although it's a shame that it took this big dispute for the pictures finally to be seen."[54]

The show was a triumph, with thirty thousand visitors streaming to the gallery, easily surpassing all previous records. But Brodie-Venart acknowledged as she prepared for the opening that the gallery's real challenge was legal, not artistic. "Art is a commodity like anything else. It's always been something that's been collected for its value, traded for its value. It's a status symbol. It's not a whole lot different than any other valuable commodity out there."[55] No one could predict the outcome of the legal battle ahead, nor where the paintings would be a year or five years or a decade after the exhibition. That awareness surely drove the attendance numbers: everyone knew *Art in Dispute* was potentially the very last chance for New Brunswickers to see many of the paintings that Beaverbrook had brought to Fredericton.

In a 2003 issue of *Tableau*, the gallery's newsletter, Timothy had waxed nostalgic about his grandfather. He recounted an episode at Arlington House, Beaverbrook's flat in central London. Timothy, just a boy, was sitting in a chair and tipping it backwards so it was balanced on only two legs. He and the chair fell, knocking over a lamp that came within two inches of damaging one of Graham Sutherland's paintings of Winston Churchill, which was awaiting shipment to Fredericton. This, he wrote, gave him a new interest in his grandfather's collection. "The gallery and its paintings should be *inclusive*, not exclusive," Timothy wrote. "The pictures are there for everyone: to stimulate, to challenge, to encourage a response, either for or against, and, above all, to rebut indifference. The artwork leads us to an outward look at the world, so that we may escape that all-too-present backyard view of life which inhibits us all; to tempt dreams of all manner of possibilities, which before seeing were un-thought-of."[56]

Two years after he wrote those words, *Art in Dispute* was granting Timothy Aitken his wish. And he had been the catalyst, though surely not in the way he would have wanted.

Maxwell Aitken arrives to testify at the arbitration hearings,
October 23, 2006.

Karen Ruet, *Telegraph-Journal*

CHAPTER ELEVEN

"One thing we can rely on is his own ego"

Kent Thomson knew the public relations war was already lost the moment he told his mother about the case. Thomson, the head of the litigation group at the blue-chip Toronto business law firm Davies Ward Phillips and Vineberg, was having one of his regular telephone chats with his mother, a retired elementary school teacher still living in his hometown in northern Ontario. She was proud of her three sons who had become lawyers in the glass-tower corporate canyons of Toronto and made a point of staying up to date on their cases. She was impressed when Kent told her he was taking on the Beaverbrook art dispute, which she had read about in the local newspaper, the *North Bay Nugget*. "She told me she really hoped that I won the case," Thomson says, "because it would be a real shame if that family actually got away with this."

In fact, he told his mother, he was representing that family and its foundation.

"You're not," she said.

Thomson assured her he was.

"Well, then," she sighed, "I really hope you lose."

Thomson had no intention of losing. His clients, Maxwell and the other family members who were trustees of the Beaverbrook U.K. Foundation, might never rehabilitate their image in Canada. But ultimately, the facts of their case were what mattered, and armed with those fact, Thomson intended to win the arbitration.

Thomson had always been competitive. As a young athlete in North Bay, Ontario, a small lumbering, mining and railway city, he had excelled in football, in track and particularly in hockey, which he'd played at the elite Triple-A level. He had not always been fascinated by the law, choosing to enrol at Queen's University law school only because his older brother had. His drive to win, however, carried over into his career, and standing at a podium before a judge or an arbitrator, he would often have one foot tapping, not with nervousness but with pent-up energy, as if in a hurry to reveal the full breadth of his argument. In the stuffy realm of legal briefs, Thomson's prose was lively, robust, even punchy: the claims of opponents were never merely doubtful or debatable, they were "remarkable" and "extraordinary." A typically confident Thomsonian assertion, made about a particular accusation by the Beaverbrook Art Gallery, was that "these are extraordinarily serious allegations of misconduct that are baseless and should never have been made." Like the man himself, his writing gave no quarter. And he was certain that once his seventy-something mother understood the facts at hand, she — like the vast majority of New Brunswickers and other Canadians who had heard about the case — would be disabused of the notion that the gallery was a weak little David being set upon by the mighty Goliath that was the Beaverbrook family.

The case was the kind of tangled, complex fight that had earned Thomson his reputation as an aggressive, intellectually rigorous lawyer. After Queen's, he joined the distinguished Toronto firm Osler, Hoskin and Harcourt, and later moved to Torys, another pillar of the Bay Street legal establishment. In 2001, he was recruited by Davies, which offered him, at a relatively young age, the job of heading the firm's litigation department. "Our goal is to achieve perfection or something close to it in the cases we handle," he says. The firm's demanding two-tier partnership structure required new recruits to excel quickly or be sent out the door. Thus Thomson had a group of lawyers as motivated as himself to draw on for the Beaverbrook arbitration, which he came to see as special. He had represented clients in a range of challenging, high-profile disputes, but, he says, "there are some cases that capture your heart more than others." Always interested in history, he saw the art dispute as "a historical jigsaw puzzle." He also genuinely liked Maxwell's gentle nature, his dignity and his commitment to the foundation's charitable work.

And then there were the facts, which could not have been clearer. Beaverbrook, whose desire for control and for documentation was "remarkable," had always transferred ownership of his gifts with elaborate precision. "He set out with as much specificity as possible what he proposed to do," Thomson wrote in his opening submission to the dispute arbitrator, Peter Cory. "He did so in writing, and typically he also undertook contemporaneous publicity to alert the world to what he had done."[1] Yet in the case of the 133 paintings that the gallery was claiming were gifts, there was no record of any offer by Beaverbrook, nor of any receipt or acknowledgement by the gallery. In fact, the opposite was true: for more than four decades — four decades, Thomson practically shouted from the pages of his submission — officials at the gallery had repeatedly described the paintings as the property of the Beaverbrook U.K. Foundation. Several precedents held that, given what Thomson called this "extraordinary" paper trail, the gallery was barred from claiming ownership at all, never mind base its claim on documents that it had held in its files throughout *those very same four decades* when it had acknowledged the foundation's ownership. On the facts and on the law, Thomson's case was solid.

Which was not to say he underestimated the talent facing him across the aisle. Larry Lowenstein was in many ways Thomson's opposite number, soft-spoken and earnest where Thomson was forceful, the office accounting manager to Thomson's campus jock. Lowenstein had been born in South Africa, the descendant of Eastern European Jews. After completing his law degree at Oxford, he had little interest in returning to Johannesburg, where a period of mandatory military service awaited him. "Among the causes I was willing to die for," Lowenstein likes to joke, "white supremacy was not high on my list." Instead he headed to Canada, to which his parents and sister had already emigrated, and moved up the ranks at Osler, Hoskin and Harcourt, the same Toronto firm Thomson had left.

Lowenstein took on the Beaverbrook case at the suggestion of Stephen Smart, the art-collecting partner at Osler who was retiring just as the dispute began. Like his courtroom persona, Lowenstein's writing style lacked Thomson's flair. He often overreached in trying to craft a colourful phrase, as when he argued that "the foundation's sabre-toothed tiger has become a paper tiger" or that contentious ownership documents were "a freak of nature in a formaldehyde bottle." But Lowenstein's methodical approach — immersing himself in the facts of the case and allowing both his intellectual and emotional reaction to point his way — told him there was something profoundly wrong with the story Kent Thomson was telling. "There was this huge disconnect in my mind between the acknowledgements [by the gallery] of foundation ownership after the death of Lord Beaverbrook and the clear indication of gift beforehand," he says. He began to shape a narrative in his mind suggesting that something had changed for Beaverbrook after he had opened the gallery. "You're proposing a theory and it must hang together internally and anticipate the facts before you even know them. It must predict the facts," he says. "When the facts start to bear out your hypothesis, that begins to gel in your mind as truth." Thomson's case — the lack of paperwork documenting the gift, the four decades of references to a loan — was not as strong as it appeared, Lowenstein concluded. "They had a very difficult time getting any sort of moral traction," he says, "and the best they could come up with was, 'What took you so long?'"

The two legal teams would cross paths throughout 2005 and 2006 at various meetings and examinations for discovery, but it was not until October 3, 2006 that they would assemble in full, along with their hundreds of binders containing tens of thousands of documents, at the Wu Centre on the University of New Brunswick campus.

Lowenstein delivered his opening statement first, a week-long opus that began with Timothy Aitken's angry letter in 2004 to David Hay and then swept back across the five-decade history of the gallery. Reconstructing that narrative had not been easy, Lowenstein told Cory. Minutes from meetings of the trustees of the Beaverbrook Foundation from 1954 to 1964 — the very documents that might have said explicitly whether the paintings were gifts or loans — were missing. Cory would thus have to infer the meaning of thousands of other documents, many drafted or vetted by Beaverbrook himself, that referred to the gallery *and the paintings inside* as his gift to New Brunswick. There was the 1958 Stuart Trueman article in *Canadian Art*, literally paid for by Beaverbrook himself, describing his donation of the gallery "and all its contents," and the piece by Michael Wardell, his faithful Fredericton acolyte, in *The Atlantic Advocate*, praising "the gift of the Gallery and the pictures." Beaverbrook's own newspaper, the *Daily Express*, reported in September 1959 that with the official opening, "the Gallery and its almost priceless collection of art treasures will cease to be the property of Lord Beaverbrook and become the property of the people of New Brunswick." A 1959 gallery catalogue referred to the building "together with its endowment" as a "gift."[2] Taken together, Lowenstein argued, it was hard to imagine that these documents, copies of which Beaverbrook had sent to many friends and acquaintances, did not reflect his own views.

And tucked away in Lowenstein's opening statement were references to other documents from that era, documents that hinted at a less public history of the gallery and of its founder. These documents, Lowenstein believed, explained the disconnect he had sensed, and supported the narrative he had been developing, which he called his "change of heart" theory. Even after months of preparation, however, the theory had still not completely taken shape. As he opened his case, Lowenstein attacked the foundation's notion of, as he put it, "a punitive, disciplinarian Lord Beaverbrook" who would want paintings taken back to England, "leaving behind a shell of a Gallery."[3] But as the weeks unfolded, this very characterization of the press baron — anathema to Lowenstein at the outset — would become central to his own case.

There were still other documents, Lowenstein said, that supported the gallery's case. Each painting on loan to the gallery in 1959 had been assigned an identification number prefixed with "L," but none of the disputed works were so labelled. (The foundation would reply

A British CD3 export form designating some paintings as "gifts."

Beaverbrook Art Gallery, exhibit G000887

that the "L" prefix was only for paintings on short-term loan.) And there were records that had been kept secret from Lowenstein. Earlier in 2006, his team had come across a treasure trove of previously unknown export forms in British archives, known as CD3s, which showed that the paintings were categorized as gifts when they were shipped out of the country.[4] The foundation's British lawyers had had the same documents a year earlier but had not disclosed them to the gallery, Lowenstein told Cory. But he gave Maxwell and Thomson the benefit of the doubt: they had not been aware of the subterfuge. Maxwell, learning at discovery that documents were not disclosed, "was embarrassed," Lowenstein said. "He was contrite."

Lowenstein's portrayal of the Aitken family would shift several times. Leading up to the hearing, he claimed former trustees of the foundations had committed a "series of abuses" to mislead the gallery about ownership — an apparent reference to Sir Max Aitken's 1970 settlement with Lady Beaverbrook over dozens of paintings that were not even part of the U.K. Foundation's claim. "Those serious allegations of misconduct were quite literally invented from whole cloth," Thomson would fume later. Lowenstein would abandon the "series of abuses" strategy in mid-hearing, just as he would abandon suggestions that the trustees wanted to sell the Turner and the Freud to underwrite foundation management fees paid to Maxwell — an argument, in effect, that he would personally profit from the sale.[5] On one family member, however, Lowenstein never wavered: he stood by his depiction of Timothy as a one-man fountain of insolence, entering into evidence the angry letters and the inflammatory comments to the media, even though neither had any bearing on ownership. Lowenstein even managed to cite as a precedent on a minor point of law — thus bringing it to the arbitrator's attention — Timothy's failed lawsuit to block the gallery from accepting provincial government money to fight the case. "That was kind of mean," Peter Cory commented. "I just lose more faith in human nature every day." Lowenstein eagerly agreed with Cory's dismay. "Can you imagine?" he said. "It's just breathtaking."

Thomson's opening statement was equally epic, and no less forceful. There was no document anywhere showing Beaverbrook's desire to give any of the paintings to the gallery, he pointed out. "He did not do so, nor did he purport to do so." Nor was there any sign the gallery ever explicitly accepted any of the paintings as gifts — another legal test of whether something actually was a gift. "That ends it," he told Cory. "As it turns out, it ends the whole of the gallery's case. If you accept my submissions on this point, the gallery's case is over." The only concession he made was that the foundation's trustees, had they been able to predict the gallery's sudden claim of ownership, might have made their intentions more explicit back in the 1950s. Even so, he noted, the gallery had acknowledged foundation ownership over and over, most obviously in lists prepared by Ian Lumsden for the foundation's U.K. auditors in June of 1969 and in subsequent "audit lists" Lumsden sent to London periodically right up until 2003.[6]

Thomson dismissed Lowenstein's contention that these acknowledgements were somehow trumped by a collection of newspaper and magazine articles. It was "extraordinary," he said, that the gallery would cite as proof of *its* ownership clippings that had been in its own files during the four decades it had been acknowledging *foundation* ownership. Indeed, a 2000 catalogue of the collection had listed the foundation as the owner of the 133 works despite citing Wardell's *Advocate* piece elsewhere. In any event, he continued, "this case does not concern a minute dissection of what the quote-unquote 'public perception' might have been in Fredericton or in New Brunswick in 1959. . . . To the extent that perception matters at all . . . the perceptions that matter are those of the people involved with the administration of the gallery and the people running the foundation." And, he said, there was no evidence of anyone at the gallery ever declaring, "'I read the article and we own the Freud.'" As for Lowenstein's argument that Beaverbrook's mailing of the stories to his friends amounted to an endorsement of their contents, Thomson reminded Cory that the press baron often exaggerated the size of his gifts and, at the time, was trying to both generate publicity for the gallery and persuade his wealthy acquaintances to donate works of art. "Lord Beaverbrook made no bones about the fact that he was, to use his own words, a 'master propagandist,'" Thomson said. "It's why he owned newspapers."

Cory looked up from his notes. "Perhaps Goebbels should never have been prosecuted as a war criminal," he told the lawyer.

Thomson, taken off guard, asked, "Pardon me?"

"Perhaps," Cory repeated, "Goebbels should never have been prosecuted as a war criminal."

"I wouldn't go that far," replied Thomson.

"Coming close," Cory said.

Thomson regained his composure and moved on. But was Peter Cory, a retired justice of the Supreme Court of Canada, actually comparing Beaverbrook to Joseph Goebbels, Hitler's minister of propaganda? "I don't understand the connection," Maxwell would comment several months later. "If he was comparing my grandfather to Goebbels — I don't think he really was — but if he was, that would be something that would surprise me."[7]

*

The witnesses began testifying on October 19. Four of them — Ron Irving, a member of the first board of governors of the gallery, Allan Aitken, a Canadian nephew of Beaverbrook with few ties to his uncle's descendants, Claire Watson-Fisher, Beaverbrook's now-frail former art advisor from Montreal, and Josephine Yorke, his travelling secretary — offered similar testimony. Each was certain that Beaverbrook's intention was to give all of the paintings in the gallery to the province as gifts. Each was forced to admit that this was only his or her impression and that they had never seen any records of the gallery or the foundation. "I know nothing about the paperwork," Yorke had admitted in an earlier media interview. "I haven't seen it."[8]

Thomson would dismiss all of their testimony as lightweight, but he was particularly contemptuous of another gallery witness, Stuart Smith, the former curator, who, in media interviews in 2004, had attributed the foundation's claim to the faltering finances of the Aitken family. Smith had a blunt and salty way of speaking, making him a lively foil for Thomson's aggressive style. "I have also stopped beating my wife," Smith retorted caustically at one point, mocking what he considered to be the lawyer's leading questions. But Thomson ended up besting him. Smith claimed at first that, when he arrived at the gallery in 1964, he interpreted the phrase "Property of the Beaverbrook Foundations" in the accession records as a reference to "where the paintings came from . . . the source of the painting that is now part of our collection." But Thomson forced him to admit that he had known the records were meant to indicate ownership. And Smith was tripped up on other facts: asked about his claims that the Aitkens wanted their paintings back to renovate Cherkley and solve their own financial troubles, he admitted he had not asked anyone about the restoration of the house, nor about whether Maxwell or members of his family were allowed to live there. "It was not a preoccupation of mine, I will tell you that," Smith said. "No, I made no inquiries."[9]

Thomson appeared to relish confronting Smith with his own words, reminding him that in 1967 he'd told the *Globe and Mail* that "legally, Lady B. or Sir Max can bring a truck to the gallery and take away at least a quarter of what we have here at a moment's notice." Smith answered that that he wasn't providing a legal opinion but was expressing the fact that the board of governors was too timid or deferential to use the power given to it by legislation. "The reality was that the custodians at that time had absolute control over that gallery," Smith said, "and they could do anything they wanted." But for Thomson, the highlight of Smith's testimony was his explanation of why he had described Beaverbrook as a "loathsome little man" when he spoke to the *Sunday Times* about the dispute. "Unfortunately just when this all came, I had just finished reading *Sunflower*," Smith said during his examination by the gallery's local lawyer, David Young. The novel by Rebecca West, he said, was "her account of her affair with Beaverbrook in 1923. . . . I was paraphrasing Rebecca West. Yes, I guess I did say that because the Rebecca West thing was in my head and that was her description of him. She added that he had hair the colour of a fox and an extremely wide mouth, but that was her."

"I don't see *that* in the *Sunday Times*," Young noted.

"No," Smith answered.[10] Lowenstein would later acknowledge that Smith's remark was an embarrassment, noting that "the gallery has never orchestrated that or supported that statement"[11] — the first time in Thomson's memory that he'd seen a lawyer disassociate himself from the direct evidence of one of his own witnesses. "Remarkable," Thomson called it.

Smith's testimony ended on a Friday; the following Monday, Maxwell, his mother, his son and his sister made their way through a crush of reporters as the most anticipated day of the hearings began. Thomson, seeking to pre-empt Lowenstein's theory that Sir Max Aitken had committed "a series of abuses," led Lady Aitken through a detailed description of her late husband's sterling character. "He cared about the gallery," she said. To undercut the gallery's argument that other descendants of Lord Beaverbrook had concealed the truth, he had her describe the foundation's behaviour as "very formal and scrupulous." She felt "complete shock and anger" at the suggestion that she herself was complicit in a cover-up. "I can't understand the vilification. It's unbelievable, besides being totally libellous." As for the idea that she and her son would benefit financially from the sale of the Turner and the Freud, "it is outrageous to suggest it. There is no question of benefiting. . . . We have never benefited from owning the paintings, not even a penny."

For sheer entertainment value, it was unlikely that anyone could have matched Lady Aitken's bravura performance on the witness stand, never mind her own son, with his calm, inscrutable demeanour. Maxwell's recollection for Thomson of the 1977 sale of *Peasant Girl Gathering Faggots* and the two Stubbs was workmanlike and effective; his account of his contacts with Riordon and the foundation's formal offer to the gallery in 2004 was perfectly straightforward. It was only when Lowenstein stepped up to the podium to cross-examine him that sparks began to fly — albeit the kind of understated sparks one might expect between a quiet lawyer with the persona of an accountant and a third-generation lord known for his placid nature. Lowenstein was never aggressive, and Maxwell remained cool and unruffled, though at the appropriate moments his face showed bafflement at just what Lowenstein was getting at.

The trustees of the foundation had not considered the impact on New Brunswick when they decided to sell *Peasant Girl* and two other works in 1977, Maxwell acknowledged. "The trustees are responsible for the foundation, not for the province of New Brunswick," he noted dryly. But surely, Lowenstein said, had the foundation known about the various magazine articles referring to the works as gifts — including one in *Newsweek* in which Beaverbrook had wanted the *Peasant Girl* mentioned specifically — "you would have investigated it."

"Well, that's your opinion," Maxwell answered. "I am the chairman of an important British foundation. We cannot start handing out assets of the foundation based on press articles of forty-five years ago." Nor was the 1959 catalogue at all relevant to his thinking. "The catalogue of the gallery is not part of the asset register of the Beaverbrook Foundation," he said. But Beaverbrook's intentions had to be relevant, Lowenstein countered, both in 1977 and again in 2004. Even on this point Maxwell would not concede. "What I was looking at was the facts of the matter, and what I looked at was the books and records of the foundation, which my grandfather was responsible for as a trustee," he said. "I was not at that time interested in intentions. I was interested in the ownership, the facts of ownership." His grandfather's dispatching of copies of the clippings and the catalogue to his friends was likewise meaningless, he said. "He was a great propagandist. No doubt he liked to receive praise and gratitude. . . . I'm sure at some points he was not distinguishing between who might own each picture. A man of his stature might not distinguish. This generosity all comes under one heading, as it were. It all emanated from him."

Lowenstein pressed ahead, trying to explore the 1970 deal between Maxwell's father, Sir Max, and Lady Beaverbrook, which saw seventy-seven paintings sold to the Beaverbrook Canadian Foundation. Lowenstein noted the clear proof that Christofor had given the gallery at least the three Sickerts, a direct contradiction of her claim. And yet, he told Maxwell, "your father decided not to take her on," failing to fulfill his duty to protect the gallery and its collection. Perhaps this was Lowenstein's bid to bolster his "series of abuses" argument about Sir Max and tie the 1970 deal to the U.K. Foundation's claim, but Cory wanted none of it. "I really don't care about the family feuds," he told Lowenstein. He had enough material to sift through in making his decision and "I don't know in the long run if that will help." Lowenstein tried to draw a parallel that hindsight was important to both cases: Sir Max's intervention, seemingly a positive gesture in 1970, had in fact put the three Sickerts at risk thirty-four years later. Cory was not persuaded. "Perhaps," he said in his congenial but firm manner, "it is a good idea to move on to other areas that could be of assistance."

Lowenstein shifted his attention to the complex realm of the foundation's finances and what its records revealed about its true motives. He had already sprinkled into his cross-examination of Maxwell several references to the £3,000 monthly salary he was being paid by the foundation he chaired for his management of the dispute litigation, an income equivalent to about $6,300. Now Lowenstein touched on it again as he turned to possible links between the Cherkley project and the proposed sale of the Turner and the Freud. Though Maxwell would note that the millions spent on Cherkley were effectively charitable spending, Lowenstein reminded him that in 2005, the foundation's gifts to the U.K. charities it traditionally supported had dropped to below £69,000. The same year, it had spent more than five times that amount on administrative costs, including Maxwell's management fees for overseeing both the dispute litigation and the Cherkley project. Overall, the Cherkley renovations combined with those overhead expenses had totalled between £800,000 and £900,000 in 2005 alone. Yet, Lowenstein said sarcastically, "I take it was the $35,000 top-up insurance cost that pushed you over the brink."

Maxwell appeared puzzled, so Lowenstein spelled it out for him: the trustees were spending more than £9 million on Cherkley overall, but claimed they could not afford the £17,500 added insurance cost for its paintings in Fredericton. "That's not what I said at all," Maxwell answered. The sale of the Turner and the Freud would increase the foundation's liquidity to help it continue its charitable work, while providing a large donation to the gallery, he said. But the sale would generate six hundred times the cost of the insurance, Lowenstein argued — hardly a fair saw-off. The fact remained, Maxwell countered, that paying for the insurance meant that the paintings in Fredericton were costing the foundation money rather than generating revenue. They had become, as he put it, "a negative yield. . . . If Cherkley does not break even when it is fully functional, the exact same scrutiny will take place."

"It sounds like you're an investment manager, sir," Lowenstein told him.

A foundation has to invest well to support charitable causes, Maxwell answered.

"The idea of negative yield," Lowenstein responded, "is diametrically opposed to your grandfather's conception."

Lowenstein and Maxwell gently sparred over other minor points, including the insults hurled by Stuart Smith and Timothy Aitken, but their confrontation was effectively over. Earlier, Maxwell had testified that he wanted the gallery to remain strong because "my name is over the door." But he also said the Turner and the Freud were not essential to his grandfather's vision. Lowenstein asked what guarantee there was that the other 131 paintings would stay in the gallery after the ten-year loan agreement expired. None at all, Maxwell answered. They might well be removed. "I have always said I hope not, and in the future, who knows?"

When Maxwell left the witness chair, a good deal of the public's and the media's interest in the hearings went with him. The two rows of seats in the room, filled to capacity during his testimony, were almost empty again. Only a couple of journalists remained now to follow the proceedings through until the end. Which is why one of the most important moments in the hearing, at least in Kent Thomson's eyes, went largely unnoticed and unreported.

Michael Marshall, a former secretary to the U.K. Foundation who had become the administrator of the Cherkley restoration, was called after Maxwell, largely to rebut Lowenstein's suggestion, made in documents he had filed, that the trustees wanted to sell the Turner and the Freud in part "to benefit the recipients of the management fees," meaning Maxwell. Lowenstein's cross-examination of Maxwell had suggested that the allegation of personal gain would be an important part of his case. But when Kent Thomson's colleague Matthew Milne-Smith began to ask Marshall about it, Lowenstein stood up. "I'm sorry, but we have made it clear since the discovery that we don't proceed on this allegation. It is there as a historic relic in the pleading." That surprised Milne-Smith, who pointed out that the pleading had been filed only a week before the hearing began. Lowenstein explained that the only reason it had remained in the document was to avoid having to renumber paragraphs. "The suggestion that any of the families personally benefited from this is not part of our case and was put in for exploratory purposes in 2005," he said. Milne-Smith was clearly skeptical but said he was "delighted to hear that it has been withdrawn, and in a public forum, at last." Thomson would later refute Lowenstein's paragraph-numbering explanation, calling it "remarkable," and condemn his inclusion of the accusation for "exploratory purposes" as nothing more than a fishing expedition — highly improper in any litigation, he would say, but particularly when the allegation is as serious as breach of trust.[12]

*

The hearing was not going well for the gallery. Its case relied on several examples of Beaverbrook's *not* calling a painting a loan — hardly proof that it was a gift. Lowenstein's "series of abuses" theory had vanished, and his probing for a financial benefit to Maxwell had yielded nothing. Stuart Smith's testimony had given Thomson new ammunition. The gallery's next witness, its director Bernard Riordon, was cornered by Thomson into admitting that the term "permanent collection" did not refer — as Riordon had testified it did — to works a gallery owned, but that it could also cover those on loan.[13] Judy Budovitch confessed on the stand to never having seen the audit lists or the accession records until the hearings began, despite the fact that she had helped draft Dan O'Brien's April 2004 letter asserting there was "no evidence" of foundation ownership. "No, I really have never seen them before these proceedings," she told Thomson.[14] Budovitch's appearance also gave Thomson the opportunity to take another swipe at the gallery's reliance on old newspaper and magazine articles that called the paintings a gift. Budovitch had helped organize the Cherish the Gift fundraising campaign in the 1980s, a time when she and other gallery officials accepted the foundation's ownership. Yet they had called the campaign Cherish the *Gift* — loosely interpreting the term to cover paintings on loan. If the gallery could use the word so loosely, so liberally, Thomson would argue, surely it was conceivable that *Time* and *Newsweek* and Stuart Trueman and Michael Wardell had done the same.

No, things did not appear to be going well at all for the gallery.

And then, with the arrival at the Wu Centre of Tom Forrestall, the core of Lowenstein's narrative — his "change of heart" theory — finally began to come into focus.

It had been more than forty-six years since Wardell had recommended, and Beaverbrook had endorsed, the firing of "poor Tom," who as assistant curator had been put in charge of maintaining the gallery's accession records before his epileptic seizures became a problem. Since his departure, Forrestall had become a successful artist whose work, described as "magic realism," was exhibited internationally. He was seventy years old when he arrived at the Wu Centre, the only artist to testify in this dispute about art. His understanding, he said, was "that these paintings belonged to the gallery and that they were part of that gift to the people of New Brunswick, kind of a totality, and it would follow through to the people of New Brunswick and the people of Canada. . . . They were all one big, great gift."[15]

He described his work on the accession records. There was a separate file for each work; the most important document in each folder was the catalogue sheet, also known as the accession sheet, a document that was sometimes typed, sometimes handwritten. Each sheet listed the work's artist, medium, size, date and history. Each file also contained a separate location sheet that recorded where, or whether, the painting was hanging in the gallery. Forrestall recognized his handwriting on location sheets David Young showed him for seventy-two of the eighty-five disputed works that had been in the gallery when he worked there. He also recognized various catalogue sheets, including one for *The Fountain of Indolence* that bore what he believed was his handwriting where the painting's size was noted.

Facing page: The catalogue sheet for *The Fountain of Indolence*.
Beaverbrook Art Gallery, exhibit G000485-D

Beaverbrook Art Gallery
CATALOGUE SHEET

Artist.... TURNER, Joseph Mallord William, RA, 1775-1851   Catalogue No. 59.259

Address..

Title of Painting....... The Fountain of Indolence.........

Date Painted.... 1834 .....Date Acquired..............

Signature on Painting......................

Medium........ Oil on canvas.....................

Source..

Gift or Purchase....... Purchase.................

Size......................... 42 x 65½ .....

Photographed: Colour.........Yes..................

     Black and White...........................

Cuts owned by Gallery: Colour.....Yes.................

     Black and White...........................

Have reproduction rights been assigned by artist?...................

Condition of Painting:

Work Carried out on Painting:

Published References to Painting:

    Sir Walter Armstrong TURNER pp.120, 122.
    C.F. Bell - EXHIBITED WORKS OF TURNER

    Tweedie, R.A.; Cogswell, Fred; MacNutt, W. Stewart; ed. "Arts in New Brunswick" (1967) Fredericton, Brunswick Press, p. 183 (reprod.)

Other Information:
    Coll: Vanderbilt Family, New York
    Exh: Royal Academy, 1834
          Metropolitan Museum, N.Y. (on loan for many years)

PROPERTY OF BEAVERBROOK FOUNDATIONS.

But the catalogue sheets listed the paintings as "Property of Beaver-brook Foundations," a designation Forrestall was certain had not been there when he had last seen the documents in 1959. "It seems to me it would change the status of the painting if it had been there," he said. There was a portrait by Graham Sutherland of Helena Rubinstein on loan to the gallery at the time, Forrestall explained, and everyone knew that made it distinct from other works. So any change in the status of others would have caught his eye. "I would have been very much aware of that," he said, "so I don't recall that being on the sheet, and I dealt with these sheets all day, every day, pretty well."[16]

This was perhaps the single most important moment for Lowenstein's case because it dovetailed with the story he needed to tell. There was no designation showing the paintings belonged to the foundations when Forrestall left the gallery, and he had left in March 1960.

Within seven months of his departure, Lowenstein recounted, Beaverbrook himself had orchestrated the destruction of the gallery's original ownership records by sending Margaret Ince to Fredericton. The implication was that she had added the designation of foundation ownership to the catalogue sheets in an attempt to change the status of the paintings retroactively from gifts to loans.

It was a stunning suggestion. But for it to hold together, Lowenstein needed to show that, before 1960, Beaverbrook had intended the paintings to be gifts, and that he had then had "a change of heart." That original intent, Lowenstein would argue, was proven not only by the newspaper and magazine articles, but by several other documents Thomson had denounced as equally meaningless: Beaverbrook's July 15, 1955 letter to his foundation, referring to its "scheme to equip an Art Gallery in Fredericton, New Brunswick," his formal offer to Premier Flemming on December 4, 1956, of a "fully equipped" gallery, the British CD3 export documents designating the paintings as gifts, and the gallery board's March 1959 report to the lieutenant-governor of New Brunswick, with its promise that Beaverbrook was continuing to buy paintings "to enhance the beauty and importance of the collection."[17]

That took care of intent, Lowenstein believed. To prove the equally essential second half of his theory — the subsequent change of heart — he pointed to an obscure, seemingly minor amendment to the wording of the trust deed of Beaverbrook's foundation, made in late 1959. This amendment would lead to the almost absurd scene of two British trust experts debating the interpretation of a single preposition.

Section 2(e) of the foundation's original trust deed, drafted in 1954, allowed for the "purchasing for or providing funds for the purchase by libraries museums or art galleries in the Province which are . . . open to the public . . . paintings prints statuary and other documents or works of art" — wording that, in Lowenstein's view, allowed the foundation only to *give* paintings as gifts, not lend them. Section 2(f), however, with its allowance for "other charitable purposes," was broad enough to cover loans. This meant Lowenstein had a double burden. To prove the paintings were gifts, he had to show that they were sent to the gallery under Section 2(e), not Section 2(f). And to prove that 2(e) had not included the power to lend before 1959, he had show that the amendment *added* the power to lend to 2(e). His expert witness on British trusts, Michael Furness, argued that, pre-1959, 2(e) did not allow loans because "if both buying to give and buying to lend were intended, then one would have expected these two activities to be distinctly authorized." Even the foundation's expert witness, Mark Herbert, said that while he considered it probable, he could not *guarantee* that the original 2(e) allowed for loans. To put it "beyond doubt," he said under cross-examination by Lowenstein, the trustees would have to execute a deed of variation — precisely what Lowenstein believed they were doing when they amended 2(e) in 1959.[18]

The amendment, which took effect on January 1, 1960, added a key phrase allowing the purchasing of paintings and other objects "for the purpose of making the same available for inspection by the public in the Province"[19] — a phrase that, Lowenstein argued, changed the clause to permit, *for the first time*, the buying of paintings to *lend* to the gallery for display. He pointed to a letter from the foundation's lawyers to its secretary, Sheila Elton, on December 9, 1959, in which Elton was told Section 2(e) was amended to extend its power to buy books and works of art "in order that they may be retained in the

HERBERT SMITH & Cº
SOLICITORS

S. SOAMES
R. C. HARE
H. W. HIGGINSON
F. A. MANN
J. G. BARKER
L. C. HARTGILL
W. G. F. BALLANTYNE
J. F. GOBLE
T. S. ENTWISTLE
H. S. MAXWELL-WOOD
A. D. SPOTTISWOODE
P. K. DRURY
G. M. LEWIS
T. W. PATERSON

Encs. By Hand.

TELEPHONE: NATIONAL 9622 (17 LINES)
TELEGRAMS:
INLAND, "PRECIS, AVE, LONDON"
OVERSEAS, "PRECIS, LONDON"

IN REPLY PLEASE QUOTE

OUR REF.   4

YOUR REF.

62, LONDON WALL,

LONDON, E.C.2.

9th December 1959

Mrs. S. Elton M.A.
The Beaverbrook Foundations.
121/8 Fleet Street,
London, E.C.4.

Dear Mrs. Elton,

THE BEAVERBROOK FOUNDATIONS.

I enclose three copies of draft Deeds amending the First and Second Beaverbrook Foundations. The amendments are :—

(a) the addition of the Province of Nova Scotia,

(b) the extension of the objects to permit the purchase of books, works of art etc. by the Foundations in order that they may be retained in the ownership of the Foundations for exhibition to the public,

(c) an extension of the power of the trustees to permit them expressly to pay expenses incurred in connection with the trusts, the example you gave me being the cost of transporting a picture to London for the trustees to see, with a view to purchase.

You will see that the extension of the power to purchase works of art etc. has been worded so that any works of art retained by the Foundations are to be made available for inspection by the public in the Province. I assume that this covers what Lord Beaverbrook desires.

I should remind you that any works of art which are retained in the ownership of the Foundations should not remain in the personal possession of Lord Beaverbrook, as this could render them liable to estate duty on his death.

Yours sincerely,

HWHigginson

The letter from the Beaverbrook U.K. Foundation's lawyers to the foundation's secretary explaining changes to the trust deed.

Beaverbrook Art Gallery, exhibit UKS4453

ownership of the Foundations."[20] "The extension which [the lawyers] are driving at is this idea that from now onwards, the foundation can actually retain ownership of the works of art that they have purchased," Michael Furness testified. This meant, Lowenstein argued, that the foundation's officials understood that they had sent paintings to Fredericton under 2(e) — and 2(e) had not allowed them to retain ownership before January 1, 1960.

This subtle, nuanced argument had powerful implications: it meant that, at a minimum, any paintings in the gallery *before* the change to 2(e) had to be considered gifts. But it was only a skeleton of a theory. To put some flesh on those bones, Lowenstein turned to Margaret Ince — "diligent, honest, warm-hearted Mrs. Ince," as Kent Thomson had called her.[21]

Not long after Forrestall left the gallery without having completed his work on the accession records, Edwy Cooke, the gallery's curator, wrote to Mrs. Ince to tell her the files remained "woefully inadequate." Because Mrs. Ince had overseen Beaverbrook's art purchases, she knew best how to fill out the documents, so Cooke began shipping catalogue sheets to London, where she would complete them and send them back to Fredericton. Eventually, Beaverbrook decided it would be simpler for Mrs. Ince to travel to Fredericton "so that the whole system will be wonderfully well organized." She arrived in October 1960 and spent most of her time in the vault, completing a card index for the collection, filling in what she called "catalogue forms," and affixing labels to the paintings. On November 7 she wrote to Beaverbrook on her progress. "I have destroyed all the old accession sheets," she told him. "And each file is now fitted with a new sheet giving all available details of the paintings."[22]

What information had Mrs. Ince destroyed? No one would ever know, Lowenstein acknowledged. It wasn't even clear which documents she was referring to, given that the catalogue sheets Tom Forrestall had worked with before her visit had evidently survived: Forrestall had recognized the sheets he was shown as the originals, albeit with the designation "Property of the Beaverbrook Foundations" added at some point after his departure. Perhaps,

GRanite 5-3371

LORD BEAVERBROOK *Hotel*

FREDERICTON, N.B.

7th November, 1960.

Dear Lord Beaverbrook,

You will have heard from Mr. Cooke that the paintings about which you wrote to Mrs. Shima, left here last Friday.

As I mentioned I have made a complete card index which will be used for reference under "accession" numbers. The files which are kept in the steel cabinet will remain in alphabetical order.

I have destroyed all the old accession sheets. And each file is now fitted out with a new sheet giving all available details of the paintings.

The job has taken me longer than I anticipated as I have had to take the small photographs of each picture which were affixed to the old sheets and fix them on the new ones. I thought it better to finish this work as I cannot see when any of the staff here were going to have time to do this.

I now go to the University to check your Collection most of which is in the Lloyd George room. There are several books on loan.

I will leave here on Friday and be in London on Saturday.

I shall not be able to finish fixing all the Lloyd George material. But I will leave a tin of fixative with the papers and so before they are taken out of the vault, they can be treated with the spray coating.

Yours sincerely,

Rt.Hon. Lord Beaverbrook.

Margaret Ince's letter to Beaverbrook telling him she had destroyed the original accession sheets.

Beaverbrook Art Gallery, exhibit G002729

Lowenstein speculated, Mrs. Ince had destroyed notes or forms, or even export documents, that said "purchased for the gallery" or "gift to the art gallery." Maybe the answer would have been found in that locked filing cabinet full of Beaverbrook's paintings correspondence, had Bob Tweedie not ordered Stuart Smith to ship it to England after Beaverbrook's death. Whatever the information Mrs. Ince had destroyed, Lowenstein did not suggest that she had acted on her own. She was following orders, he said: Lord Beaverbrook's orders.[23]

So Lowenstein's story had four elements: Beaverbrook's intention to give paintings to the gallery, at least up until its opening; his decision to change the trust deed so that his foundation could begin lending paintings in January 1960; the mysterious addition of foundation ownership to the records after March of 1960; and Mrs. Ince's destruction of older records when she came to Fredericton in October 1960. At first glance, the notion that Beaverbrook had retroactively tried to turn his gifts into loans was tenuous — hardly enough to undo four decades of gallery documents acknowledging foundation ownership. But it might be enough to plant a seed of doubt about those acknowledgements in the mind of the arbitrator, Peter Cory. Maybe those acknowledgements had been based on records that had been altered on Beaverbrook's instructions.

Left unsaid was what might have prompted the "change of heart." Lowenstein did not have to speculate about a reason; all he had to show was that it had happened. Perhaps Christofor, who made her own questionable claims on paintings she had given the gallery, was manipulating her new companion to do the same. Perhaps he had begun to fret about losing control: there was a letter from George Millar in 1961 explaining that the foundation was lending the paintings because Beaverbrook wanted "to provide the Foundation with authority and power after his death to compel the Gallery in Fredericton to behave itself, should occasion arise." And later that year Beaverbrook told his Fredericton lawyer, Charles Hughes, that he felt several members of the gallery board "were of no value."[24] Whether these growing doubts about local authority over the gallery prompted Beaverbrook's change of heart more than a year earlier is unclear — if that change of heart even occurred.

All Lowenstein could offer was a suggestion that, later in 1960, there was scrutiny of Beaverbrook's actions from a surprising quarter. Michael Wardell, Beaverbrook's "captain," wrote to Beaverbrook in December that he had met with New Brunswick's comptroller-general and that the gallery was required, ahead of its provincial audit, to list the paintings in the gallery "with statement of ownership in every case. . . . In those cases where the pictures do not belong to the gallery, as indicated by the new labels, a statement will be required as to the terms and conditions under which they are on exhibit at the gallery." In London, Beaverbrook told Millar that the gallery's contents were not subject to the comptroller's audit requirements and were "none of his business."[25] Lowenstein read this as evidence that Wardell knew the new labels attached by Mrs. Ince just a month or two earlier were misleading, that he was trying, albeit diffidently, to compel Beaverbrook to correct them, and that Beaverbrook wanted to avoid outside scrutiny. But Wardell didn't push, perhaps because he wrongly believed — as he had when Beaverbrook sold the *Synnot Children* painting without telling the board — that his patron had absolute power to do whatever he pleased at the gallery. Or perhaps Wardell's dependence on Beaverbrook simply ruled out anything more than a half-hearted objection. Whatever the explanation, the Wardell letter was, in the gallery's eyes, more evidence of Beaverbrook's change of heart.

There was one troubling consequence of Lowenstein's theory for the gallery's case. True, it provided an at least potentially plausible explanation for ownership of the eighty-five works delivered *before* the end of 1959. But it could not apply to the forty-eight that had arrived *after* the trust deed amendment that gave the foundation the power to lend paintings instead of giving them. In fact, the "change of heart" theory, while bolstering the claim to pre-1960 paintings, undermined the gallery's claim to the post-1960 works. Lowenstein could only argue that, if the latter group was made up of loans, the foundation had intended *permanent* loans that it could not now revoke unilaterally.[26] It was a much weaker argument — Kent Thomson called it "remarkable" — but Lowenstein would accept the trade-off. Almost all of the most interesting and valuable paintings in dispute, including

Turner's *The Fountain of Indolence* and Freud's *Hotel Bedroom*, had arrived before the change of heart. They were covered by the much more compelling argument that they could only be gifts.

Kent Thomson dismissed Lowenstein's entire theory as "of no moment whatsoever in this case. . . . [It] is simply not sustainable, and is a complete red herring." One of the lawyers on Thomson's all-star Davies team, Timothy Youdan, happened to be both British and an expert on trust law, and he told Cory the change to Section 2(e) of the trust deed was "a minor amendment for a purpose that appears never to have had any real significance." The phrase about making the paintings "available for inspection by the public in the Province" was probably inserted to allow them to tour locations other than art galleries, museums or libraries, he said. Of the December 1959 letter that said the amendment allowed the foundation to retain ownership, Youdan said, "Frankly, to put it perhaps colloquially, I don't get it. I don't see what significance can be derived from this letter. To me this is a commonplace letter that's a covering letter from a firm of solicitors."[27]

But never mind the 1960 amendment: Thomson was convinced Lowenstein's theory was flawed at a more fundamental level, at its very foundation, in the original 1954 version of Section 2(e). Along the lines of Bill Clinton's famous declaration that "it depends on what the meaning of the word 'is' is," Thomson disputed what the trustees had used the word "for" for. The gallery's trust expert, Michael Furness, had testified that the key elements of the phrasing – "purchasing for . . . art galleries" — referred to gifts, not loans, because "for" meant "for the benefit of" the gallery. Thomson's trust expert, Mark Herbert, agreed with that interpretation of "for" but "the difference between us is that I would suggest that a gratuitous loan of paintings is 'for the benefit of' a gallery, perhaps not as much of a benefit to the gallery as an outright gift, but that it is, nevertheless, a benefit."[28] This meant that the entire case might turn on the meaning of a single preposition: if Cory accepted Herbert's reading of the original 2(e) — a broader interpretation of "for" that did not preclude lending paintings — Lowenstein's "change of heart" theory would evaporate.

Mrs. Ince's destruction of gallery records was similarly unremark-able, Thomson argued. There was no evidence, he noted, that the destroyed documents contained anything different from their surviv-ing replacements. "It was no doubt perfectly sensible to her to destroy old sheets, having just created new ones containing all the available information," he argued. "It would have been duplicative and pot-entially confusing to have two sets of records." And, he pointed out, there was no evidence that the curator, Edwy Cooke, or anyone else at the gallery or on its board, objected to what she had done, nor to her affixing new labels to the frames of the paintings saying they were owned by the foundation. Wardell's veiled objection in his December 1960 letter was nothing of the sort, Thomson insisted. That he never pressed Beaverbrook was a reflection not of his subservience, but of the fact "that he saw nothing to challenge." And as for Tom Forrestall's seemingly critical testimony, it was hardly surprising that the notations about foundation ownership had been added to the rec-ords after he left the gallery, Thomson said. His firing had cut short his own efforts to complete the accession documents, so it was logical that work would have been done on them afterwards.[29]

For good measure, Thomson professed indignation at the gallery's dragging of the saintly Mrs. Ince into the dispute. Lowenstein had not even mentioned her supposedly crucial letter during his questioning of Maxwell at the discovery examination in the summer of 2005, Thomson said. It was only when Judy Budovitch was questioned by the foundation in November 2005 that Lowenstein revealed that "we have a concern that the information on the old sheets was differ-ent from the new sheets. . . . We have grave concerns that records were changed and then destroyed." His description of Mrs. Ince as an "instrument of what appears to have been a breach of trust" by the trustees of the foundation was a "startling" and "remarkable" al-legation that was, Thomson said, contradicted by witnesses including Lady Violet Aitken, who had testified that Mrs. Ince "would never, never do anything wrong, it wouldn't matter what Lord Beaverbrook told her."[30]

Thomson mounted a robust attack on the other elements of the gallery's case. He repeated that newspaper and magazine articles from the 1950s could not be trusted, and that, in any event, the gallery had had those articles in their files during the four decades in which it had formally cited the foundation's ownership over and over again. Helpfully, Thomson listed about fifty of these acknowledgements in his closing brief. To shoot down the importance of the Bank of England CD3 export forms, which listed many of the paintings as gifts, Thomson tracked down Anthony Parker, a former official at the bank, who had literally written the book on exchange control law. Parker, too frail to travel from his home in New Zealand, filed a report to the hearing to say that any exports of goods from the U.K. that did not involve payment and that lacked a date of return, such as an indefinite loan of paintings, "were treated as gifts at that time because the Bank of England had no way of policing whether the loan was repaid or not."[31]

Thomson did not play defence for the entire hearing. He had his own documents to introduce, some of which were not easily explained away. The most powerful was a list of British paintings in the collection in June 1959 that appeared to indicate that almost all of the disputed works were owned by the foundation.

In May 1959, the foundation had prepared a nine-page schedule of paintings in a format similar to the one used for other, undisputed paintings that were sent to the gallery as gifts in later years. The schedule listed paintings acquired by the foundation before September 1958. But the document was never signed or sent to Fredericton. "This near-gift is perhaps the best evidence that no gift ever occurred," Thomson argued. A month later, in June 1959, what would become known as "the asterisk list" was created. Its authorship — indeed, the very continent on which it was drafted — became another key disagreement. Colin B. Mackay, the president of the university and a member of the board of governors, had asked Beaverbrook for "a list of Gallery paintings." The result, labelled "List of paintings now in custody of Beaverbrook Art Gallery," itemized 234 works, of which ninety, almost all of them works in dispute, were marked with asterisks indicating "property of First and Second Beaverbrook Foundations and on extended loan to Beaverbrook Gallery."[32]

Thomson presented expert evidence showing that the list was

7.

216. WHISTLER, J. McNeil	Drawings (2)
217. WIGGINS, W. Guy	(FIFTH Avenue Snow Storm (American Artist))}
218. WILLIAMS, D.	(DAFODDAY) OR WINDLAWN
219. WILSON, G. P.	Paintings in Six Related Rhythms
220. WINT, Peter de	Old Shipyard, Jarrow *
221. WOLSTENHOLME, D.	Harbour Scene (drawing)
222. WOOD, Christopher	The Essex Hunt *
223. WOOD, Christopher	Window, St. Ives *
224. WOOD, Christopher	Two Nudes, Paris *
225. WOOD, Christopher	Two Sailors - drawing
226. WOOTTON, J.	Nude Girl with Flowers *
227. WRIGHT, Joseph	General Onslow *
228. SMITH, J. R.	The Synnot Children *
	Engraving of the Synnot Children after WRIGHT.
229. MINIATURE	Unknown Man
230. ARTIST UNKNOWN	Woman with children)
231. ARTIST UNKNOWN	Interior of a Church) Withdrawn from Collection
232. ARTIST UNKNOWN	Flight into Egypt)
233. ARTIST UNKNOWN	Portrait of a Lady
233A. do.	RUWRY VILLAGE (FIRST WORLD WAR)
234. MALIAVIN, P.	Portrait of Trotsky. (Pencil and chalk)

* Property of First and Second Beaverbrook Foundations and on extended loan to Beaverbrook Gallery.

The last page of the "asterisk list."
Beaverbrook Art Gallery, exhibit 1251

prepared on Canadian paper, using a typeface found on a Canadian typewriter at the time. This was critical, because if Thomson could persuade Cory that the author of the list was Bob Tweedie, it would show that the gallery had acknowledged foundation ownership of the works *before* the opening of the gallery and, more importantly, before the supposed change of heart by Beaverbrook. It appeared, Thomson argued, that Tweedie gave the list to Beaverbrook, who was in Fredericton when it was prepared, because Beaverbrook handed it to Mrs. Ince when he returned to London later in June. Thomson surmised that Mrs. Ince later sent the list back to Tweedie so that he could prepare "clean lists" of paintings in the gallery without any ownership designations.[33] What Tweedie knew, the gallery knew, Thomson argued, and Tweedie had known when he typed the list that those paintings were on loan.

Lowenstein thus had to "keep the asterisk list . . . out of Mr. Tweedie's hands," as Thomson put it. Lowenstein could not refute the expert analysis that it had been drafted in Canada, on a Canadian typewriter, so he argued that *anyone* in Fredericton, not necessarily Tweedie, could have typed it on Beaverbrook's instructions while he was in the city. And, Lowenstein added, when Tweedie contacted Mrs. Ince in London later in June to obtain the list requested by Mackay, Beaverbrook told her to send Tweedie a list "without any marks on it"[34] — meaning that, even if he *had* planned to designate the asterisk-marked paintings as loans, Beaverbrook decided to keep secret, or perhaps remove, these designations. The list, Lowenstein contended, "represents nothing more than Beaverbrook's private ruminations," never acted upon. The foundation, he said, would have to live with the consequences: by not sending the asterisked list, Beaverbrook had allowed the works to be seen as gifts, and the gallery had accepted them on that understanding.

It was on this and other subtle and obscure points — the meaning of the word "for," the conjectured contents of documents destroyed by a loyal secretary forty-six years earlier — that Peter Cory would be forced to base his decision.

As if to jolt everyone involved in the case out of this murk, the final witness to testify in Fredericton injected a note of the bizarre and outlandish into the proceedings. Paul Hachey had arrived at the gallery in 1971 to work as assistant curator and had stayed seventeen years, during which, he testified, he had little interaction with either the board of governors or members of the Aitken family. Although his understanding had been that the paintings were on loan, "we were very shocked when the three pictures were removed," he said, referring to the Gainsborough, *Peasant Girl Gathering Faggots*, and the two Stubbses, *White Dog in a Landscape* and *Hunters Out at Grass*. "I didn't know they could be removed until they were removed."

Hachey conceded on his cross-examination by Thomson's colleague Matthew Milne-Smith that Ian Lumsden, the author of most of the acknowledgements of foundation ownership over the years, was the most reliable authority on the status of the paintings. But, Hachey added, Lumsden had also "complained that the family had very much a hands-on attitude towards the collection, and they were very grabby." When Milne-Smith asked him to confirm that Lumsden had never mentioned any concerns about document tampering, Hachey stunned him and everyone in the room by answering, "Oh, yes, he did. . . . What I can tell you is that Ian Lumsden told me that Sir Max had come in one Saturday morning with a workman with a hacksaw and that they cut open file cabinets in an office belonging to Bob Tweedie. Never to this moment have I been able to find out why it was done."

As he told the story, Hachey asked to see some copies of the accession records, and he pointed to one example where, he said, the words "property of Beaverbrook Foundation" appeared not to have come from the same typewriter as the rest of the page. On another page, the designation was crooked, suggesting it had been added after the fact. "You're not an expert in chemical or document analysis," Milne-Smith pointed out. Hachey agreed; it just seemed logical to assume, he said, that these apparent changes to the records "had something to do with breaking into the filing cabinet."

Sir Max in the gallery with a hacksaw: this image was disastrous for the foundation. As he left the room after his testimony, Hachey smirked, as if pleased that he had thrown a last-minute wrench into the foundation's legal gears. As it turned out, both Milne-Smith and

Lowenstein knew what Hachey was referring to: the decision by the gallery board in 1970 to have a locksmith open Tweedie's filing cabinet while he was out of town, as the struggle with Lady Beaverbrook reached its climax. Sir Max had not been there, and there was no hacksaw involved; the story had apparently become embellished as it filtered through several decades and various tellers. That the Fredericton testimony would conclude on this absurd note illustrated just how much of the case relied on imprecise perceptions that had evolved into myth.

*

After a brief session in Toronto to hear from art experts about the minutiae of accession records and other gallery document-keeping, Lowenstein and Thomson had a month's break to prepare their closing arguments for Peter Cory. They returned to Fredericton at the end of November, each hoping to synthesize his sprawling case into a coherent and persuasive narrative.

Lowenstein went through his "change of heart" theory again, but with a subtle difference. Earlier, he had claimed "the trustees" of the foundation had committed a breach of trust. Now Lowenstein blamed Beaverbrook himself in his role as head of the foundation. Mrs. Ince had admitted to destroying records, he said, but she was "following orders from Lord Beaverbrook — the grand pooh-bah of the gallery and the grand pooh-bah of the foundation." What those records contained was lost to history, but that was not the gallery's problem. "It's her letter," Lowenstein said. "It's the foundation's letter. It's incumbent on them to tell us." If they could not, then, he said, Cory was compelled to rule that the eighty-five paintings in dispute delivered before 1960 were gifts, despite Beaverbrook's efforts to retroactively turn them into loans. The other forty-eight, delivered after 1960, he continued, had to be considered permanent, indefinite, irrevocable loans. "One thing we can rely on is his own ego," Lowenstein said. "He was the ultimate hometown boy made good. He dominated this city. This is where he could be seen in his best light." It was not credible that, at the end of his life, Beaverbrook would have allowed the possibility — even in theory — that any part of his legacy might be taken back to England the day after he died.

Thomson, too, recapped his entire case, citing again the dozens of times the gallery had said the foundation owned the paintings. He also pounced on what he now saw as a major concession by the gallery: Lowenstein's admission that forty-eight paintings were loans. The gallery had effectively abandoned its claim to paintings sent after the end of 1959, he said, "presumably because that claim was literally crushed under an avalanche of evidence." And it had undermined its case for the pre-1959 group as well: the gallery had pointed out early in the hearing that the paintings in dispute did not have identification numbers with the prefix "L" for loan, as other works on loan did. Now the gallery was acknowledging that the post-1959 group *were* loans — even though they were not marked with an "L." If a post-1959 work could be a loan despite the absence of an "L," then the lack of an "L" was meaningless for the pre-1959 group as well.

But Thomson had a problem in the form of Peter Cory. As he tried to demolish Lowenstein's case, the arbitrator repeatedly interrupted him to challenge his logic. Beaverbrook "should have said something, perhaps along these lines: 'These are a loan, not part of my generous gift, and can be recalled at any time,'" Cory told Thomson. "Why wouldn't a man like Lord Beaverbrook, who took such notice of detail, not make a notice of disclosure? Why the silence?" Cory was also troubled that the "asterisk list" had not been sent to the gallery from London. "Here we have a list circulating that is clearly marked with asterisks to verify the ownership of paintings, but what goes to the board of governors? A blank list. . . . This is concealment, not disclosure."[35] When Thomson argued that several of the gallery's witnesses were "peripheral" to the case, Cory stopped him again. "Does that apply to Mrs. Watson-Fisher?" he asked, meaning Beaverbrook's Canadian art advisor.

"Yes," Thomson said.

"Really?" Cory asked.

None of them had seen the foundation's records, Thomson told him. None had any great involvement with the gallery.

Cory didn't consider Claire Watson-Fisher peripheral at all. "I will retain my high impression of her while recognizing her limitations," he said. "She's a very credible, decent witness. She walked with him and talked with him, like in the old hymn: 'He walked with me and talked with me and told me of his dreams.' I found that moving evidence and credible evidence."

"It's an involvement issue," Thomson said, carrying the debate perhaps one sentence too far.

Cory uttered a trademark "All righty," then paused. "I won't scratch her completely from my list. I'll keep her and treasure her."

Thomson fell back on more persuasive arguments: there was no document in which Beaverbrook explicitly donated any of the paintings to the gallery, and no document in which the gallery had explicitly accepted any of them as donations. There was no way such an impressive gift could "slip through the cracks" like that, Thomson argued. And based on legal precedent and legislation, the time limitation on the gallery's ability to claim otherwise had passed decades ago — particularly because the documents it was relying on in 2006 had been available to it in the 1960s.[36] Of course, the gallery's response was that those limitations did not apply because it had been deceived. But this argument, too, was unfair to the foundation, an example of "extraordinary" prejudice. "It's a case where even the most innocuous facts have been cast in a sinister light with a view toward proving misconduct fifty years after the fact," Thomson said. "If the gallery is going to stand up fifty years later and allege non-disclosure in a case of this nature, where all of the relevant witnesses are dead and the documents that have survived are manifestly incomplete, how in the world can [the foundation] meet the legal burden?"[37]

It sounded like a last-ditch plea. Cory's interventions did not bode well for Thomson's case. And when Lowenstein returned to the podium for his half-day rebuttal of Thomson's closing arguments, the retired judge signalled again that the foundation was in trouble. Supposing, Cory asked Lowenstein in mid-argument, that the pre-1960 group of eighty-five paintings were gifts. What about the argument that the post-1960 batch should have been *explicitly* designated as an irrevocable loan? Lowenstein returned to his dubious argument about Beaverbrook's ego — the idea that he would not have wanted *any* of the paintings removed — but the foundation lawyers shifted nervously in their seats. For several minutes, Cory quizzed Lowenstein on the implications of the "change of heart" theory, a sign that he was, at least, seeing the case in the gallery's terms. He was willing to ponder, at least hypothetically, that the change of heart had been real. "There seems little doubt that [gifts were] part of his original intention," Cory told Lowenstein. "But as you point out — it's your case — things change."

Indeed. Over two years, Lowenstein's case had evolved as it roamed through the generations of the Aitken family, blaming first a "series of abuses" by Sir Max, then a desire for management fees by Maxwell. But as he summed up, Lowenstein pointed the finger at Beaverbrook himself. He shed his earnest lawyer's demeanour; his jaw was set, his face visibly angry. The foundation's entire case, he said, had been based on "a question of character." Thomson had been indignant that anyone had dared impugn the reputation of Sir Max or Mrs. Ince, Lowenstein said sarcastically. "We heard how fastidious they were, how scrupulous they were. Everybody in this room knows you cannot say that about the man himself. . . . They want to prop him up by his advisors."

In his opening brief, Lowenstein had dismissed "the concept of a punitive, disciplinarian Lord Beaverbrook" who would leave behind "a shell of a gallery." Now he accused the great man of far worse — of committing a deliberate, fraudulent concealment, a breach of his duties as a trustee of the foundation he had created, which had made this painful dispute inevitable. It was as if Beaverbrook himself, dead for four decades, was suddenly on trial — a surreal turn of events in a province where so many buildings and monuments bore his name, and where a premier had once told Bob Tweedie, "We must remember the greatness of the man."

This new, less flattering image of the great benefactor was not the gallery's fault, Lowenstein said. No, it was Timothy and Maxwell who had brought this upon their grandfather's name. "We have heard that Lord Beaverbrook left Canada in financial disgrace and came back to New Brunswick in triumph and eventually decided to open the art gallery he always dreamed about," Lowenstein told Cory. "Now, his two grandsons have required him to be exhumed and forensically dissected in a way from which his reputation in this province will probably never recover. They have done great harm to Beaverbrook's reputation."

He would not, he added, waste Peter Cory's time by asking the arbitrator to salvage that reputation. "It is not a worthwhile endeavour."

Bernard Riordon, director of the Beaverbrook Art Gallery, with
The Fountain of Indolence by J.M.W. Turner, December 8, 2006.
Nigel Dickson

CHAPTER TWELVE

"He did not act in the best interests of the gallery"

It was the second week of December when the arbitration hearing ended. Fredericton, the little capital that once hung on Beaverbrook's every word, settled in to wait for a verdict on his legacy. Down on Queen Street, next to the gallery, workers were toiling behind tarps that covered the old grey Lord Beaverbrook Hotel. Its new owners had decided to rebrand it as a Crowne Plaza franchise, and the dreary pewter-coloured facade was being transformed with a brighter cream-and-red design. The hotel would officially be known as the Crowne Plaza Lord Beaverbrook, but the older part of its name, chiselled into the stone over the door, was barely visible below the chain's bold, modern logo. No one protested that the Beaverbrook name was losing the prominence it once had. It was an afterthought, a vestige of an era as ancient as Rome.

Peter Cory, the arbitrator, had told the two teams of lawyers that he hoped to have his decision written by the end of February, or by mid-March at the very latest. Then he ambled out of the room, and Larry Lowenstein and Kent Thomson shook hands, congratulating each other on their efforts. Their colleagues, too, mingled and chatted amiably as they packed up their briefcases and prepared to rush to the airport to catch the next flight home to Toronto. They had waged a long and exhausting battle for Beaverbrook's art, and this was a moment of well-earned relaxation and collegiality. But it lasted only a moment: Thomson was already thinking ahead to how he would craft an appeal, in the event that Cory found in favour of the gallery. He would soon be fuming again about another burst of media coverage; springing from the hearing's conclusion, it revived the idea that Maxwell and his family were out for personal gain.

Still, the heavy lifting was over for Thomson. Not so for Lowenstein: he was also representing the gallery in its parallel dispute with Timothy Aitken's Beaverbrook Canadian Foundation, a suit that remained mired in preliminary procedural skirmishes before the Court of Queen's Bench of New Brunswick. There was no trial on the horizon before 2008 at the earliest because the two sides had agreed to put that process on hold until the arbitration was resolved; after the hearings at the Wu Centre wrapped up, players from both sides speculated privately about whether Cory's decision might prompt the gallery or the foundation to agree to a settlement. After all, neither side had bottomless pockets, though the New Brunswick government announced before Christmas it would lend the gallery an additional $3.5 million to help it keep up with its legal bills. Whether he was facing a far-off trial or imminent settlement negotiations, Lowenstein had to be prepared.

The Canadian Foundation case seemed refreshingly straightforward compared to the sprawling epic of the arbitration. At its core was the legitimacy of the deal Sir Max Aitken had engineered in 1970 to put an end to Christofor's harassment of the gallery: the purchase by the Canadian Foundation of seventy-seven paintings that she claimed belonged to her and to the Sir James Dunn Foundation, which she controlled. The gallery would have to prove that the paintings had not been hers, or her foundation's, to sell, a seemingly simple question.

But nothing was simple in this war of the Beaverbrooks. Throughout 2005 and 2006, the lawyers battled on a variety of fronts. The foundation's counsel, Rodney Gillis, of Saint John, accused the gallery of failing to provide a promised list of paintings it alleged had been removed by Sir Max. The gallery, meanwhile, suggested that Gillis had asked to see thousands of unnecessary documents, forcing employees into a cumbersome and comical shuttling of boxes through the gallery's loading dock to the nearby hotel, where discovery hearings were taking place. A judge had to rule on the routine question of whether Judy Budovitch's discovery could be rescheduled so she could visit her ailing mother in Cape Breton; another ruling was needed to establish that it was up to the gallery, not the foundation, to decide whether Timothy would be examined in London or would have to travel to Fredericton.[1] By early 2007 his discovery had still not taken place. "I'm making it as hard as I possibly can for them," Timothy admitted in London in March, "and I don't actually have the time or the patience to waste my time with them."[2]

Despite the poisoned atmosphere, the outline of each side's case was clear. The foundation would argue, as its U.K. counterpart had during the arbitration, that the proof was right there in the gallery's own files. In this case, the single most compelling piece of evidence was a letter that the board's chairman, Wallace Bird, had sent to Sir Max in 1970 to thank him for having the foundation spend $250,000 to buy the paintings from Christofor. This was the clearest possible indication that the gallery had accepted, rather than contested, the legitimacy of Christofor's earlier ownership and the foundation's purchase. The gallery, however, argued that the clarity of those documents ignored a practical reality that was hard to deny. "None of the staff or Governors of the Gallery were in a position to challenge Sir Maxwell or Lady Beaverbrook in relation to the dispute," the gallery's Fredericton lawyer, David Young, wrote in one document, "as they enjoyed dominant positions in relation to the Gallery's staff and Board of Governors." Sir Max and Christofor, he said, had ignored their legal duty, as co-custodians of the gallery, to protect its interests by disclosing their own conflicts of interest and by urging the gallery to get independent legal advice.[3]

The gallery also argued that the 1970 agreement had stipulated that the gallery would be the sole beneficiary of the sale and that the paintings would become part of the Beaverbrook Art Gallery's permanent collection. In fact, Young argued, Lady Beaverbrook had agreed to the sale "only on the condition" that the paintings remained in the gallery in Fredericton.[4] But the more fundamental point was that the paintings the foundation bought in 1970 "were not in fact in the possession of the sellers," Lowenstein's colleague, Ahab Abdel-Aziz, said during discovery hearings in 2006. "They didn't have the ownership to pass. So, being aware of that, we are suspect of these documents. . . . She purported to sell to the Canadian Foundation works that she could not possibly have owned . . . These transactions are a sham."[5]

For three of the disputed paintings, the gallery could rely on the affidavit Sir Alec Martin of Christie's had drafted in September 1959, after Christofor had told Beaverbrook she had loaned "her" Sickerts to the gallery only for his lifetime. Martin had written that Christofor had acknowledged at least three times that the portraits — *Sir James Dunn, Viscount Castlerosse*, and *H.M. King Edward VIII* — were gifts. But matters were considerably murkier for other works. During discovery, Gillis, the foundation's lawyer, clashed at length with Abdel-Aziz over the gallery's suggestion that there were multiple, contradictory purchase records for a painting by James Tissot. One showed the Sir James Dunn Foundation buying it from a dealer in 1960; another recorded the foundation buying it from Christofor in 1964. A third identified it as a 1961 gift to the gallery, purchased by Beaverbrook with money donated by the industrialist Eric Bowater. "I rather suspect the answer is that Lady Beaverbrook created documents and caused records of transactions to take place without caring much about the truth of those transactions, because she clearly understood that she was asking for records to be created that were contradictory to what had already taken place," Abdel-Aziz told Gillis. "I don't know how you would purport to rely on a series of ledgers that manifestly record a falsehood to suggest that, when it's convenient to the case you'd like to make, they ought to be believed."[6]

Given the ambiguity and the rancour, the idea of a settlement seemed far-fetched. During our interview for this book in March 2007, however, Timothy Aitken — though as animated and combative as ever — sounded at times like a man wishing he could wash his hands of the dispute. "New Brunswick as far as I'm concerned can go to hell," he said. "I'm not very interested in the whole thing anymore. I believe the whole thing is disgraceful. The Canadian Foundation has a better case, I think, by anybody's standard, than the English foundation, because *it bought the bloody pictures*." His preoccupation now

- 2 -

gallery. She said to me did I really mean that and I told her yes and that I knew Lord Beaverbrook would be tremendously grateful if she would kindly consent to give these pictures to the gallery. She then said she would.

When I reached Fredericton to hang the exhibition, I met Lady Dunn the day I arrived and we discussed not only the great picture by Dali that she had given, but I also told her that before I could complete the hanging of the pictures I should want to have the three Sickert pictures at the gallery. She told me that her sister did not like the pictures leaving the house and that she had had some difficulty with her sister about them. I pointed out that she had already kindly and generously promised to give them to the gallery and that the gallery without them would, to my mind, be very much impoverished. She then said she would send them along and after some delay I eventually got them along and they now hang in the gallery, and I think make an extraordinary attraction to the gallery. Her picture by Dali, of course, hangs prominently in the centre gallery, a blaze of blue, but I think that the three Sickert pictures are outstanding of their kind and will, to my mind, go down as three of the great possessions of the gallery.

When I had completed the hanging of the exhibition, I was asked by the press to give my views about the collection and having in mind that I must include the

A page from Sir Alec Martin's affidavit with two confirmations that Christofor gave the Sickert paintings to the gallery.
Beaverbrook U.K. Foundation, exhibit 14-1924

was not the Fredericton gallery but a centre for media ethics that the foundation had endowed at McGill University in Montreal. "That's what life is about for me. I'm interested in my grandfather's name being kept alive in people, not statues or pictures or any other rubbish. I think I'm on to something that makes a good deal of sense."[7]

Timothy's comments came in response to a theory I put to him: as the wealthier of the Beaverbrook grandsons, he had opted against arbitration because he had deep enough pockets to fund a more protracted and expensive battle in court. "We haven't spent any significant money yet and I'm really not inclined to do so," he replied. He pointed out that the Beaverbrook Canadian Foundation was represented by Rodney Gillis — one of New Brunswick's best litigators, but not nearly as pricey as the blue-chip Toronto firm that his cousin had hired. "I don't think we need to employ top firms," Timothy said. "I think we do it on the merits of the facts and that's it. We are using a law firm in New Brunswick that is not mega-expensive. . . . So I'm not inclined to spend money. In fact, I will stop the money being spent. . . . I won't use expensive Toronto law firms to do things which are garbage. The case is what it is. [Gillis] can present that very simply and straightforwardly."[8]

While Timothy was inclined by early 2007 to dismiss the entire dispute as inconsequential, his cousin Maxwell remained preoccupied with persuading New Brunswickers and Canadians that he was not the ogre he had been made out to be. This may have been a natural reaction to the bad publicity that continued to plague him: in January he was forced to shut down a website, CheekyMoon, owned by a company he ran. The site, with its self-described "traditional British end-of-the-pier saucy humour," featured games such as Naughty Netball and promised players the chance to win the services of "delectable guys and gals" known as CheekyButlers and CheekyMaids.[9] The British papers, as well as Canadian media that had followed the art dispute, gleefully reported the site's demise. "You get some wrong, you get some right," Maxwell told a reporter. "I've done both."[10] There had been other negative headlines several months earlier about the Bank of Scotland going after him again for unpaid debts. The situation was nowhere near as dire as his 1992 bankruptcy, he said.

His finances, he told me in our interview, were "very strong, I would say, in fact, probably stronger than ever."[11]

Nonetheless, at the end of February, the deadline Peter Cory had given for the release of his decision, Maxwell travelled to Canada and gave a series of media interviews "to try to get a fair and reasonable balance of what happened," as he put it to the *Globe and Mail*. He explained again the sensible offer the foundation had made to Riordon and the gallery. He clarified again that he and his family did not live at Cherkley and could not benefit from the restoration.[12] But on the most critical question of all — the fate of the paintings — Maxwell's public-relations blitz raised more questions than it answered. The very last paragraph of Kent Thomson's closing submission to Peter Cory in December had said that if the U.K. Foundation won the case, its trustees were "committed irrevocably to abide by the terms of the loan agreement provided to the Gallery in January 2004, and seek only the immediate return of the paintings by Turner and Freud."[13] In his round of interviews, Maxwell said the proposal he had made to Riordon was "no longer in existence"[14] — a remark that opened the door for the foundation to remove all the paintings immediately if it won ownership.

"When you get into this sort of fight," Maxwell explained during our interview, "all bets are off." But that was not what Kent Thomson's submission to Cory had said, I pointed out. "What I'm saying," he answered, "is that we have not said we are going to sell the Turner and the Freud. We've gone right away from that and we have not made a decision on what would be sold. What we have said, and Mr. Thomson is absolutely correct, is we're not just going to take the collection out of the gallery and leave the gallery with some empty space. Whether we give them the six million that they wanted towards their endowment fund is another matter. We've been forced to spend more than that on legal fees. So that, we'll have to see about. It's clearly not in our interest to see the gallery diminished and denuded. We share a name. I share a name with the foundation and the foundation shares a name with the gallery. So you have to plan for the peace."

That plan, he hinted, might require some heads to roll at the Beaverbrook Art Gallery, though he would not specify whose. "Would you leave a hundred million with people who tried to steal it from you?" he asked. "So you either change the arrangement or you change the people." Then Maxwell — who said he was "surprised" when Cory compared his grandfather to the Nazi propagandist Joseph Goebbels — appeared to draw a similar parallel of his own between the gallery administration and Hitler's regime. "We do not control who runs the gallery, but I imagine in 1945 it was important that there not be civil disorder in Germany, and peace was planned around that. Equally, we'd like to find a way forward. Our collection has to stay somewhere. I can't hang it in here," he said, gesturing around the small office the foundation rented from Timothy's company in London's Knightsbridge district. "For us to have an ongoing relationship, we'll need to mend some fences. And there may be some people there whom it will be very difficult to mend fences with both ways."[15]

*

My London interviews with Timothy and Maxwell Aitken were six days apart. One morning between those two appointments, I travelled by commuter train from the cacophony of London's Victoria Station to a small, old-fashioned brick train station in the bucolic village of Leatherhead, forty minutes from the city. It was a mild, sunny March day. Anna Nelson, an attractive blonde woman in her forties, met me outside and took me on a five-minute drive out of the village and into the Surrey countryside. Just off a roundabout, we turned onto a private road that cut across a broad field. We passed rows of saplings and two small houses before rounding a small hill, where Cherkley Court materialized in front of us.

Nelson had been the property manager for the Royal Horticultural Society, overseeing the visits of 700,000 people per year to its gardens and greenhouses, when she was approached by a headhunter working for the Beaverbrook U.K. Foundation. The trustees wanted someone with solid credentials to oversee the running of Cherkley, which would finally open to the public at Easter 2007, a month after my visit. Nelson, who had been looking for a change of pace, accepted their offer. She knew little about Beaverbrook — "I think everyone in England knows that he was a press baron, but not much more than that," she said — but her expertise with facilities management was exactly what the foundation needed, even if her advice was occasionally dismaying. To avoid legal liability, she had told the trustees that a grotto below the house decorated entirely in sea shells — a costly and painstaking effort — had to be chained off to prevent garden tourists from venturing inside. "People would just cut their heads open and children would cut their hands on these shells," she told me as landscapers groomed some walking paths nearby. Maxwell was more easily persuaded on some of the other modern tourist conventions: though he was anxious to avoid kitsch, he had agreed to the printing of two tasteful postcards that could be sold to visitors.[16]

The art dispute in Canada was not the only drama associated with the Cherkley restoration. In another example of the adversity besetting the foundation, people living near the estate had fought the project. "Neighbours, such as they are — they're not exactly on top of each other — had come to find it agreeable to have a reclusive old lady and her sister living there, because that didn't create any traffic or disturbance or any change, really," Maxwell told me. "It got very personal, talking as if I wanted to have wild parties there and so on and so forth. Outrageous allegations." The local council agreed that the transformation from private residence to public site would inevitably increase traffic, and it demanded the construction of a second access road to avoid congestion at the entrance to the property, which was just a hundred feet away from a roundabout. Then homeowners overlooking the field that would be bisected by the new road objected. "Things like, they'd be disturbed by headlights at night coming down there," Maxwell said. "Now we have the very same people asking if they can have a private look around because they're hearing that it's so marvellous and all the rest of it."[17] The neighbours were eventually soothed by the imposition of several conditions: the house itself can be booked for a maximum of fifty events a year, there are to be no tents, "and we can't land helicopters," Nelson said.

The house itself had been restored to its former glory, its exterior walls a bright cream colour, the main hall's magnificent marble columns and Victorian furniture bathed in natural light from the dome in the roof. There were no signs of the stains created by the water that had leaked in. Nelson led me through the drawing room and the cinema and the breakfast room, identifying which would be available for events and which would not. Two weddings were already scheduled at Cherkley for 2007, with two others tentatively booked. The foundation's hope was that, given its proximity to Heathrow Airport, the house would become a popular venue for European conferences and symposia — an ironic target market, given Beaverbrook's vehement opposition to Britain forging closer ties to the continent. Holding a function at Cherkley would not be cheap: rates for the least expensive room, the morning room, were £700 a day, or more than $1,500 Canadian, while the priciest, the Orangery, would cost £1,700 a day, about $3,800. In peak season, the entire house could be had for £8,000 a day, or $18,000. The foundation was clearly determined that this aspect of Beaverbrook's legacy would not become, as Maxwell had said of the paintings in Fredericton, "a negative yield."

Nelson showed me into the dining room, where my eyes were drawn to a painting on the wall, a bright if indistinct smudge of colour that resembled Venice. I was about to speak when she said, "It's not a real Turner." "I know," I replied. It had to be the fake Turner, *View from the Giudecca*, which had once hung in the gallery in Fredericton. This was one of the paintings Le Roux Smith Le Roux had urged Beaverbrook to buy, setting in motion his eventual firing as the press baron's art advisor. "So he actually bought it as a *real* Turner," Nelson said when I told her the story. "Oh my."

She pointed over my shoulder. "Now that's a real Stubbs, as I understand it," she said, "but not a very good one, apparently." I turned and realized I was looking at *White Dog in a Landscape*, one of the three works Sir Max had called back from the gallery in 1977. *White Dog* was the one that had failed to sell at auction, and here it was in front of my eyes, still in the foundation's possession thirty years later — easy enough to find, it occurred to me, in the event that Peter Cory decided it was owned by the Beaverbrook Art Gallery.

For sheer historical voyeurism, however, nothing could match Cherkley's library, lined with signed first editions by many of the most prominent British authors of the twentieth century. It led out onto the legendary terrace where Beaverbrook had entertained his famous guests. Further adding to its romance, the library was not one of the rooms available for rent; the public would never be able to leaf through Cherkley's guest book, as Anna Nelson allowed me to do. There were the signatures of the famous, such as Winston Churchill and Joseph Kennedy, as well as many of those who were present at the creation of the Beaverbrook Art Gallery: the premier of New Brunswick, Hugh John Flemming, Robert Tweedie, Michael Wardell, and Sir James Dunn and Christofor. "I want to come back," Dunn wrote during one visit. "So do I please," his wife added. "I find it hard to leave this refuge," Dunn jotted on another page. "Too short a story," he wrote on a third.

On a left-hand page toward the end of the book, Michael Wardell's final visit to Cherkley was noted, in his precise penmanship, as "May 24-June 8, 1964," the latter date the eve of Beaverbrook's death. Next to it, also in his hand, was an addition, "June 9-28." Other than two entries for July, the rest of the page was blank. On the facing page, there are four entries from October 1965, from Christofor and three members of her family. She signed as "M. Beaverbrook, St. Andrews, N.B." Next to the date was a one-word remark: "Hurrah!!!"

*

Returning to London, I walked from Victoria Station to Tate Britain, the art gallery that is home to more than 150 works by J.M.W. Turner. That morning on the way to Cherkley, a headline in the *Times* had caught my eye: "Boy raids his piggy-bank to save a Turner." In the accompanying photograph, eight-year-old Matthew Hughes glanced up at a Turner watercolour, *The Blue Rigi*, which, the Tate had announced the previous day, had been saved from being exported out of England. "The 1842 painting is regarded as one of the finest achievements not only of Turner but of any artist working in watercolour," the story said.[18]

The shimmering work was one of three in a series Turner had painted of Mount Rigi, a mountain above Lucerne, Switzerland. It had been sold by Christie's in June 2006 for £5.8 million, nearly tripling the previous record for a Turner watercolour.[19] The winning bidder was a foreign buyer, and the British government delayed the required export permit, declaring the work "of special significance for the study of the work of Turner and, in particular, his final master-pieces." The Tate was given until March 20, 2007 to raise enough money to match the auction price, and the gallery teamed up with the Art Fund, a charity devoted to keeping British works in the country, for a public appeal.[20] They devised an innovative Internet-based "Buy a Brushstroke" campaign that allowed donors to sponsor one pixel of an online image of *The Blue Rigi*. Donors who bought enough pixels could spell out their names in the sky above Turner's Rigi. The money poured in — from a retired couple who had spent their honeymoon in Lucerne, from a man whose parents had visited the mountain after the Second World War, and from young Matthew Hughes, who emp-tied his piggy bank of its £9.20 to help save the Turner. Nineteen days ahead of the deadline, the Tate declared victory, and the painting joined its vast Turner collection.[21]

On its first full day as a rescued national treasure, *The Blue Rigi* was attracting steady traffic in a small gallery at the opposite end of the Tate from the rest of its Turners. The gallery had borrowed the two other works in the series, *The Red Rigi* and *The Dark Rigi*, and like other visitors, I waited patiently for my turn to look at the luminescent trio up close. "Is J.M.W. Turner our favourite painter?" a reader wondered in the *Guardian*'s weekly You Asked feature. "The public has come to love Turner as no other painter of his era," replied art expert Maev Kennedy. "The miserable git had an ability, out of what often seems a singularly joyless life, to lock joy into his can-vas or paper." Kennedy recalled that when *The Blue Rigi* appeal was launched, many wondered if it was "one Turner too many." But the campaign had captured the public imagination, and, Kennedy noted, the controversial increase in the projected cost of London's 2012 Olympic Games would have paid for 1,667 *Rigi*s. "The Turner," she concluded, "was cheap at the price."[22]

It was a coincidence that this Turner had been "saved" just as I arrived in London to research the Beaverbrook dispute, not an omen. But if it had been an omen, what would it have portended? That *The Fountain of Indolence* would return to Turner-loving England, as the Beaverbrook U.K. Foundation intended? Or that it would remain on public display, as the Beaverbrook Art Gallery wanted?

This was not quite the dilemma, as the Tate's rescue of *The Blue Rigi* made clear. Turner was undoubtedly hot; if *The Fountain of Indolence* ever did go on the market, it would likely fetch or exceed the price Sotheby's had predicted in 2002 — roughly twice that of *The Blue Rigi*. And the *Rigi* campaign had been the largest, most ambitious and unlikeliest fundraising effort of its kind in British history. Not even the Tate would be able to afford *The Fountain of Indolence*, and the painting would probably end up in a private collection, perhaps outside the U.K. The only way the public was certain to have a chance to enjoy it would be for it to remain in the little gallery that Lord Beaverbrook had built in New Brunswick.

*

That evening I left London for Manchester. The next morning I found the Manchester Art Gallery, just off St. Peter's Square in the heart of the city, and hurried up the broad stone steps to its main entrance. Floor plan in hand, I made my way impatiently to the second floor. In a small gallery devoted to portraits and landscapes of eighteenth-century Britain, I found her: Beaverbrook's favourite painting of all, Thomas Gainsborough's *Peasant Girl Gathering Faggots*.

Despite the humility or — perhaps this was my imagination — the touch of sadness in her face, she dominated the room. The only work that dared to compete with her for the visitor's attention was a Stubbs, *Cheetah and Stag with Two Indians*, on the opposite wall. The rest of the room was filled with smaller canvases by Sir Joshua Reynolds, Joseph Wright of Derby, William Hogarth, and Gainsborough himself. But the *Peasant Girl* outshone them all. The colours were darker than they had appeared in reproductions I had seen, but they were richer and more vibrant. The trees were a mustier green, the sky a darker, more brooding violet. Stepping closer, I could see some cracking of the paint near the girl's right arm, but otherwise the painting appeared to be in fine condition.

Her arrival in Manchester was not nearly as contentious as the eventual dispute over her departure from Fredericton, but it did set tongues wagging in the city. Thomas Agnew and Sons, the venerable London art dealers, had bought the painting at the July 1977 Sotheby's auction for £92,000. After restoring it, they put it up for sale for £200,000, then offered it to the city-owned gallery in Manchester at a reduced price of £170,000, realizing a profit of eighty-five per cent. Manchester's elected council was criticized for approving the purchase in April 1978, just a month after raising local taxes. The *Daily Express,* which had touted its proprietor's purchase of the painting in 1956, and which had been under non-Beaverbrook ownership for less than a year, adopted a populist tone, sarcastically referring to the "special" price, the "sound investment" and the council's claim that the *Peasant Girl* would "help to attract people and business back into the city." Its headline was more literal: "Portrait of big spenders."[23]

A family of four came into the gallery while I was looking at the painting. "See that pretty lady?" the mother asked her young daughter, pointing at the *Peasant Girl*. "She's a ballerina." The little girl was too clever for that. "She's not a *ballerina*," she protested, sounding exasperated.

No, she is a peasant girl, wearing a look of gratitude and servility towards a benevolent noble. And that made her exile to Manchester an irresistible metaphor for what had befallen the Beaverbrook name in New Brunswick: a loss of prestige, the vanishing of deference. The more charitable view of the old man's love of the painting, and of the province, was that he simply wanted people to enjoy the art. And given his adoration for this work above all the others he had ever acquired, I sensed as I stood there looking at her that — regardless of the overwhelming logic of the foundation's case — Beaverbrook would have seen this exile as the ultimate shattering of his legacy. He would not have wanted this, of all paintings, to be in this gallery or in any other, but only in the one he had so lovingly built in Fredericton.

I went downstairs to the gallery gift shop to buy a postcard of the *Peasant Girl* to bring home to New Brunswick.

They were sold out.

*

Peter Cory's first promised delivery date, the end of February, had already come and gone. His at-the-latest deadline of mid-March passed as well, and still there was no decision. Bernard Riordon, the director of the gallery in Fredericton, was naturally anxious. His contract as director, originally for five years, had been extended by another three with the hope that, once the dispute was resolved, he could get his strategic plan back on track and, as he had put it, "make the mummies dance." As the days ticked towards the end of March with no word from Cory, Riordon began feeling physically ill. He concluded that the stress of the wait was getting to him until he and his doctor noticed that he had mistakenly been prescribed a half-strength dose of the medication he took for the high blood pressure that ran in his family.

For the Aitkens, meanwhile, life went on: on Sunday, March 25, the *Daily Telegraph* reported that Maxwell's son, also named Max, was engaged to marry Inés Nieto Gómez-Valencia, whom he had met one night when he accidentally locked himself out of his flat. Young Max, the fourth in his line to have that name and the next Lord Beaverbrook, had invested a year earlier in *The Sportsman*, a new daily aimed at the lucrative sports gambling market. It failed within months, and Max resigned as managing director, prompting newspaper stories contrasting the collapse with his great-grandfather's success. So word of his pending wedding was a much more pleasant bit of publicity. Ms. Gómez-Valencia, the *Telegraph* noted, was "a delightful art dealer who specialized in Old Masters from her native Spain."[24]

And then the agonizing wait was over.

The day after young Max's engagement made news, Peter Cory sent his 114-page decision to Larry Lowenstein and Kent Thomson. In their respective offices, both men read through the document quickly and came to the same conclusion: it was a sweeping victory for the gallery.

With one notable exception, Cory had accepted Lowenstein's narrative in its entirety. The newspaper articles — meaningless, in Thomson's view — were clear evidence that Beaverbrook considered the paintings to be gifts, Cory said. "Not only did Lord Beaverbrook adopt the articles, he was proud of them and made a point of sending them to friends," he wrote. "A great propagandist cannot escape, any more than any other citizen, the consequences of authorizing and adopting public statements that indicate his intent to make a gift." The export documents' use of the same word, "gift" — a generic designation that applied to loans, the foundation had argued — further confirmed Beaverbrook's intentions, Cory found. The change to Section 2(e) of the trust deed in 1960 provided more corroboration: by adding the power to lend, the foundation was implicitly acknowledging that paintings previously sent to Fredericton had been gifts. "No matter how heavy or strict the onus may be on those arguing that a gift was made, the Gallery has more than satisfied it," Cory wrote. "The evidence taken together has a cumulative effect and irrefutably establishes that a gift was made." In the unlikely event that Beaverbrook truly did intend to lend the paintings, he "participated in a massive misrepresentation" and was bound by his own characterization of the works as a gift.[25]

More importantly, Cory ruled that the foundation itself was bound to honour that same characterization. He accepted Lowenstein's view that Beaverbrook's intentions and the foundation's intentions were, in legal terms, one and the same. In hiding information from the gallery — the infamous and never-delivered "asterisk list" and Mrs. Ince's changes to the records in 1960 — Beaverbrook had breached the duty he owed to the gallery, a breach for which the foundation was responsible. "I cannot speculate as to what was destroyed by Mrs. Ince," Cory wrote. "However, the fact remains that the destruction of the old records was selective and was carried out pursuant to the directions of Lord Beaverbrook. In those circumstances it would, if necessary, be appropriate for me to draw adverse inferences as to what was destroyed." The foundation had to be held accountable for the changes — and that meant not only an award of ownership to the gallery of all the paintings it had held when it opened, but also a finding that Gainsborough's *Peasant Girl Gathering Faggots* and Stubbs's *White Dog in a Landscape* and *Hunters Out at Grass* had been the property of the gallery when they were removed. The gallery's apparent consent in 1977 "was not an effective and informed consent as a result of Lord Beaverbrook's breaches of the fiduciary duty he owed the Gallery," Cory said.[26] Though *White Dog* was still at Cherkley, the arbitrator acknowledged that the other two works had been sold and were now beyond the gallery's reach. He ordered the foundation to compensate the gallery for the agreed-upon value of those two paintings and several lesser works that had also been removed.

This notion of Beaverbrook's breach of his duties also nullified Thomson's argument on time limitations. The gallery's four-decade long acknowledgement of a loan could not prevent it from claiming ownership now, Cory said. "If there was any change with regard to his understanding of ownership then he had a duty to disclose it to the Gallery," Cory wrote. "Common decency required no less. More importantly, the law required no less. Yet he carefully concealed, until Mrs. Ince had made the changes in the records in the vault of the Gallery, any indication that in his opinion a very substantial portion of his magnificent gift was, in reality, no more than a loan that could be recalled at any moment."[27]

Though couched in Cory's style — an idiosyncratic blend of legalisms and expressions of his congenial personality — the decision amounted to a harsh indictment of a man who had once been above reproach in New Brunswick. "It cannot be forgotten that Lord Beaverbrook insisted that the Gallery Act provide that he would be a member of the Gallery Board of Governors and the Custodian of the Gallery. He sought and obtained the position which imposed upon him the fiduciary duties that the law rightly recognizes are strict and onerous," Cory wrote. "It was the lack of disclosure and calculated concealment by Lord Beaverbrook himself which led to the problems presented in this case. He did not act in the best interests of the Gallery. . . . It was his actions and his failure to disclose pertinent facts which gave rise to this unfortunate situation and the ensuing litigation."[28]

The only silver lining for the foundation was that Cory's acceptance of Lowenstein's "change of heart" theory meant that the forty-eight paintings sent to the gallery after the 1960 trust deed amendment had to be on loan. Cory could find no evidence to support the gallery's argument that these were somehow permanent, irrevocable loans, and he awarded ownership of them to the foundation. At first glance, this made Cory's decision appear to be a saw-off, with more than one-third of the works awarded to the foundation. But with only a handful of exceptions — among them paintings by Botticelli and Claude Joseph Vernet — they did not represent a major loss to the gallery, either artistically or in their value. Turner's *The Fountain of Indolence*, Freud's *Hotel Bedroom*, the other Gainsborough, *Lieutenant Colonel Edmund Nugent*, as well as several Sickerts, Sutherlands and Sargents, were all staying put. "We can live with it," Dan O'Brien, the chair of the gallery board, said with considerable understatement at a news conference the day Cory released his decision.

Even after such a long and painful quest for clarity, O'Brien gave an explanation of the decision and its implications that was remarkably muddled. He apparently had not read the arbitration documents that listed the location of all the works removed from the gallery by the foundation; he told the assembled journalists that "whether they are in the possession of the foundation remains to be determined." When a curious reporter asked their value, O'Brien answered, "I'm not sure we're prepared to talk about that today," even though both sides had agreed to a figure, $2.4 million, which was contained in arbitration documents available to the public on the gallery's web site. He also said there was "all sorts of evidence" using the word gift, when in fact there had been precious little. And asked to explain Cory's eighty-five/forty-eight split, O'Brien said lawyers "for the other side" had established there were changes to the trust deed — when it was the gallery's own counsel that had made this crucial argument.[29] O'Brien, who had retired from his job as a university president, managed to mangle nearly every aspect of the gallery's triumph.

Many questions remained unanswered. Cory's decision left each side in possession of something that belonged to the other. The foundation had been ordered to pay the gallery $2.4 million, while the gallery held forty-eight paintings that now belonged to the foundation. Each, therefore, had an incentive to comply with Cory's ruling. Might a trade be possible in which the foundation would give some of the forty-eight works to the gallery in return for a reduction in, or cancellation of, the compensation it was now obligated to pay? And given that one painting that belonged to the gallery — *White Dog in a Landscape* — was hanging in the dining room at Cherkley, would it be part of such a deal? The *Peasant Girl* was lost forever, but after three decades, might the *White Dog* come home to Fredericton?

A more profound question lurked in the background: had Maxwell and Timothy, in laying claim to one part of their grandfather's legacy, gambled another? The foundation had spent seven million dollars on the case.[30] As the instigator and the loser, it would have to pay its own legal bills and potentially some or all of the gallery's, plus the $2.4 million in compensation for the paintings it had removed and sold. Yet its most recent financial statements, entered into evidence at the arbitration, had shown it had only £1.1 million in cash in 2005 — about $2.4 million Canadian — and about four times that amount in shares. Its biggest asset was Cherkley itself, valued at £11.9 million in 2005. Maxwell had acknowledged during the hearings that the foundation was willing to treat the estate with the same financial ruthlessness as the paintings in Fredericton, with their "negative yield." "If Cherkley does not break even when it is fully functional," he had said, "the exact same scrutiny will take place."[31] If the foundation's funds were severely depleted by the cost of Cory's decision, Maxwell might be forced to scrutinize Cherkley in a different way: as an asset to be sold to keep the foundation alive.

An appeal of the ruling by the foundation would raise the stakes even more, piling on more legal bills that the foundation would have to pay if it lost again. But an appeal was precisely what Maxwell announced within hours of O'Brien's news conference. Cory's decision, he said in a prepared statement, was "inconsistent with a great deal of evidence that was not referred to in the decision" and "contrary to the uninterrupted and uniform consensus between the parties that existed for at least four decades."[32] The foundation would invoke the appeal process it and the gallery had agreed upon in 2004: each would select one retired appellate-level Canadian judge, and those two jurists would in turn select a third, forming a panel to hear arguments on whether Cory had made legal errors or not properly weighed the evidence. Kent Thomson would argue that he had done both, by dismissing the foundation's contention that it was too late for the gallery to contradict its own records and by completely ignoring several elements of the foundation's case. And, the appeal document would say, Cory "gave the appearance of failing to give even-handed justice" when he compared Beaverbrook to Goebbels.[33]

On two fronts — the U.K. Foundation's appeal and the Canadian Foundation's court case — the story would continue. The gallery's victory might be reversed. But that would never erase the resounding condemnation of Lord Beaverbrook contained in Peter Cory's decision. No less than a retired Supreme Court of Canada judge had blamed the entire fiasco on the man himself. This indictment would become part of the historical record of Beaverbrook's life, another of the many contradictions that defined the man. He had helped Churchill save humanity, but at the most personal level he was a user, and abuser, of men like Michael Wardell and Bob Tweedie. Among the tremendous gifts he had given to the province he called home was a great art gallery, which he had then, through his need for control, nearly wrecked. Beaverbrook had outsmarted himself and set a trap for his descendants. Acting half a century later on what they sincerely believed was his foundation's claim to the paintings, they ended up exposing his vanity and trickery for all to see.

Beaverbrook emerged from the dispute a diminished giant, a figure whose time, like that of his beloved British Empire, had passed. The little province that had treated him like a god had grown up, and its deference, like that of his precious *Peasant Girl*, was gone. The province and the gallery would have to stand on their own. Maxwell's choice of words in our London interview in March 2007 was telling: while he had remarked at the hearings in October that "my name is over the door," he told me that "I share a name with the foundation and the foundation shares a name with the gallery" — a new degree of separation. New Brunswick's connection to his family was now severed, likely for good. Among the province's people, that name over the door, Beaverbrook, now invited skepticism and ridicule.

Yet it was not the name or the family line that had done such profound damage. It was one man, Lord Beaverbrook himself, who had built and shattered a great legacy. In his memorable 1963 article for *Maclean's* on the province's cult-like devotion to Beaverbrook, Malcolm Muggeridge had drawn what he acknowledged was a "preposterous" parallel to Stalin, citing "the passion of a human ego to occupy the wide open spaces of history, to ensure that the notice achieved or enforced in life shall endure after death. . . . The one hacked and killed his way into history, the other has tried to buy his way in." Muggeridge had also predicted that, like Stalin, Beaverbrook would eventually face a day of reckoning. "History itself may take a quite different course from the one he has envisaged," he wrote. "These seemingly mighty pillars round which his ego has twined itself like ivy . . . may themselves prove pasteboard, and the seemingly mighty events . . . turn out to deserve, not whole chapters, but only a meagre footnote."[34]

There would be no Eastern Europe-style pulling down of Beaverbrook's statue in Officer's Square, but in their own quiet way, New Brunswickers had turned their backs on an era and on the man who had personified it.

His day of reckoning had come.

ACKNOWLEDGEMENTS

Researching and writing this book would have been impossible to contemplate without the cooperation of the two main antagonists, the Beaverbrook U.K. Foundation and the Beaverbrook Art Gallery. Therefore my first thanks must go to the current Lord Beaverbrook, chairman of the foundation, and to Bernard Riordon, the gallery director. In the midst of a long and difficult legal battle, both men recognized the historical value of an independent, journalistic account of the dispute and offered me their full assistance, with no conditions attached.

At the gallery, Brian Perry, Laura Ritchie and Laurie Glenn Norris granted me access to files and records, and Laura in particular was patient with me as I did my last-minute fact-checking and tied up other inevitable loose ends. With Bernard Riordon's approval, the gallery's counsel, Larry Lowenstein, provided me with all the case documents I asked for. His associate Jennifer Fairfax helped amass them, and Larry also patiently answered many of my questions about the details of the case. Jean-Marc Leclerc kindly clarified some questions about accession records very close to deadline.

At the foundation, Lord Beaverbrook gave me access to the foundation's mountain of arbitration documents. Its lead lawyer in Canada, Kent Thomson, made them available to me. Like Larry Lowenstein, Kent took time to help me understand the complexities and nuances of the case he was advancing. I am also grateful to Debra Bilous, for organizing the large amount of material I requested, and to Matthew Milne-Smith, for his assistance. Lord Beaverbrook also granted me permission to quote from the correspondence and writings of his grandfather for which he and the

281

foundation hold the copyright. In addition, he allowed me to visit Cherkley Court during my research trip to England, a once-in-a-lifetime experience for which I am grateful. Thanks as well to Anna Nelson, the house manager at Cherkley, for showing me the property and for indulging my long-held desire to visit the grave of R.B. Bennett in nearby Mickleham.

Archivists and librarians, the custodians of our history and our collective memory, were a great help to me. Patricia Belier, head of archives and special collections at the Harriet Irving Library at the University of New Brunswick, was my Sherpa. The material I gathered up there on the fifth floor forms the backbone of the first half of this book, and I owe a large debt to her and her staff. At the Provincial Archives of New Brunswick, Fred Farrell and his colleagues helped me track down Bob Tweedie's correspondence as well as a number of photographs. The staff of the Legislative Library at the New Brunswick Legislature were, as always, cheerfully helpful. I also thank Annie Pinder at the House of Lords Records Office in London for arranging for my visit and the staff of the search room for their quick and efficient assistance.

At the CBC, my boss, Mary-Pat Schutta, as well as Susan Mitton and Esther Enkin, allowed me to take on this project, agreed to a leave of absence, and permitted me to quote from my CBC reporting on the dispute, and my colleagues in Fredericton, particularly Myfanwy Davies and Alan White, accommodated my work on the book. In the library, Elizabeth Thompson was a great help, and Barbara Roberts used her encyclopedic knowledge of Fredericton to help me contact several people for interviews, most notably Helen Parker.

At St. Thomas University, Philip Lee, the director of the school of journalism, invited me to teach a course that coincided precisely with my book leave, an offer that made the proposition somewhat more affordable. My students in Journalism 2033 kept my reporting reflexes sharp during the semester and reminded me of the excitement and curiosity that is at the heart of any reporter's work.

Thanks also to James Boudreau of the Halifax law firm Wickwire Holm, who generously provided quick and concise legal advice on the manuscript, Karen Ruet, my former *Telegraph-Journal* colleague, who helped me track down photographs, and Chris McCreery, from the office of Senator Noel Kinsella, who found information on Beaverbrook's commissioning of war artists during the First World War.

In the UK, Filipa Vasconcelos of Aitken Alexander Associates Ltd. and Georgia Glover of David Higham Associates speedily granted me permission to quote from two Beaverbrook biographies. Melva Croal of the

Manchester Art Gallery send me documents from the gallery's files on Thomas Gainsborough's *Peasant Girl Gathering Faggots*.

My old friend Laura Scanga, a newspaper colleague from the heady days of post-communist Prague, and her husband Paul opened their home to me in Manchester so I could view the *Peasant Girl* during my research trip.

Another old friend, Kevin Fram, first made me aware of the fascinating life of the original Lord Beaverbrook, and his enthusiasm for a book about the art dispute propelled me forward. Kevin copied several documents and lent me hard-to-find books from his collection of Beaverbrook materials, he reviewed my first draft of Chapter Two, and he gave me a photocopy of Beaverbrook's will. This copy came to him from Peter Glennie, now a judge, who, as a young lawyer, found the original in the mechanics' liens files in Newcastle, New Brunswick, where it had been misplaced for several years.

I am happy that I allowed Susanne Alexander of Goose Lane Editions to persuade me that this book was doable; I got to immerse myself in a terrific story, and I enjoyed working with her, Julie Scriver, and the rest of the team at Goose Lane once more. Being able to work again with Laurel Boone was one of my main motivations for agreeing to the project. I wish she could edit everything I write.

The support of my in-laws, Gail and André Goguen, made a significant contribution to this book.

My wife Giselle Goguen is my ultimate friend and collaborator. I thought her support for my first book was extraordinary, but that was before we had two children; she never wavered in her willingness to help me with this one, whether I had to travel to England for a week or simply devote a couple of hours on a Saturday afternoon to writing. Giselle's enthusiasm was constant and without parallel. Any success that I have, I owe to her.

THE HOUSE OF BEAVERBROOK

A partial family tree

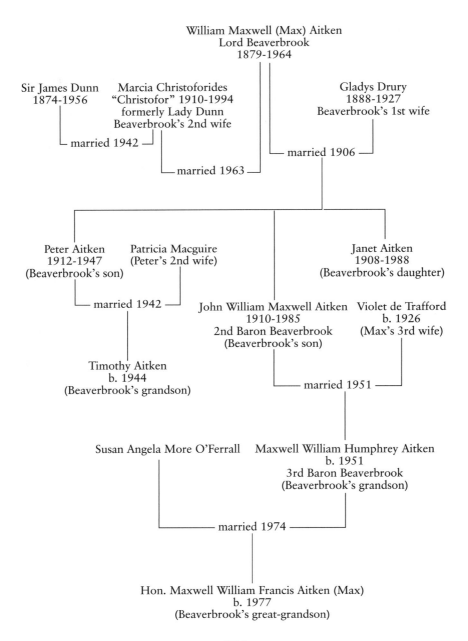

William Maxwell (Max) Aitken
Lord Beaverbrook
1879-1964

Sir James Dunn
1874-1956

Marcia Christoforides
"Christofor" 1910-1994
formerly Lady Dunn
Beaverbrook's 2nd wife

Gladys Drury
1888-1927
Beaverbrook's 1st wife

└─ married 1942 ─┘

└─ married 1906 ─┘

└─ married 1963 ─┘

Peter Aitken
1912-1947
(Beaverbrook's son)

Patricia Macguire
(Peter's 2nd wife)

Janet Aitken
1908-1988
(Beaverbrook's daughter)

└─ married 1942 ─┘

John William Maxwell Aitken
1910-1985
2nd Baron Beaverbrook
(Beaverbrook's son)

Violet de Trafford
b. 1926
(Max's 3rd wife)

Timothy Aitken
b. 1944
(Beaverbrook's grandson)

└─ married 1951 ─┘

Susan Angela More O'Ferrall

Maxwell William Humphrey Aitken
b. 1951
3rd Baron Beaverbrook
(Beaverbrook's grandson)

└─ married 1974 ─┘

Hon. Maxwell William Francis Aitken (Max)
b. 1977
(Beaverbrook's great-grandson)

Aitken, William Maxwell: Lord Beaverbrook.
Aitken, Janet (Janet Aitken Kidd): Beaverbrook's oldest child and sister of John William Maxwell Aitken.
Aitken, John William Maxwell ["Sir Max Aitken"]: Second child and first son of the first Lord Beaverbrook. He inherited but renounced the title Lord Beaverbrook.
Aitken, Jonathan: Grandson of Beaverbrook's brother Magnus and son of his nephew William; MP in the British House of Commons and cabinet minister in the John Major government.
Aitken, Maxwell William Humphrey ["Maxwell"]: Son of Sir Max and Lady Violet Aitken and the first Lord Beaverbrook's grandson; inherited the title Lord Beaverbrook after the death of his father, Sir Max, in 1985; chair of the Beaverbrook U.K. Foundation at the time of the dispute.
Aitken, Peter: Third child of Lord Beaverbrook.
Aitken, Timothy: Lord Beaverbrook's grandson, son of Peter, nephew of Sir Max and cousin of Maxwell; chair of the Beaverbrook Canadian Foundation and member of the board of the Beaverbrook Art Gallery at the time of the dispute.
Aitken, Lady Violet: Third wife of Sir Max and mother of Maxwell and Laura Aitken Levi.
Andrus, Donald: Assistant curator of the Beaverbrook Art Gallery from 1964 to 1967.
Bird, Richard: Son of Wallace Bird; Fredericton lawyer and chair of the Board of Governors of the Beaverbrook Art Gallery from 1974 to 1987.

Bird, Wallace: Lieutenant-Governor of New Brunswick and chair of the
    Board of Governors of the Beaverbrook Art Gallery from 1968 to
    1971.
Budovitch, Judith: Long-time member of the Beaverbrook Art Gallery
    Board of Governors and chair of the Board of Governors from 1991
    to 2001.
Christoforides, Marcia Anastasia ("Christofor"): Third wife of Sir James
    Dunn, thus Lady Dunn, and then second wife of Lord Beaverbrook,
    thus Lady Beaverbrook.
Constable, W.G.: Curator of paintings at the Museum of Fine Arts,
    Boston, and advisor to Beaverbrook leading up to the opening of the
    Beaverbrook Art Gallery.
Cooke, Edwy: Curator of the Beaverbrook Art Gallery from 1959 to 1964.
Dunn, Sir James: New Brunswick-born business tycoon, friend of Lord
    Beaverbrook, and first husband of Christofor.
Elton, Sheila: First secretary of the Beaverbrook U.K. Foundation.
Flemming, Hugh John: Premier of New Brunswick from 1952 to 1960.
Ince, Margaret: Secretary to the office of Lord Beaverbrook.
Lumsden, Ian: Curator of the Beaverbrook Art Gallery from 1969 to 1983
    and Director from 1983 to 2001.
Mackay, Colin B.: President of the University of New Brunswick during the
    establishment of the Beaverbrook Art Gallery.
Martin, Sir Alec: Chairman of Christie's, the auction house, from 1940 to
    1958.
McNair, John: Former premier of New Brunswick who served as
    Lieutenant-Governor of the province and chair of the Board of
    Governors of the Beaverbrook Art Gallery from 1965 to 1968.
Millar, A.G. (George): Lord Beaverbrook's accountant and advisor.
Parker, Helen (Savage): A secretary at the Beaverbrook Art Gallery in its
    early years.
Robichaud, Louis: Premier of New Brunswick from 1960 to 1970.
Smith, Stuart: Curator of the Beaverbrook Art Gallery from 1964 to 1969.
Tweedie, Robert (Bob): Political assistant assigned to support Lord
    Beaverbrook's activities in New Brunswick; later held a variety
    of posts including secretary to the Board of Governors of the
    Beaverbrook Art Gallery, secretary to the Beaverbrook Foundations,
    secretary to the Sir James Dunn Foundation, and secretary to the
    board of the Playhouse.
Wardell, Michael: Former employee of Lord Beaverbrook; publisher of the
    Fredericton *Daily Gleaner* during the creation of the Beaverbrook Art
    Gallery.

CHAPTER ONE: *"I thought we had friends in New Brunswick"*
Material in this chapter, unless otherwise noted, is drawn from my own reporting on the dispute in October 2006, including interviews gathered for the CBC program *The Current*.

1   A.J.P. Taylor, *Beaverbrook* (London: Hamish Hamilton, 1972), p. 671.
2   James Thomson, "The Castle of Indolence." *Representative Poetry Online* (University of Toronto, public domain), http://rpo.library.utoronto.ca/poem/2206.html.
3   Tate Online, *Lucian Freud* (2002 exhibition), audio clip of Caroline Blackwood, http://www.tate.org.uk/britain/exhibitions/freud/work_hotelbedroom.htm.
4   Beaverbrook U.K. Foundation, Closing Submissions, Nov. 26, 2006, p. 6.
5   Interview with Maxwell Aitken.
6   David Fukumoto, "Yee-Sun Wu Memorial Tribute," http://www.fukubonsai.com.

CHAPTER TWO: *"This was his hour"*
1   Lord Beaverbrook, *My Early Life* (Fredericton: Brunswick Press, 1965), p. 78.
2   Lord Beaverbrook, *Friends: Sixty Years of Personal Intimate Relations with Richard Bedford Bennett* (London: Heinemann, 1959), p. 4.
3   Beaverbrook, *My Early Life*, p. 86.
4   P.B. Waite, *The Loner: Three Sketches of the Personal Life and Ideas*

of R.B. Bennett, 1870-1947 (Toronto: University of Toronto Press, 1992), p. 32.

5   *Close-Up*, CBC Television, Oct. 29, 1959.
6   Beaverbrook, *My Early Life*, p. 75.
7   Anne Chisholm and Michael Davie, *Beaverbrook: A Life* (London: Hutchinson, 1992), p. 28.
8   Taylor, p. 6.
9   Beaverbrook, *My Early Life*, p. 24.
10 Beaverbrook, *My Early Life*, p. 48.
11 Chisholm and Davie, p. 25.
12 Waite, p. 32.
13 Beaverbrook, *My Early Life*, p. 107
14 Beaverbrook, *My Early Life*, p. 150.
15 Chisholm and Davie, p. 529.
16 Gregory Marchildon, *Profits and Politics: Beaverbrook and the Gilded Age of Canadian Finance* (Toronto: University of Toronto Press, 1996), p. 179-180.
17 Taylor, p. 38.
18 Taylor, p. 61.
19 Chisholm and Davie, p. 94.
20 Janet Aitken Kidd, *The Beaverbrook Girl* (London: Collins, 1987), pp. 19, 37.
21 Beaverbrook U.K. Foundation, Closing Submissions, p. 230.
22 Chisholm and Davie, pp. 107, 144.
23 Chisholm and Davie, p. 158.
24 Taylor, p. 155.
25 Chisholm and Davie, p. 224.
26 David Leitch, "Not For Gropers in the Mud," *Times* (London), Dec. 14, 1988.
27 Taylor, p. 171
28 Chisholm and Davie, p. 516.
29 Chisholm and Davie, p. 276.
30 Chisholm and Davie, p. 306.
31 Taylor, p. 293
32 Chisholm and Davie, p. 298.
33 Beaverbrook, *Friends*, p. 58.
34 Chisholm and Davie, p. 335.
35 *Close-Up*, CBC Television, Oct. 29, 1959.
36 Kidd, p. 152.
37 Chisholm and Davie, p. 349.
38 Taylor, p. 395
39 *Close-Up*, CBC Television, October 29, 1959..
40 Chisholm and Davie, p. 376.

41 Quoted in Michael Wardell, "Beaverbrook: His Supreme Service," in Beaverbrook, *My Early Life*, p. 190.
42 Taylor, pp. 24-25
43 Beaverbrook, *My Early Life*, p. 144
44 Kidd, pp. 62-63.
45 Chisholm and Davie, p. 317.
46 Kidd, p. 31.
47 Chisholm and Davie, pp. 317, 314-315.
48 Kidd, pp. 159, 31, 23.
49 Chisholm and Davie, p. 446.

CHAPTER THREE: *"We must remember the greatness of the man"*
1 Taylor, pp. 276, 170.
2 Beaverbrook, *Friends*, p. 122
3 Beaverbrook, *Friends*, p. 103.
4 Rhianna Edwards and William G. Godfrey, "R.B. Bennett Project: Archival Research Report" (Ottawa: Parks Canada, 1999), pp. 14-16.
5 Ian Sclanders, "The Beaver Comes Home," *Maclean's*, Jan. 15, 1948, p. 45.
6 Geoffrey Stevens, *The Player: The Life and Times of Dalton Camp*, (Toronto: Key Porter, 2003), p. 52.
7 Dalton Camp, *Gentlemen, Players and Politicians* (Toronto: McClelland and Stewart, 1970), p. 24
8 Stevens, p. 60.
9 House of Lords Record Office (HLRO), BBK/K/1/70, Dec. 14, 1957.
10 Sclanders, p. 8.
11 Chisholm and Davie, p. 465.
12 Robert Tweedie, *On with the Dance: A New Brunswick Memoir 1935-1960* (Fredericton: New Ireland Press, 1986), pp. 162-163.
13 Tweedie, pp. 164-165.
14 Tweedie, pp. 159, 161.
15 Letter of Robert Tweedie to Hugh John Flemming, May 9, 1959, Robert Tweedie correspondence, Provincial Archives of New Brunswick (PANB).
16 Beaverbrook Canadian Correspondence, Archives and Special Collections, Harriet Irving Library, University of New Brunswick (BCC), case 128 (b) file 1h, no. 79213.
17 Richard Shone and Ian Lumsden, *Sargent to Freud: Modern British Paintings and Drawings in the Beaverbrook Collection* (Fredericton: Beaverbrook Art Gallery, 1998), p. 39.
18 Chisholm and Davie, p. 466.

19 John DeMont, *Citizens Irving* (Toronto: Doubleday Canada, 1991),
        p. 103.
20 Chisholm and Davie, p. 468.
21 Camp, p. 24.
22 Chisholm and Davie, p. 468.
23 BCC, case 135, file 16, no. 83578; case 135, file 16, no. 83593;
        case 128, file 1f, no. 78980.
24 BCC, case 130, file 1a, no. 80050; case 136, file 20, no. 83611.
25 BCC, case 128, file 1f, no. 78947; case 128, file 1f, no. 78954.
26 BCC, case 128, file 1f, no. 78976; case 128, file 1f, no. 78975.
27 BCC, case 128, file 1f, no. 78971;, case 128, file 1f, no. 78999.
28 BCC, case 128, file 1f, no. 79005; case 128, file 1f, no. 79006.
29 Michael Wardell, "Beaverbrook: A Study in Frustration by Tom
        Driberg," *Daily Gleaner* (Fredericton), undated clipping, BCC,
        case 128(b), file 1h, no. 79242.
30 BCC, case 128 (b) file 1h, no. 79174; case 129, file 1a, no. 79289.
31 Tweedie, p. 194
32 Tweedie, pp. 141, 143-144, 130.
33 BCC, case 44, file 7, no. 27430; case 42, file 5, no. 26026.
34 BCC, case 42, file 5, no. 26060.
35 BCC, case 42, file 5, no. 26093; case 44, file 5, no. 27329.

CHAPTER FOUR: *"The rich man loose in the art market has a lot to learn"*
1   Beaverbrook Art Gallery, Memorandum of Opening Statement, exhibit
        G000968.
2   Michael Wardell, "The Beaverbrook Art Gallery," *Atlantic Advocate*
        (Sept. 1959), p. 47.
3   Taylor, p. 624.
4   Beaverbrook U.K. Foundation, Opening Submissions, Oct. 10, 2006,
        p. 23.
5   Beaverbrook Art Gallery, Memorandum of Opening Statement, Oct. 3,
        2006, p. 40.
6   Beaverbrook U.K. Foundation, Opening Submissions, p. 24.
7   Beaverbrook Art Gallery, Memorandum of Opening Statement, p. 42.
8   Beaverbrook Art Gallery, Memorandum of Opening Statement, exhibit
        G001242.
9   Beaverbrook U.K. Foundation, Opening Submissions, p. 29.
10 Beaverbrook Art Gallery, Memorandum of Opening Statement, exhibit
        GS005841.
11 Taylor, p. 612.
12 Beaverbrook Art Gallery, Memorandum of Opening Statement, exhibit
        0089.

13 Shone and Lumsden, p. 38.
14 Taylor, p. 624.
15 Chisholm and Davie, p. 484.
16 Chisholm and Davie, pp. 487-488.
17 Tweedie, p. 173.
18 "Lord Beaverbrook Collection of Art on Display Today," *Evening Times-Globe* (Saint John), Nov. 8 1954.
19 Letter of Le Roux Smith Le Roux to Robert Tweedie, July 13, 1955, Robert Tweedie collection, PANB.
20 Tweedie, p. 173.
21 Ian G. Lumsden, Curtis Joseph Collins and Laurie Glenn, *The Beaverbrook Art Gallery Collection: Selected Works* (Fredericton: Beaverbrook Art Gallery, 2000), p. 15.
22 BCC, case 128, file 1g, no. 79130.
23 BCC, case 136, file 19, no. 83769; case 42, file 6, no. 26206.
24 Shone and Lumsden, p. 50.
25 David Alan Mellor, *Interpreting Lucian Freud* (London: Tate Publishing, 2002), pp. 12-14.
26 Caroline Blackwood et. al., *Lucian Freud: Early Works* (New York: Robert Miller Gallery, 1993), pp. 16, 14.
27 Ian Lumsden, Beaverbrook Art Gallery accession records for *Hotel Bedroom*.
28 "Beaverbrook Art Display Lauded: Nearly 1,000 At Opening," *Daily Gleaner* (Fredericton), Oct. 20, 1955.
29 BCC, case 139, file 16, no. 86178.
30 Letter of Margaret Ince to Robert Tweedie, Nov. 17, 1955, Robert Tweedie correspondence, Provincial Archives of New Brunswick.
31 Shone and Lumsden, p. 56.
32 BCC, case 25, file 1, no. 15155; case 25, file 1, no. 15156.
33 BCC, case 25, file 1, no. 14937.
34 W.G. Constable, oral history interview, Smithsonian Archives of American Art, July 1972-June 1973.
35 W.G. Constable, "Epoch-making Gift to Maritimes" (text of speech), *Daily Gleaner* (Fredericton), Oct. 19 1956.
36 BCC, case 26, file 1, no. 15492; case 25, file 1, no. 14975; case 26, file 1, no. 15542; case 26, file 1, no. 15574.
37 BCC, case 25, file 1, no. 14897.
38 BCC, case 25, file 1, no. 15301.
39 "Fragonard Work in Suit for $45,000," *New York Times*, Sept. 30, 1955.
40 BCC, case 139, file 18, No. 86335.
41 Manchester Art Gallery, notes on *Peasant Girl Gathering Faggots*, http://www.manchestergalleries.org/the-collections

42   Stephen Butler, *Gainsborough* (London: Studio Editions, 1992), pp. 6, 5.

43   Manchester Art Gallery, accession records for *Peasant Girl Gathering Faggots*.

44   BCC, case 25, file 1, no. 15038.

45   BCC, case 25, file 1, no. 15036; case 25, file 1, no. 15037; case 25, file 1, no. 15035; case 25, file 1, no. 15078; case 25, file 1, no. 14906.

46   BCC, case 25, file 1, no. 14908; case 25, file 1, no. 14966.

47   BCC, case 25, file 1, no. 15285.

48   BCC, case 25, file 1, no. 15133; case 25, file 1, no. 14964; case 26, file 1, no. 15713.

49   BCC, case 25, file 1, no. 15077; case 26, file 1, *no.* 15418; case 26, file 1, *no.* 15421.

50   BCC, case 139, file 11, no. 85870; BCC, case 25, file 1, no. 14911; case 26, file 1, *no.* 15820.

51   Martin Butlin and Evelyn Joll, *The Paintings of J.M.W. Turner* (New Haven: Yale University Press, 1977), p. 186.

52   Butlin and Joll, pp. 206-207.

53   BCC, case 139, file 14, no. 85923; case 139, file 14, no. 86023.

54   Testimony of Claire Watson-Fisher, Oct. 20, 2006.

55   BCC, case 27, file 1, *no.* 16220; case 27, file 1, *no.* 16247.

56   BCC case 139, file 15, no. 86093; case 139, file 15, no. 86125; case 139, file 15, no. 86129.

57   Lord Beaverbrook, *Courage: The Story of Sir James Dunn* (Fredericton: Brunswick Press, 1961), p. 249.

58   BCC, case 25, file 1, *no.* 15510; case 139, file 14, no. 86061; case 29, file 1, no. 16911.

59   Beaverbrook Art Gallery, Memorandum of Closing Argument, Nov. 24, 2006, exhibit 0332.

60   Beaverbrook Art Gallery, Memorandum of Closing Argument, exhibit G000364-Q; GS005966; GS005354.

61   Chisholm and Davie, p. 486.

62   W.G. Constable, oral history interview.

CHAPTER FIVE: *"The way is dark, and the dark is very dark"*

1   Tweedie, p. 171.

2   BCC, case 29, file 1, no. 16911.

3   BCC, case 129, file 1a, no. 79251.

4   John Leroux. "Architecture of the Spirit: Modernism in 1950s and 1960s Fredericton," *Journal of Canadian Art History* 28 (2007), pp. 8-37.

5 BCC, case 139, file 14, no. 85921; case 139, file 14, no. 85922.
6 W.G. Constable, oral history interview.
7 BCC, case 42, file 6, no. 26204.
8 BCC, case 136, file 22, no. 83873.
9 Tweedie, p. 174.
10 Tweedie, pp. 167-70.
11 BCC, case 129, file 1f, no. 79936; case 44, file 7, no. 27517; case 44, file 7, no. 27518.
12 BCC, case 44, file 7, no. 27547; case 44, file 7, no. 27537; case 129, file 1f, no. 79965.
13 BCC, case 25, file 1, no. 15507; case 129, file 1f, no. 79979.
14 BCC, case 27, file 1, no. 15920; case 29, file 1, no. 17056; case 29, file 1, no. 16801.
15 BCC, case 146, file 2, no. 91064.
16 BCC, case 130, file 1, no. 80004.
17 Beaverbrook Art Gallery, Memorandum of Closing Argument, exhibit GS005968.
18 BCC, case 119, file 1, no. 72849; case 119, file 1, no. 72961; case 31, file 3, no. 17911.
19 BCC, case 29, file 1, no. 16911; BCC, case 29, file 1, no. 16958.
20 Chisholm and Davie, p. 487.
21 Beaverbrook U.K. Foundation, Opening Submissions, p. 80; BCC, case 119, file 1, no. 72877; case 119, file 1, no. 72962.
22 BCC case 146, file 2, no. 91426; case 29, file 1, no. 16926; case 146, file 2, no. 91478.
23 BCC, case 31, file 3, no. 17951; case 31, file 3, no. 17952; case 146, file 2, no. 91439; case 146, file 2, no. 91473.
24 BCC, case 119, file 1, no. 72821; case 119, file 1, no. 72799; case 119, file 1, nos. 72660-72663.
25 BCC, case 31, file 3, no. 18035.
26 BCC, case 31, file 4, no. 18122; case 31, file 4, no. 18134; case 31, file 4, no. 18125; case 31, file 3, no. 17907.
27 Letter of Lord Beaverbrook to Hugh John Flemming, Feb. 27, 1959, Robert Tweedie correspondence, Provincial Archives of New Brunswick.
28 Taylor, pp. 643-644.
29 Beaverbrook Art Gallery, Memorandum of Opening Statement, pp. 20-23, 25-26.
30 Jenkins, pp. 889-890; Chisholm and Davie, p. 486.
31 BCC, case 109, file 4, no. 65598.
32 Geraldine Norman, "Sutherland Felt At the Mercy of his Sitter," *Times* (London), Jan. 27, 1978.
33 Shone and Lumsden, p. 44.

34 Beaverbrook Art Gallery, Memorandum of Opening Statement, p. 28.
35 Beaverbrook Art Gallery, Memorandum of Opening Statement,
       pp. 28-29.
36 Ian Aitken, "The Day that Enriches a Nation," *Daily Express*
       (London), Sept. 17, 1959.
37 Beaverbrook Art Gallery, Memorandum of Closing Argument,
       exhibit G002289.
38 Geoffrey Crowe, "Incomparable Gift to Arts in Canada," *Evening
       Times-Globe* (Saint John), Sept 17, 1959.
39 Beaverbrook Art Gallery, Memorandum of Closing Argument,
       exhibit G002337.
40 *Close-Up*, CBC Television, Oct. 29, 1959.

CHAPTER SIX: *"Let them come and see the paintings where they belong"*
1   Tweedie, p. 176.
2   BCC, case 32, file 5, no. 18847.
3   Tweedie, p. 177
4   BCC, case 33, file 3, no. 19152.
5   BCC, case 140, file 15, no. 86854; case 140, file 12, no. 86730.
6   BCC, case 140, file 16, no. 86885.
7   Interview with Helen Parker.
8   BCC, case 12, file 2, no. 6830; case 12, file 1, no. 6618.
9   BCC, case 12, file 2, no. 6841; case 12, file 2, no. 6847; case 12,
       file 2, no. 6893.
10 BCC, case 32, file 5, no. HIL 18847.
11 Beaverbrook U.K. Foundation, Closing Submissions, exhibit 13-1902;
       exhibit 13-1918; exhibit 13-1909.
12 BCC, case 131, file 1a, no. 80484; case 131, file 1a, no. 80523.
13 BCC, case 109, file 4, no. 65550; case 12, file 1, no. 6808; case 130,
       file 1, no. 80353.
14 Beaverbrook Art Gallery, Memorandum of Opening Statement, exhibit
       GS005493; exhibit 1851.
15 BCC, case 115a, file 3, no. 68722.
16 BCC, case 130, file 1, no. 80179.
17 BCC, case 130, file 1, no. 80221; case 136, file 21, no. 83820.
18 BCC, case 132, file 1d, no. 81339.
19 Taylor, pp. 645, 647.
20 Taylor, p. 654.
21 Taylor, p. 661.
22 BCC, case 15a, file 2, no. 8712.
23 BCC, case 115a, file 3, no. 8847; case 132, file 1d, no. 81613;
       case 15a, file 2, no. 8979; case 15a, file 2, no. 8818.

24 BCC, case 109, file 1f, no. 64338; case 109, file 1f, no. 64348.
25 Malcolm Muggeridge, "The Cult the Beaver Built," *Maclean's*, Nov. 2, 1963, p. 20-21, 60-64.
26 BCC, case 132, file 1d, no. 81925; case 109, file 1f, no. 64330.
27 Taylor, p. 660.
28 BCC, case 30, file 1, no. 80402; case 131, file 1a, no. 80486.
29 Michael Wardel, "Reply to Muggeridge," *Atlantic Advocate*, Nov. 1963, p. 14-15.
30 BCC, case 132, file 1d, no. 81981; case 132, file 1d, no. 82007.
31 BCC, case 109, file 1f, no. 64315.
32 Michael Wardell, in Beaverbrook, *My Early Life*, p. 188; Chisholm and Davie, p. 523.
33 BCC, case 109, file 1f, no 64321.
34 Kidd, p. 215.
35 Taylor, p. 669; Kidd, p. 215.
36 Chisholm and Davie, p. 524.
37 Tweedie, p. 192.
38 Chisholm and Davie, p. 524; "Newcastle Churches Pay Tribute to Beaverbrook," *Times* (Moncton), June 15, 1964.
39 Chisholm and Davie, pp. 526-527.
40 Taylor, p. 670.
41 *Time* (Canada), Sept. 14, 1962.
42 Chisholm and Davie, p. 526.

CHAPTER SEVEN: *"I will strive to climb the mountains"*
1 Lord Beaverbrook, *Courage*, pp. 121-128.
2 HLRO, BBK/K/1/70, letter of Oct. 7, 1956.
3 Beaverbrook, *Courage*, pp. 128-132, 147, 154-155.
4 Beaverbrook, *Courage*, pp. 156-158.
5 Beaverbrook, *Courage*, pp. 207-218.
6 Beaverbrook, *Courage*, pp. 242-243.
7 Beaverbrook, *Courage*, pp. 267-268.
8 BCC, case 128b, file 1h, no. 79191; case 128b, file 1h, no. 21956.
9 HLRO, BBK/K/1/70, letter of Sept. 29, 1956.
10 Taylor, p. 639.
11 Letter of Robert Tweedie to Lord Beaverbrook, March 9, 1959. Robert Tweedie collection, PANB.
12 BCC, case 119, file 1, no. 72867; case 130, file 1, no. 80163.
13 BCC, case 130, file 1, no. 80185.
14 *Daily Gleaner* (Fredericton), Oct. 17, 1960.
15 Beaverbrook Art Gallery, Memorandum of Opening Statement, exhibit G002832.

16 BCC, case 131, file 1a, no. 80489.
17 BCC, case 131, file 1a, no. 80525; case 140, file 2, no. 86498; case 140, file 16, no. 86885.
18 Taylor, p. 638.
19 Beaverbrook Art Gallery, exhibit G005542/1; exhibit GS005545/1. Shown to the author by Claude Roussel.
20 BCC, case 15a, file 2, no. 8752; case 15a, file 2, no. 8810.
21 Kidd, pp. 213-214.
22 BCC, case 132, file 1d, no. 81893; case 132, file 1d, no. 81896; case 15a, file 2, no. 8961.
23 Interview with Timothy Aitken.
24 Kidd, p. 216.
25 Interview with Timothy Aitken.
26 Testimony of Stuart Smith, Oct. 19, 2006; Letter of Margaret Ince to Robert Tweedie, June 9, 1959. Robert Tweedie collection, PANB.
27 Testimony of Stuart Smith, Oct. 19, 2006. In this chapter, all subsequent comments attributed to Smith and information about Smith's part in the dispute are from this testimony unless otherwise noted.
28 Aviva Boxer, "One Heart, One Mind, One Soul," *New Brunswick Reader*, Dec. 10, 1994, p. 9.
29 HLRO, BBK/A/301, letter of Nov. 7, 1966.
30 Interview with Claude Roussel.
31 Robert Pichette, "Remembering a Memorable Woman," *Telegraph Journal* (Saint John), March 10, 1995.
32 BCC, case 132, file 1d, no. 81601.
33 HLRO, BBK/A/301, letters of Oct. 23, 1964 and June 14, 1965.
34 "Text of Michael Wardell's Statement at Playhouse Patrons' General Meeting," *Daily Gleaner* (Fredericton), Sept. 9, 1965.
35 HLRO, BBK/A/301, letter of Sept. 14, 1965; telegram of Sept. 16, 1965.
36 DeMont, p. 83.
37 BCC, case 15a, file 2, no. 8847.
38 May 12, 1967. Robert Tweedie collection, PANB.
39 Beaverbrook U.K. Foundation, Closing Submissions, exhibit 25-3770.
40 Robert Tweedie letter, July 8, 1969, quoted in transcript of examination for discovery of Judith Budovitch, November 2005, New Brunswick Court of Queen's Bench file F/C/407/04.
41 Beaverbrook U.K. Foundation, Closing Submissions, exhibit 26-3881.
42 Beaverbrook U.K. Foundation, Closing Submissions, exhibit 26-3885.
43 Testimony of Lady Violet Aitken, Oct. 23, 2006.
44 Lady Beaverbrook letter, Jan. 8, 1970, quoted in transcript of examination for discovery of Judith Budovitch.

45 Letter of Lady Beaverbrook to Robert Tweedie, Sept. 7, 1966. Robert Tweedie collection, PANB.
46 Letter of Robert Tweedie to Ian Lumsden, Jan. 26, 1970. Robert Tweedie collection, PANB.
47 Beaverbrook U.K. Foundation, Closing Submissions, exhibit 26-3954.
48 Beaverbrook U.K. Foundation, Closing Submissions, exhibit 26-4130
49 Beaverbrook U.K. Foundation, Closing Submissions, exhibit 26-3961; exhibit 26-3966.
50 Tweedie, p. 194.
51 Beaverbrook U.K. Foundation, Closing Submissions, exhibit 27-4001; exhibit 27-4026; exhibit 27-4030; exhibit 27-4040.
52 Letter of Feb. 4, 1971, cited in examination for discovery of Judith Budovitch, November, 2005.
53 Reuben Cohen, *A Time to Tell* (Toronto: Key Porter, 1998), pp. 192-194.
54 Interview with Timothy Aitken.
55 Interview with Maxwell Aitken.
56 "The Dowager Lady Beaverbrook: Obituary," *Times* (London), Oct. 31, 1994.
57 Boxer, "One Heart, One Mind, One Soul," pp. 10, 11.
58 Testimony of Lady Violet Aitken, Oct. 23, 2006.
59 Testimony of Michael Marshall, Oct. 24, 2006.
60 Interview with Maxwell Aitken.
61 Testimony of Michael Marshall, Oct. 24, 2006.
62 Aviva Boxer, "Lady Beaverbrook Rewards the Faithful," *Telegraph Journal* (Saint John), Feb. 15, 1995, p. A1.
63 Interview with Marc Leger.
64 Transcript of examination for discovery of Judith Budovitch, November 2005.

CHAPTER EIGHT: *"He's not at the centre of anything"*

1 Interview with Timothy Aitken.
2 Interview with Maxwell Aitken.
3 Kidd, pp. 170, 205.
4 Interview with Timothy Aitken.
5 HLRO, BBK/K/1/52, exchange of letters, Oct. 1957; BBK/K/1/52, letter of Timothy Aitken, Sept. 15, 1957; BKK/K/1/54, letter of Lord Beaverbrook, Sept. 16, 1959.
6 HLRO, BBK/H/204, letter of Lord Beaverbrook, April 20, 1959; BBK/K/1/53, note from tutor, Jan. 6, 1958; BBK/K/1/53, report card of Timothy Aitken, 1958; BBK/K/1/53, letter of Lord Beaverbrook, Oct. 24, 1958.

7   HLRO, BBK/H/226, letter of Lord Beaverbrook, March 14, 1963.
8   Interview with Timothy Aitken.
9   Chisholm and Davie, p. 473.
10 HLRO, BBK/H/121, letter of John Gordon, Dec. 9, 1947.
11 Taylor, pp. 666, 671.
12 Lewis Chester and Jonathan Fenby. *The Fall of the House of Beaverbrook* (London: Andre Deutsch, 1979), pp. 42, 12-14.
13 Chisholm and Davie, p. 518.
14 HLRO, BBK/K/1/53, letter of Lady Violet Aitken, Jan. 8, 1958.
15 Interview with Maxwell Aitken.
16 Chester and Fenby, p. 79.
17 Interview with Maxwell Aitken.
18 Interview with Timothy Aitken.
19 Chester and Fenby, p. 78.
20 Chester and Fenby, pp. 78, 120, 121, 124.
21 Chester and Fenby, p. 225.
22 Chester and Fenby, p. 236.
23 Chester and Fenby, pp. 237, 238.
24 Interview with Maxwell Aitken.
25 Chester and Fenby, p. 239.
26 Beaverbrook U.K. Foundation, Closing Submissions, exhibit 30-4490.
27 Beaverbrook U.K. Foundation, Closing Submissions, exhibit 30-4528.
28 Letter of Sir Max Aitken to Stuart Smith, Oct. 26 1967, Robert Tweedie collection, PANB.
29 Beaverbrook U.K. Foundation, Closing Submissions, exhibit 30-4528; exhibit 30-4537.
30 Beaverbrook U.K. Foundation, Closing Submissions, exhibit 30-4538.
31 Joint Documents Brief, exhibit JDB-CHRON30-4539-1.
32 Beaverbrook U.K. Foundation, Closing Submissions, exhibit 31-4563.
33 Beaverbrook U.K. Foundation, Closing Submissions, exhibit 31-4563.
34 Interview with Maxwell Aitken.
35 Beaverbrook U.K. Foundation, Closing Submissions, exhibit 31-4584.
36 Beaverbrook U.K. Foundation, Closing Submissions, exhibit 31-4593; exhibit 31-4606.
37 Interview with Timothy Aitken.
38 Interview with Maxwell Aitken.
39 BCC, case 25, file 1, no. 14906.
40 Testimony of Lady Violet Aitken, Oct. 23, 2006.
41 Kidd, p. 234; interview with Maxwell Aitken.
42 Interview with Timothy Aitken.
43 Interview with Maxwell Aitken.
44 Interview with Timothy Aitken.

CHAPTER NINE: *"Families are absolutely a necessary evil"*
1   HLRO, BBK/K/1/59, letter of March 22, 1963; BBK/K/1/59, letter of April 18, 1963.
2   Michael Leapman, "Money Splits a Family Dynasty," *Times* (London), Feb. 3, 1986.
3   Malcolm Brown, "Long Knives Spice a Tale of Two Cousins," *Sunday Times* (London), Nov. 24, 1985.
4   Leapman; Philip Robinson, "Feud Fuels Aitken Bid Rumours," *Sunday Times* (London), Dec. 22, 1985.
5   Richard Evans, "Aitken's Role in a Boardroom 'Soap,'" *Times* (London), Feb. 25, 1988.
6   Interview with Timothy Aitken.
7   John Jay and Ivan Fallon, "Cursing Cousins: Jonathan and Timothy Aitken," *Sunday Times* (London), Feb. 28, 1988.
8   Edward Pearce, "Where Has All the Talent Gone?: The Crisis Facing Conservatives in the House of Lords," *Sunday Times*, Dec. 20, 1987.
9   Interview with Timothy Aitken.
10 Interview with Maxwell Aitken.
11 Interview with Maxwell Aitken.
12 Craig Seton, "Insolvent Peer Vows to Recover His Fortune," *Times* (London), Sept. 3, 1992.
13 Ivan Fallon and Janine di Giovanni, "From Clogs to Clogs," *Sunday Times* (London), Sept. 6, 1992.
14 Jonathan Dalrymple, "Beaverbrook Tells of 'Crazy' Fall from Grace," *Sunday Times* (London), Nov. 1, 1992.
15 Dalrymple.
16 Interview with Timothy Aitken.
17 HLRO, BBK/K/1/60, letter of Feb. 9, 1964.
18 Richard Norton-Taylor and Kamal Ahmed, "How the Golden World of a Man Who Would Be King Turned to Dust," *Guardian* (London), June 21, 1997.
19 Jonathan Aitken, "The Simple Sword of Truth" (text of statement), *Guardian* (London), April 11, 1995.
20 Luke Harding and David Pallister, "He Lied and Lied and Lied," *Guardian* (London), June 21, 1997.
21 David Pallister, David Leigh and Jamie Wilson, "Aitken, the Fixer and the Secret Multi-Million Pound Arms Deals," *Guardian* (London), March 5, 1999.
22 Interview with Timothy Aitken.
23 Interview with Timothy Aitken.
24 Robert Tweedie, Report to board of governors of the Beaverbrook Art Gallery, March 9, 1970. Robert Tweedie collection, PANB.
25 Lumsden, Collins and Glenn, pp. 27-28.

26   Ian Lumsden, "Futures Report: The Beaverbrook Art Gallery,"
      Jan. 8, 1988.
27   Timothy Aitken, "Art was Beaverbrook's Passion," *National Post*
      (Toronto), Aug. 19, 2004.
28   Interview with Timothy Aitken.
29   Interview with Maxwell Aitken.
30   Interview with Timothy Aitken.
31   Ray Cronin, "Beaverbrook Art Gallery in Tune with the Times," *Daily
      Gleaner* (Fredericton), May 23, 1998.
32   Beaverbrook U.K. Foundation, Closing Submissions, p. 235.
33   Testimony of Maxwell Aitken, Oct. 23, 2006.
34   Testimony of Judith Budovitch, Oct. 26, 2006.

CHAPTER TEN: *"You really don't want to deal with my cousin"*
1   Beaverbrook Art Gallery, Memorandum of Opening Statement, exhibit
      4207.
2   Interview with Timothy Aitken.
3   Interview with Timothy Aitken.
4   Transcript of examination for discovery of Judith Budovitch,
      Dec. 7, 2005.
5   Beaverbrook U.K. Foundation, Opening Submissions, p. 173.
6   Beaverbrook Art Gallery, Memorandum of Opening Statement, p. 9.
7   Testimony of Maxwell Aitken, Oct. 23, 2006.
8   Beaverbrook U.K. Foundation, Opening Submissions, p. 174.
9   Testimony of Maxwell Aitken, Oct. 23, 2006.
10   Beaverbrook U.K. Foundation, Opening Submissions, p. 174.
11   Ian MacLeod and Joel Chenier, "Nazi Looting Saved Art from
      Bombings, Gallery Director Says," *Citizen* (Ottawa), Jan. 4, 2001.
12   Interview with Timothy Aitken.
13   Beaverbrook U.K. Foundation, Opening Submissions, exhibit
      41-5483.
14   Interview with Timothy Aitken.
15   Interview with Timothy Aitken.
16   Joint Document Brief, exhibit 42-5514.
17   Interview with Bernard Riordon.
18   Beaverbrook U.K. Foundation, Closing Submissions, p. 237.
19   Interview with Timothy Aitken.
20   Interview with Maxwell Aitken.
21   Testimony of Maxwell Aitken, Oct. 23, 2006.
22   Beaverbrook U.K. Foundation, Closing Submissions, exhibit
      42-5525.

23 Beaverbrook Art Gallery, Memorandum of Opening Statement, exhibit CF1186.
24 Beaverbrook U.K. Foundation, Closing Submissions, p. 229.
25 Testimony of Michael Marshall, Oct. 24, 2006.
26 Interview with Maxwell Aitken.
27 Testimony of Maxwell Aitken, Oct. 24, 2006.
28 Timothy Aitken interview, *Information Morning*, CBC Radio, Fredericton, NB, August 26, 2004.
29 Interview with Timothy Aitken.
30 Interview with Maxwell Aitken.
31 Interview with Maxwell Aitken.
32 Beaverbrook U.K. Foundation, Opening Submissions, exhibit 42-5546.
33 Beaverbrook Art Gallery, Memorandum of Opening Statement, exhibit G005171.
34 Beaverbrook U.K. Foundation, Opening Submissions, exhibit 42-5549; exhibit 42-5558.
35 Beaverbrook Art Gallery, Memorandum of Opening Statement, exhibit G005174; exhibit 4196; exhibit G005175.
36 "Beaverbrook Paintings in Dispute," *Toronto Star*, March 24, 2004; Stuart Smith, "Give (and Take) in Fredericton," *National Post* (Toronto), Aug. 10, 2004; Siri Agrell, "N.B. Art Gallery at War over 'World-class' Paintings," *National Post* (Toronto), March 22, 2004.
37 Undated audio archive of CBC Radio interview with Vincent Prager, 2004.
38 Nina Chiarelli, "N.B. Silent in Dispute, Says Gallery Official," *Telegraph-Journal* (Saint John), April 9, 2004.
39 Timothy Aitken interview, *Information Morning*, CBC Radio, Fredericton, N.B., August 26, 2004.
40 Timothy Aitken, answers to written questions in lieu of discovery, June 1, 2006.
41 Interview with Timothy Aitken.
42 Marty Klinkenberg, "Beaverbrook Board Shocked by Boorish Behaviour," *Telegraph-Journal* (Saint John), Oct. 27, 2006.
43 "Dispute can be resolved: Lord Beaverbrook," CBC New Brunswick website, April 16, 2004.
44 Interview with Timothy Aitken.
45 Beaverbrook Art Gallery, Memorandum of Opening Statement, exhibit G005191.
46 Timothy Aitken interview, *Information Morning*, CBC Radio, Fredericton, N.B., August 26, 2004.
47 Beaverbrook Art Gallery, Memorandum of Opening Statement, exhibit G005191; exhibit G005205.

48 Timothy Aitken interview, *Information Morning*, CBC Radio,
    Fredericton, N.B., August 26, 2004.
49 Patrick Windle, affidavit, June 18, 2004, New Brunswick Court of
    Queen's Bench File No. F/C/256/04.
50 Timothy Aitken interview, *Information Morning*, CBC Radio,
    Fredericton, N.B., August 26, 2004.
51 Timothy Aitken, letter of Sept. 15, 2004.
52 "Beaverbrook Gallery Shows 'Art in Dispute,'" CBC New Brunswick
    web site, June 30, 2005.
53 "Beaverbrook's Disputed Art Draws More Visitors." CBC New
    Brunswick website, August 30, 2004.
54 "Beaverbrook Gallery Shows 'Art in Dispute,'" CBC New Brunswick
    web site, June 30, 2005.
55 "Beaverbrook Gallery Shows 'Art in Dispute,'" CBC New Brunswick
    web site, June 30, 2005.
56 Timothy Aitken, "Custodian's Message," *Tableau*, May-August 2003.

CHAPTER ELEVEN: *"One thing we can rely on is his own ego"*
In addition to the following sources, this chapter also draws on my own
    reporting of the arbitration hearing, Oct.-Dec. 2006.

1   Beaverbrook U.K. Foundation, Opening Submissions, p. 51.
2   Beaverbrook Art Gallery, Memorandum of Opening Statement,
    pp. 17, 19, 29, 32.
3   Beaverbrook Art Gallery, Memorandum of Opening Statement, p. 95.
4   Beaverbrook Art Gallery, Memorandum of Opening Statement, exhibit
    G000887.
5   Beaverbrook U.K. Foundation, Closing Submissions, pp. 6, 226-227.
6   Beaverbrook U.K. Foundation, Closing Submissions, pp. 68, 148-149.
7   Interview with Maxwell Aitken.
8   Beaverbrook U.K. Foundation, Closing Submissions, p. 115.
9   Beaverbrook U.K. Foundation, Closing Submissions, pp. 170-171.
10 Testimony of Stuart Smith, Oct. 20, 2006; Oct. 19, 2006.
11 Testimony of Maxwell Aitken, Oct. 24, 2006.
12 Beaverbrook U.K. Foundation, Closing Submissions, pp. 226-228.
13 Beaverbrook U.K. Foundation, Closing Submissions, p. 226.
14 Transcript of testimony of Judith Budovitch, Oct. 26, 2006.
15 Transcript of testimony of Tom Forrestall, Oct. 25, 2006.
16 Transcript of testimony of Tom Forrestall, Oct. 25, 2006.
17 Beaverbrook Art Gallery, Memorandum of Closing Argument, exhibit
    4268-D; pp. 61, 83.

18 Beaverbrook Art Gallery, Memorandum of Closing Argument, pp. 4, 7, 8.
19 Beaverbrook U.K. Foundation, Closing Submissions, p. 264.
20 Beaverbrook Art Gallery, Memorandum of Closing Argument, p. 14.
21 Beaverbrook U.K. Foundation, Opening Submissions, p. 107.
22 Beaverbrook Art Gallery, Memorandum of Closing Argument, p. 139; exhibit G002729.
23 Beaverbrook Art Gallery, Memorandum of Closing Argument, pp. 140, 143.
24 Beaverbrook Art Gallery, Memorandum of Closing Argument, exhibit G002847; exhibit G003035.
25 Beaverbrook Art Gallery, Memorandum of Closing Argument, pp. 149-150.
26 Beaverbrook Art Gallery, Memorandum of Closing Argument, p. 158.
27 Beaverbrook Art Gallery, Memorandum of Closing Argument, pp. 4-5, 15-16.
28 Beaverbrook U.K. Foundation, Closing Submissions, p. 259.
29 Beaverbrook U.K. Foundation, Closing Submissions, pp. 141-145, 151, 117.
30 Beaverbrook U.K. Foundation, Closing Submissions, pp. 142, 143.
31 Beaverbrook U.K. Foundation, Closing Submissions, p. 24.
32 Beaverbrook U.K. Foundation, Opening Submissions, pp. 78, 87-88.
33 Beaverbrook U.K. Foundation, Opening Submissions, pp. 88, 89-90.
34 Beaverbrook Art Gallery, Memorandum of Closing Argument, pp. 93, 94.
35 Marty Klinkenberg, "U.K. Foundation's Case under Fire," *Telegraph-Journal* (Saint John), Dec. 6, 2006.
36 Beaverbrook U.K. Foundation, Closing Submissions, pp. 310-311.
37 Marty Klinkenberg, "Colour-coded Proof of Ownership Handed to Art Dispute Mediator," *Telegraph-Journal* (Saint John), Dec. 7, 2006.

CHAPTER TWELVE: *"He did not act in the best interests of the gallery"*
1 The Beaverbrook Canadian Foundation vs. The Beaverbrook Art Gallery, New Brunswick Court of Queen's Bench file F/C/407/04.
2 Interview with Timothy Aitken.
3 Beaverbrook Art Gallery, amended statement of defence and counter-claim, June 13, 2006, Court of Queen's Bench file F/C/407/04.
4 Beaverbrook Art Gallery, amended statement of defence and counter-claim.
5 Transcript of examination for discovery of Judith Budovitch, November 2005.

6   Transcript of examination for discovery of Judith Budovitch, November 2005.
7   Interview with Timothy Aitken.
8   Interview with Timothy Aitken.
9   CheekyMoon press release, Jan. 6, 2006.
10 Marty Klinkenberg, "Aitken-led Gambling Website May Fold," Daily Gleaner (Fredericton), Feb. 24, 2007.
11 Interview with Maxwell Aitken.
12 Sarah Hampson, "'We Expect to Win,'" Globe and Mail (Toronto), Feb. 24, 2007.
13 Beaverbrook U.K. Foundation, Closing Submissions, p. 351.
14 CTV Atlantic 6 p.m. news, Feb. 14, 2007.
15 Interview with Maxwell Aitken.
16 Except where noted, the description of my tour of Cherkley Court, including comments by Anna Nelson, is based on notes I made during my visit on March 2, 2007.
17 Interview with Maxwell Aitken.
18 David Alberge, "Boy Raids His Piggy-bank to Save a Turner," Times (London), March 2, 2007.
19 Nigel Reynolds, "Turner Watercolour Fetches Record £5.8m," Daily Telegraph (London), June 6, 2006.
20 Tate Britain, J.M.W. Turner: The Three Rigis (London: Tate Britain, 2007).
21 Alberge.
22 Maev Kennedy, "Is J.M.W. Turner Our Favourite Painter?" Guardian (London), March 3, 2007.
23 "Portrait of Big Spenders," Daily Express (London), April 20, 1978.
24 "Aitken Reigns in Spain," Daily Telegraph (London), March 25, 2007.
25 Peter Cory, Arbitration Award, March 20, 2007, pp. 28-29, 7, 30-31.
26 Cory, pp. 86, 7.
27 Cory, p. 94.
28 Cory, pp. 106-107.
29 CBC audio recording of news conference by Daniel O'Brien, March 26, 2007.
30 Hampson.
31 Testimony of Maxwell Aitken, Oct. 24, 2006.
32 Maxwell Aitken, prepared statement, March 26, 2007.
33 Beaverbrook U.K. Foundation, Notice of Appeal and Appellants' Certificate, April 19, 2007.
34 Muggeridge, p. 64.

PRIMARY SOURCES

Beaverbrook Art Gallery accession records, *Hotel Bedroom*. Notes by Ian G. Lumsden.

Beaverbrook Canadian Correspondence, Archives and Special Collections, Harriet Irving Library, University of New Brunswick, Fredericton (BCC).

Beaverbrook, Lord. Last Will. Jan. 10, 1964. Registry of Deeds for Northumberland County, New Brunswick.

Beaverbrook Papers, House of Lords Record Office (HLRO), London.

Charities (Accounts and Reports) Regulations 2000, Statutory Instrument 2000 No. 2868, Government of the United Kingdom.

Constable, W.G. Oral history interview. Smithsonian Archives of American Art, July 1972-June 1973.

Flemming, Hugh John. Correspondence. Provincial Archives of New Brunswick (PANB).

Manchester Art Gallery accession records, *Peasant Girl Gathering Faggots*

Tweedie, Robert. Correspondence. Provincial Archives of New Brunswick (PANB).

Arbitration Documents: The Beaverbrook Art Gallery vs. The Beaverbrook U.K. Foundation

    Beaverbrook Art Gallery: Memorandum of Opening Submission and exhibits, Oct. 3, 2006.

    Beaverbrook Art Gallery: Memorandum of Closing Argument and exhibits, Nov. 24, 2006.

Beaverbrook U.K. Foundation: Opening Submissions and exhibits,
    Oct. 10, 2006.
Beaverbrook U.K. Foundation: Closing Submissions and exhibits,
    Nov. 24, 2006.
Beaverbrook U.K. Foundation: Notice of Appeal and Appellants'
    Certificate, April 19, 2007.
Cory, Peter. Arbitration Award, March 26, 2007.
Transcript of testimony of Maxwell Aitken, Oct. 23-24, 2006;
    Transcript of testimony of Tom Forrestall, Oct. 25, 2006;
    Transcript of testimony of Stuart Smith, Oct. 19-20, 2006.

Court of Queen's Bench (New Brunswick) Documents: The Beaverbrook
Art Gallery vs. The Beaverbrook Canadian Foundation
    Amended statement of defence and counterclaim of the Beaverbrook
        Art Gallery, Court of Queen's Bench file F/C/407/04, June 13,
        2006.
    The Beaverbrook Canadian Foundation vs. The Beaverbrook
        Art Gallery, New Brunswick Court of Queen's Bench file F/
        C/407/04.
    Budovitch, Judith. Transcript of examination for discovery, Court of
        Queen's Bench file F/C/407/04, November 2005.
    Windle, Patrick. Affidavit. New Brunswick Court of Queen's Bench
        File No. F/C/256/04, June 18, 2004.

SECONDARY SOURCES
Beaverbrook, Lord. *Courage: The Story of Sir James Dunn*. Fredericton:
    Brunswick Press, 1961.
———— . *Friends: Sixty Years of Personal Intimate Relations with Richard
    Bedford Bennett*. London: Heinemann, 1959.
———— . *My Early Life*. Fredericton: Brunswick Press, 1965.
Blackwood, Caroline, et. al. *Lucian Freud: Early Works*. New York: Robert
    Miller Gallery, 1993.
Butler, Stephen. *Gainsborough*. London: Studio Editions, 1992.
Butlin, Martin and Evelyn Joll. *The Paintings of J.M.W. Turner*. New
    Haven: Yale University Press, 1977.
Camp, Dalton. *Gentlemen, Players and Politicians*. Toronto: McClelland
    and Stewart, 1970.
Chester, Lewis and Jonathan Fenby. *The Fall of the House of Beaverbrook*.
    London: Andre Deutsch, 1979.
CBC New Brunswick website. http://www.cbc.ca/nb
Chisholm, Anne, and Michael Davie. *Beaverbrook: A Life*. London:
    Hutchinson, 1992.

Cohen, Reuben. *A Time To Tell*. Toronto: Key Porter, 1998.

DeMont, John. *Citizens Irving*. Toronto: Doubleday Canada, 1991.

Edwards, Rhianna, and William G. Godfrey. "R.B. Bennett Project: Archival Research Report." Ottawa: Parks Canada, 1999.

Jenkins, Roy. *Churchill*. London: Pan Books, 2002.

Kidd, Janet Aitken. *The Beaverbrook Girl*. London: Collins, 1987.

Lumsden, Ian G., Curtis Joseph Collins and Laurie Glenn, *The Beaverbrook Art Gallery Collection: Selected Works*. Fredericton: Beaverbrook Art Gallery, 2000.

Marchildon, Gregory. *Profits and Politics: Beaverbrook and the Gilded Age of Canadian Finance*. Toronto: University of Toronto Press, 1996.

Manchester Art Gallery. Notes on *Peasant Girl Gathering Faggots*. http://www.manchestergalleries.org/

Mellor, David Alan. *Interpreting Lucian Freud*. London: Tate Publishing, 2002.

Shone, Richard, and Ian G. Lumsden. *Sargent to Freud: Modern British Paintings and Drawings in the Beaverbrook Collection*. Fredericton: Beaverbrook Art Gallery, 1998.

Stevens, Geoffrey. *The Player: The Life and Times of Dalton Camp*. Toronto: Key Porter, 2003.

Tate Britain. *J.M.W. Turner: The Three Rigis*. London: Tate Britain, 2007.

Tate Online. *Lucian Freud* (2002 exhibition). http://www.tate.org.uk/britain/exhibitions/freud/

Taylor, A.J.P. *Beaverbrook*. London: Hamish Hamilton, 1972.

Tweedie, Robert. *On with the Dance: A New Brunswick Memoir, 1935-1960*. Fredericton: New Ireland Press, 1986.

Waite, P.B. *The Loner: Three Sketches of the Personal Life and Ideas of R.B. Bennett, 1870-1947*. Toronto: University of Toronto Press, 1992.

INTERVIEWS

Maxwell Aitken (March 6, 2007, London)
Timothy Aitken (Feb. 28, 2007, London)
Donald Andrus (Feb. 15, 2007, by telephone)
Judith Budovitch (Jan. 26, 2007, Fredericton)
David Hay (Feb. 23, 2007, Fredericton)
Sinclair Healy (Feb. 8, 2007, by telephone)
Henry Irwin (Feb. 22, 2007, by telephone)
Marc Leger (March 15, 2007, by telephone)
Larry Lowenstein (March 27, 2007, by telephone)
George MacBeath (Jan. 10, 2007, Fredericton)
Anna Nelson (March 2, 2007, Leatherhead, England)
Helen (Savage) Parker (March 30, 2007, Fredericton)

Vincent Prager (Jan. 26, 2007, by telephone)
Bernard Riordon (March 28, 2007, Fredericton)
Claude Roussel (Feb. 27, 2007, Cap-Pelé, NB)
Kent Thomson (March 28, 2007, by telephone)
Colleen Thompson (Feb. 14, 2007, by e-mail)
Jackie Webster (March 22, 2007, Fredericton)

Note: Two former gallery officials and one acquaintance of Robert Tweedie granted interviews on the condition of anonymity. Ian Lumsden did not respond to requests for an interview and Richard Bird refused several requests for an interview.

University of New Brunswick 13, 14,
19, 28, 48, 50, 52-53, 66, 70, 74,
77, 97, 140, 154, 160, 164, 178,
212, 226, 286
University Press 55, 57, 123

V
Vanderbilt family 88
Vaughan, David 191
Vaughan, Marguerite Pillow 191
Vaughan, Murray 119
Vaughan Foundation 191
Ventech Corporation 193
Vernet, Claude Joseph 276
View from the Giudecca 75, 76, 268
Viscount Castlerosse 117, 262

W
Walker, Horatio 89
Wardell, Michael 19, 36, 46, 53,
54-60, 61, 62, 65, 69, 72-73, 81,
93, 95, 96-98, 100, 105, 106,
109, 115, 119-120, 121, 122-
123, 126, 128, 129-130, 131,
132, 142-144, 145, 146, 147,
151, 152-153, 157, 227, 230,
238, 246, 248, 269, 278, 287
Warkworth Castle, Northumberland
87
Watson, Claire 89-90, 98
Watson, Homer 107
Watson, William 89
Watson-Fisher, Claire 231, 254
Webster, Jackie 56, 61, 66
Weir, Elizabeth 213
Wells, H.G. 36
Westminster UK 18, 190
Westover, Anne 174, 191
White Dog in a Landscape 112, 174,
178, 252, 268, 275, 277
Wilson, Peter 174, 176
Wilson's Printing 55
Windsor, Duchess of (Wallis Warfield
Simpson) 40, 55, 128
Windsor, Duke of (Edward VIII) 40,
55, 62, 106, 110, 128, 169
Wing Lung Bank 28

World War I. *See* First World War
World War II. *See* Second World War
Wright, H.S. 74
Wright, Joseph 121, 271
Wu Centre 28, 226, 238, 260
Wu Yee-Sun 28

Y
Yeats, W.B. 36
Yorke, Josephine 86, 231
Youdan, Timothy 247
Young, David 232, 238, 261
Young Artists Exhibition 22

Z
Zinkeisen, Doris 151